PROPAGANDA
AND
PERSUASION

PEOPLE AND COMMUNICATION

Series Editor: PETER CLARKE   *University of Michigan*

Volumes in this series:

PROPAGANDA AND PERSUASION

by
GARTH S. JOWETT
and
VICTORIA O'DONNELL

SAGE PUBLICATIONS
The Publishers of Professional Social Science
Newbury Park   Beverly Hills   London   New Delhi

To Ada and May, who lived through two World Wars and who, in another time and place, took me to the movies.

Garth S. Jowett

Just as this book was nearing completion, my mother's life came to a close. My portion of this book is dedicated to Helen A. O'Donnell in memory of a special woman who loved life, people, pets, movies, and me.

Victoria O'Donnell

For information address:

SAGE Publications, Inc.
275 South Beverly Drive
Beverly Hills, California 90212

SAGE Publications Inc.   SAGE Publications Ltd.
2111 West Hillcrest Drive   28 Banner Street
Newbury Park   London EC1Y 8QE
California 91320   England

SAGE PUBLICATIONS India Pvt. Ltd.
M-32 Market
Greater Kailash I
New Delhi 110 048 India

Printed in the United States of America

Library of Congress Cataloging-in-Publication Data

Main entry under title:

Jowett, Garth.
    Propaganda and persuasion.

(People and communication ; v. 18)
    Bibliography: p.
    Includes indexes.
    1. Propaganda.   2. Persuasion (Psychology)
I. O'Donnell, Victoria.   II. Title.   III. Series.
HM263.J69   1986   303.3'75   85-30441
ISBN 0-8039-2398-8
ISBN-0-8039-2399-6 (pbk.)

THIRD PRINTING, 1987

CONTENTS

ACKNOWLEDGMENTS

The preparation of this book has taken longer than anticipated; we would therefore like to thank our publishers for their seemingly infinite patience over the years, especially those at Sage Publications who had the arduous duty of prodding us along as we waded through the labyrinths of the vast literature of propaganda, and traveled up and down highway 145 between Houston and Denton.

Specifically for assistance along the way we would like to thank Terry Book for being so supportive and helpful, Gail Sadlowski for helping us draft the model of propaganda in Chapter 8; Cydney Foote for typing some of the manuscript; Marlina Gonzalez for research assistance; Richard Nelson for his encouragement; and Patricia Marsh Cavanaugh for research assistance as well as for preparing and typing the bibliography, and for just being there when her presence made some of the darker days much brighter.

PREFACE

This book grew out of the discovery that both of the authors were interested in the study of propaganda; however, we come to this interest from the perspectives of different academic disciplines: Professor Jowett from that of communications history and Professor O'Donnell from persuasion and rhetoric. To any discerning reader, this will make the primary authorship of the individual chapters obvious, but to keep the record straight Professor Jowett wrote Chapters 2, 3, and 5; Professor O'Donnell was responsible for Chapters 1, 4, and 6. Chapters 7 and 8 are the result of the joint exchange of ideas.

We were both intrigued with how poorly propaganda had fared in recent years as part of general communication studies, and further informal investigations revealed that few students were being given the opportunity or encouragement to examine this subject in a systematic manner. When we questioned our colleagues, we were assured that propaganda as a topic within the communications curriculum still held great interest, but because the subject was so vast in scope, it was difficult to cover it in anything but the most cursory way. This problem was compounded by the lack of suitable classroom materials designed to allow a systematic treatment, without forcing the student to consult a wide array of disparate sources. This book was written with a view to solving some of these problems by presenting an overview of the history of propaganda as well as a review of the social scientific research on its effects and an examination of its applications. We have tried to restrict the narrative so that it will serve as a guide to further reading on specific issues rather than be encyclopedic in scope.

In the past seventy years there have been many hundreds of books dealing with various aspects of propaganda. There have also been almost an equal number of books and journal articles dealing with persuasion, and very often these two subjects have come to be regarded as synonymous. With the growth in the study of persuasion in the last two decades, propaganda has received scant attention as a subject in its own right within the spectrum of communication studies. With the advent of a whole range of new communication technologies, and the imminent promise of a myriad of channels for disseminating information, the opportunities for increased propaganda activities are obvious. For this reason we believe that the time has come to revive the study of propaganda as a separate topic, and of great significance at this particular point in time.

This book is offered as a modest treatment of a very old subject, and we trust that the reader will be sympathetic to the fact that we could not include a detailed history of propaganda nor a lengthy review of all of the research ever done to evaluate its effectiveness in specific campaigns. Our aim was to provide the reader with a challenge to become involved in the fascinating world of propaganda in the hope that it would stimulate further research and discussion. We both owe an intellectual debt to T. H. Qualter (1962), whose excellent slim volume *Propaganda and Psychological Warfare* was all that was available for a long time, and whose recent detailed monograph *Opinion Control in the Democracies* (1985) is a landmark study, but that unfortunately was only received after this volume had been sent to the printer. Other than Qualter and the important work by David L. Altheide and John M. Johnson (1980) *Bureaucratic Propaganda,* the three-volume compilation of important articles by Harold D. Laswell, Daniel Lerner, and Hans Speir, *Propaganda and Communication in World History* (1979), and Richard A. Nelson's (1986) forthcoming detailed bibliography on the subject, there have been very few systematic examinations of propaganda in recent years, and it is our intention that this book fill some of the gaps in the current literature.

What may appear to the reader to be a relatively short book is, in fact, the result of several years of reviewing a vast literature, which is unfortunately reflected only in a minor way in the bibliography. We chose to present in this book both a digest of important and classic ideas on the subject and our original ideas. It has been our goal to produce a work that, we hope, will enable students of modern-day propaganda to recognize, analyze, and evaluate propaganda in their midst while giving them an appreciation of its history and development. Although respectful of the work of Jacques Ellul, we could not incorporate many of his ideas within the text of this book. We aimed to clarify and distinguish propaganda as a form of communication, but found that we could not do so with Ellul's view of the pervasiveness of propaganda. Also, advertising, although presented as the most prevalent form of propaganda in the United States, does not receive extensive treatment. We felt that advertising as propaganda is such a complex and extensive subject that it required an entire series of studies in itself and that such a treatment was beyond the scope of this book.

Writing a book should always be a learning experience, and this book taught us that we all have a great deal to learn about the role and practice of propaganda in our everyday society. We have also learned that in order not to fear propaganda, we must first understand it.

Garth S. Jowett   Victoria O'Donnell
Houston, Texas   Denton, Texas

1

WHAT IS PROPAGANDA AND HOW DOES IT DIFFER FROM PERSUASION?

Propaganda is a form of communication that is different from persuasion because it attempts to achieve a response that furthers the desired intent of the propagandist. Persuasion is interactive and attempts to satisfy the needs of both persuader and persuadee. A model of propaganda depicts how elements of informative and persuasive communication may be incorporated in propagandistic communication. References are made to past theories of rhetoric that indicate that propaganda has had few systematic theoretical treatments prior to the twentieth century. Public opinion and behavior change can be affected by propaganda.

The study of propaganda has been approached as history, political science, sociology, and psychology. To study propaganda as history is to examine the practices of propagandists as events and the subsequent events as possible effects of propaganda. To examine propaganda in light of political science is to analyze the ideologies of the practitioners and the dissemination of public opinion. To approach propaganda as sociology is to look at social movements and the counterpropaganda that emerges in opposition. A more recent trend has been to examine propaganda as mass culture and the ways in which propaganda is disseminated as ideas and practices in the culture. This book approaches the study of propaganda as communication. Persuasion, a subset of communication, is also examined in this book. The two terms "propaganda" and "persuasion" have been used interchangeably in the literature on propaganda as well as in common usage. There is a certain amount of overlap, but the two terms can be differentiated. A communication approach to the study of propaganda enables us to isolate its communicative variables, to determine the relationship of message to context, to examine the responses and responsibilities of the audience, and to trace the development of propagandistic communication as a process.

We believe that there is a need to evaluate propaganda in a modern context free from value-laden definitions. Our objectives are to (1) provide a concise examination of propaganda and persuasion, (2) examine the role of propaganda as an aspect of communication studies, and (3) analyze propaganda as part of the social system.

COMMUNICATION DEFINED

Communication has been defined quite simply as that which happens when A communicates to B about X (Westley and MacLean, 1977). A may be a person, a group, or a social system. B may be a person, a group, or a social system as well. In any case, A is commonly referred to as the "sender" and B as the "receiver." Communication is often a face-to-face interaction, but it is also often a mediated interaction whereby A communicates to B through C about X. Here C is a gatekeeper, an encoder of a message, or, quite possibly, an agent for B (Westley and MacLean, 1977). Communication involves attempts to share meaning through a process of symbolic interaction between and among human beings. Communication is a convergence process in which sender and receiver, either through mediated or nonmediated means, create and share information. In a convergence process, there is a tendency for the sender and receiver to move toward one point, or for one to move toward the other, or to unite in a common interest or focus. The communication elements that enable convergence to occur are (1) a communicator, (2) a message, (3) a channel, and (4) an audience. Other important aspects are (5) feedback and (6) effects of the message. All of these elements must be examined in light of the context in which they occur, both in a specific and immediate sense and in the social-cultural framework of the times.

PROPAGANDA DEFINED

Propaganda, in the most neutral sense, means to disseminate or promote particular ideas. It is from Latin—"congregation de propaganda fide"—meaning congregation for propagating the faith of the Roman Catholic Church. Usage has rendered the word "propaganda" pejorative. To identify a message as propaganda is to suggest something negative and dishonest. Words frequently used as synonyms for "propaganda" are "lies," "distortion," "deceit," "manipulation," "psychological warfare," and "brainwashing." Many of these synonyms are suggestive of techniques of message production rather than purpose or process.

When usage emphasizes purpose, propaganda is associated with control and is regarded as a deliberate attempt to alter or maintain a balance of power that is advantageous to the propagandist. Deliberate attempt is linked with a clear institutional ideology and objective. In fact, the purpose of propaganda is to send out an ideology to an audience with a related objective. Whether it is a government agency attempting to instill a massive wave of patriotism in a national audience to sustain a war effort, a military leader attempting to frighten the enemy by exaggerating his or her strength, or a corporation attempting to promote its image in order to maintain its legitimacy among its clientele, there is a careful and predetermined plan of prefabricated symbol manipulation to communicate to an audience in order to fulfill an objective. The objective that is sought requires the audience to reinforce or modify attitudes and/or behavior.

According to Leo Bogart's (1976: 195-196) study of the U.S. Information Agency, "Propaganda is an art requiring special talent. It is not mechanical, scientific work. Influencing attitudes requires experience, area knowledge, and instinctive 'judgment of what is the best argument for the audience.' No manual can guide the propagandist. He must have 'a good mind, genius, sensitivity, and knowledge of how that audience thinks and reacts.''' (The quotations enclosed are from the original five-volume study of the USIA that Bogart's work condenses.) Furthermore, according to Terence H. Qualter (1962: xii), "Propaganda, to be effective, must be seen, remembered, understood, and acted upon . . . adapted to particular needs of the situation and the audience to which it is aimed." Influencing attitudes, anticipating audience reaction, adaptation to the situation and audience, and being seen, remembered, understood, and acted upon are important elements of the communicative process.

Our definition of propaganda focuses on the communicative process and most specifically on the purpose of the process: *Propaganda is the deliberate and systematic attempt to shape perceptions, manipulate cognitions, and direct behavior to achieve a response that furthers the desired intent of the propagandist.* Propaganda is an attempt at directive communication with an objective that has been established a priori. Further, propaganda seeks to contain information in a specific area, and responses to propaganda are manipulated in an attempt to keep them in the contained area. The recipient of the propaganda message is discouraged from asking about anything outside the contained area. Yet contemporary technology is capable of instantaneous transmission of messages around the world, and because there has been a tremendous expansion of exposure to all of the mass media throughout the world, it is, as Bogart (1976: xviii) has pointed out, "increasingly difficult to maintain a country in isolation from ideas and information that are common in the rest of the world." Furthermore, propaganda itself, as a form of communication, is influenced by the technological devices for sending messages that are available in a given time.

The study of contemporary propaganda in both oppressed and free societies is a complex endeavor. We acknowledge that one's perception of a form of communication determines what is self-evident and what is controversial. One person's propaganda may be another person's education. The elements of deliberateness and manipulation along with a systematic plan to achieve a purpose that is advantageous to the propagandist, however, distinguish propaganda from a free and open exchange of ideas.

FORMS OF PROPAGANDA

Although propaganda takes many forms, it is almost always in some form of activated ideology. Sometimes propaganda is agitative where attempts are made to arouse an audience to certain ends; sometimes it is integrative where attempts are made to render an audience passive, to be accepting and nonchallenging (Szanto, 1978: 10). Propaganda is also described as white, gray, or black in relationship to an acknowledgment of its source and its accuracy of information.

White propaganda is when the source is identified correctly and the information in the message tends to be accurate. This is what one hears on Radio Moscow and the Voice of America during peacetime. Although what listeners hear is reasonably close to the truth, it is presented in a manner that attempts to convince the audience that the sender is the "good guy" with the best ideas and political ideology. White propaganda attempts to build credibility with the audience, for this could have usefulness at some point in the future.

During the 1984 Olympics, there were many complaints of "biased" coverage by the American reporters, particularly from the British Broadcasting Corporation. The absence of the Russians in Los Angeles provoked a less than enthusiastic reaction to the multiple victories of Americans from non-American news sources. While the former gold medalists of past games lauded American performances, the home countries of the other athletes cried "unfair." Daley Thompson, the decathlon winner from Great Britain, appeared on television wearing a t-shirt that read, "But what about the coverage?"

The American Broadcasting Company's coverage was objective reporting of the events and white propaganda. They appeared to stir up American patriotism deliberately while being genuinely excited about the American athletes' achievements. Doubtlessly, this was also intended to convey a message to the Russian government that said, "We do not need you at the Games."

Gray propaganda is when the source may or may not be correctly identified and the accuracy of information is uncertain. In 1961, when the Bay of Pigs invasion took place in Cuba, the Voice of America moved over into the gray area when it denied any American involvement in the CIA-backed activities. When

Russia invaded Afghanistan, Radio Moscow utilized gray propaganda when it attempted to justify the action. Gray propaganda is also used to embarrass an enemy or competitor. Radio Moscow took advantage of the assassinations of Martin Luther King and John F. Kennedy to derogate the United States. The Voice of America did not miss the opportunity to offer similar commentaries about the Russian invasion of Afghanistan or the arrests of Jewish dissidents.

Black propaganda is when a false source is given and lies, fabrications, and deceptions are spread. Black propaganda is the "big lie," including all types of creative deceit. During World War II, prior to Hitler's planned invasion of Britain, a radio station known as "The New English Broadcasting Station," supposedly run by discontented British subjects, ran half-hour length programs throughout the day, opening with "Loch Lomond" and closing with "God Save the King." The station's programming consisted of "war news." This was actually a German undercover operation determined to reduce the morale of the British people throughout the Battle of Britain.

Radio Free Hungary made its appearance ten years later. This station attracted world attention and sympathy in 1956 when the Russians sent their tanks into Budapest to squelch the popular revolution that tried to overthrow the Communist regime. Radio Free Hungary's fervent pleas for help from the United States aroused sympathy from the free world. The atrocities of the Russians were described in hideous detail, and the Russians were cursed and denounced in every transmission. The station was actually a totally brilliant fake operated by the KGB with the intention of embarrassing the United States. There was little chance that the United States would send troops to Hungary, even though Radio Free Europe had suggested that Americans would support a popular uprising in Hungary. Russia used Radio Free Hungary to demonstrate that the United States could not be relied upon to help a country in revolt. Radio Free Hungary was so effective that the United States Central Intelligence Agency did not know that it was a Russian propaganda device until after it ceased broadcasting.

Another term used to describe propaganda is *disinformation*. It is usually considered black propaganda because it is covert and uses false information. Disinformation is made up of news stories designed to weaken adversaries. News stories are planted in newspapers by journalists who are actually secret agents of a foreign country. Ladislav Bittmann, former deputy chief of the Disinformation Department of the Czechoslovak Intelligence Service, in testimony before the House Committee on Intelligence of the United States Congress in February 1980, said, "If somebody had at this moment the magic key that would open the Soviet bloc intelligence safes and looked into the files of secret agents operating in Western countries, he would be surprised. A relatively high percentage of secret agents are journalists . . . . There are newspapers around the world penetrated by the Communist Intelligence services" (*Washington Inquirer*, May 4, 1984). Allan C. Brownfeld (1984), reporter for the *Washington Inquirer*, wrote,

> The documentation of the manner in which Moscow has placed false stories in the non-Communist press is massive. In one instance, Alezander Kasnechev, the senior KGB officer in Rangoon, Burma, who defected to the U.S. in 1959, described the Soviet effort to plant such stories. His department was responsible for receiving drafts of articles from Moscow, translating them into Burmese, and then seeing that they were placed in local publications to appear as if they had been written by Burmese authors. The final step was to send copies back to Moscow. From there they were quoted in Soviet broadcasts of publications as evidence of 'Burmese opinion' that favored the Communist line" (1984).

He also cites Senator Daniel P. Moynihan, who said,

> The technique is used variously to influence the confidence of foreign populations in their leaders and institutions, discredit individuals and groups opposed to Soviet policies, deceive foreigners about Soviet intentions and conditions within the Soviet Union itself, and at times simply to obscure the motives or authors of Soviet-sponsored activities around the world. Sometimes disinformation is quite subtly done, so much so that we can never be certain with any degree of confidence that it is disinformation at all.

Propaganda thus runs the gamut from truth to deception. It is, at the same time, always value- and ideology-laden. The means may vary from a mild slanting of information to outright deception, but the ends are always predetermined in favor of the propagandist.

Subpropaganda

Another dimension of propaganda is what Doob (1948) called "subpropaganda." This is when the propagandist's task is to spread an unfamiliar doctrine, for which a considerable period of time is needed to build a frame of mind in the audience toward acceptance of the doctrine. In order to gain the target audience's favor, various stimuli are used to arouse the attention of the audience and the related encoders and agents who mediate communication. L. John Martin (1971: 62), who was a research administrator in the U.S. Information Agency for nine years, calls subpropaganda "facilitative communication," that is, an activity that is designed to keep lines open and to maintain contacts against the day when they will be needed for propaganda purposes. Facilitative communication most frequently takes the form of radio newscasts, press releases, books, pamphlets, periodicals, cultural programs, exhibits, films, seminars, language classes, reference services, and personal social contacts. These are all arranged in an effort to create a friendly atmosphere toward those who may be needed later on. W. Phillips Davison (1971) gives examples of influencing journalists to give favorable press to the United States by offering rides and other services such as office space provided by the U.S. Committee on Public Information, parties, conducted tours of foreign cities, and news scoops.

Facilitative communication itself may not be propaganda, but it is communication that is designed to render a positive attitude toward a potential propagandist. In 1969, 450 active registrations of agencies distributing propaganda were on file with U.S. government on behalf of foreign agencies. Davison points out that most were concerned with tourism, investment, or trade. This did not include embassies or consulates' activities, nor did it include mail and short-wave radio from abroad. Meanwhile, the U.S. International Communication Agency (USICA) employs a staff of 8,758 employees who work in 126 countries at a cost of $433 million per year "to give foreign peoples the best possible understanding of U.S. policies and intentions" (*U.S. News and World Report*, 1979: 47). This agency alone publishes 12 magazines in 22 languages, produces more than 90 films a year, operates a radio-teletype network, and broadcasts more than 800 hours a week through the Voice of America in 37 languages to an estimated 75 million listeners. The use of propaganda is certainly not on the decline. Communication networks have expanded and changed, and information tends to be more accessible, but modern society still retains the need to deliberately manipulate responses.

A MODEL OF PROPAGANDA

The literature of propaganda often refers to "mass persuasion," suggesting that propaganda is persuasion on a one-to-many basis. Propaganda tends to be linked with a general societal process, whereas persuasion is regarded as an individual psychological process. Propaganda has not been successfully differentiated from persuasion. The model in Figure 1.1 is an attempt not so much to differentiate but to demonstrate a separation according to purpose and process. The model also reveals the overlap between the two processes as an overlap of techniques with subtle differences of technique according to purpose.

Propaganda and Information

Communication has been defined as a convergence process in which sender and receiver, either through mediated or non-mediated means, create and share information. When the information is used to accomplish a purpose of sharing, explaining, or instructing, this is considered to be informative communication. People seek information when they need to understand their environment. Once gained, information tends to reduce uncertainty. Uncertainty reduction is normally acquired through the communication of messages; thus messages can be analyzed in terms of the amount of uncertainty they remove from the situation being communicated about. Informative messages have an impact upon receivers by allowing them to acquire information, understand the environment, and learn. Generally speaking, informative communication is thought to be neutral because it is a very special and limited use of language. Informative discourse is communication about subject

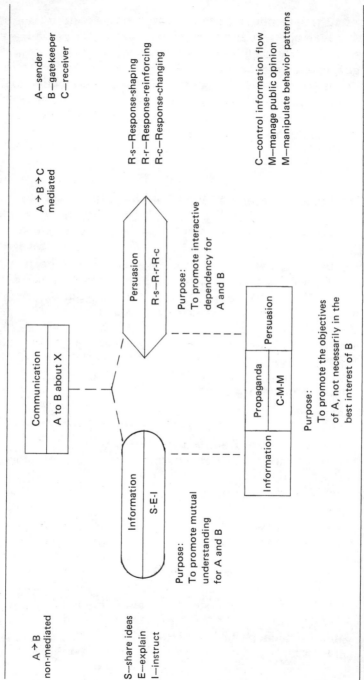

Figure 1.1 A Purpose Model of Propaganda

matter that has attained the privileged status of being beyond dispute. Whenever information is regarded as disputable by either the sender or receiver, it is difficult for the communication to proceed as information. An informative communicator differs from other kinds of communicators by having the purpose of creating mutual understanding of data that are considered to be accurate, of concepts that are considered to be indisputable, and of ideas that are based on facts.

Propaganda utilizes informative communication in a similar fashion. The difference is that the purpose exceeds the notion of mutual understanding. The purpose of propaganda is to promote a partisan or competitive cause in the best interest of the propagandist but not necessarily in the best interest of the recipient. The recipient, however, may believe that the communication is merely informative. Often white propaganda is very similar to informative communication. Information is imparted from an identifiable source, and the information is accurate. The distinction between white propaganda and informative communication is that white propaganda intends to promote a partisan cause or the informative communication would not have taken place. Techniques of informative communication are also used in gray and black propaganda, but the information is not likely to be accurate or even based in reality.

Many writers grapple with the distinction between propaganda and informative communication in educational practices that include the communicative purpose of instructing for mutual understanding. Elliot Aronson (1980: 60) questions whether educators are merely imparting knowledge or skill in American history. He asks, "What about the vast majority of high-school textbooks in American history that ignore the contributions of blacks and other minorities to the American scene? Is this merely imparting knowledge?" Another subject area that Aronson questions is arithmetic. He also points out that most of the examples in elementary school arithmetic texts deal with buying, selling, renting, working for wages, and computing interest. He also cites Zimbardo et al. (1977) who feel that these examples do more than simply reflect the capitalistic system in which education is occurring. The point is that arithmetic problems with a capitalistic ideological base endorse the system, legitimize it, and suggest that it is the natural

and normal way. Aronson says that interpretation of an instructional practice depends largely on the values of the person who
is interpreting it. William E. Griffith, in his essay on Communist
propaganda, refers to "propaganda" and "education" interchangeably. He says that educating the masses is the same as
propaganda. In fact, Soviet reform propaganda, he says, resulted in more educated Soviet officials (in Lasswell et al., 1980:
vol. 2, 239-258).

By evaluating educational practices according to their ends
rather than their means, however, one can observe the use of
informative communication as a means of achieving a propagandistic end in practices such as the ones described above.

PROPAGANDA AND PERSUASION:
PERSUASION DEFINED

Persuasion as a subset of communication is usually defined
as a communicative process the purpose of which is to influence. A persuasive message has a point of view or a desired behavior for the recipient to adopt in a voluntary fashion. Victoria
O'Donnell and June Kable (1982:9) define persuasion as "a
complex, continuing, interactive process in which a sender and
a receiver are linked by symbols, verbal and nonverbal, through
which the persuader attempts to influence the persuadee to
adopt a change in a given attitude or behavior because the persuadee has had perceptions enlarged or changed." Persuasion
has the effect, when it is successful, of resulting in a reaction
such as, "I never saw it that way before." What happens is that
the recipient of the persuasive interaction relates or contrasts
the message to his or her existing repertoire of information. The
process of persuasion is an interactive one in which the recipient sees the fulfillment of a need or desire if the persuasive purpose is adopted. Because both persuader and persuadee stand
to have their needs fulfilled, "persuasion" is a more neutral
term than "propaganda."

Persuasion Is Transactional

People respond to persuasion that promises to help them in
some way by satisfying a want or need. That is why the persuader must think in terms of the persuadee's needs as well as

his or her own. Persuasion is a reciprocal process in which both parties are dependent upon one another. It is a situation of interactive dependency. The persuader who understands that persuasion is a transaction in which both parties approach a message-event and use it to attempt to fulfill needs will never assume a passive audience. It is an active audience that seeks to have its needs fulfilled by the persuader, and it is an active persuader who knows that he or she must appeal to audience needs in order to ask the audience to fill his or her needs by adopting the message-purpose. A politician seeking votes must address the needs of the voters. If the voters are convinced that the politician will fulfill their needs, then they will fulfill the needs of the politician by casting positive votes at election time.

Responses to Persuasion

Persuasion attempts to evoke a specific change in the attitude or behavior of an audience. The change sought is a specific response from the audience. There are three different forms of response that are possible (Roloff and Miller, 1980: 16).

First, there is response shaping. This is similar to learning, wherein the persuader is a teacher and the audience is a pupil. A persuader may attempt to shape the response of an audience by teaching it how to behave and offer positive reinforcement for learning. If audience responses favorable to the persuader's purpose are reinforced by rewards to the audience, positive attitudes are developed toward what is learned. The audience has a need for positive reinforcement filled, and the persuader has a need for a desired response from the audience filled.

Second, there is response reinforcing. If the people in the audience already have positive attitudes toward a subject, the persuader reminds them about the positive attitudes and stimulates them to feel even more strongly by demonstrating their attitudes through specified forms of behavior. Much persuasion in today's society is response reinforcing (blood drives, fund raising, pep rallies, helping others, and so on), but people have to be motivated to go out and do these things year after year. There is little controversy in these situations, but people's emotional needs have to be aroused to get them to get out and give blood or money or team support, and so on.

Third, there is response changing. This is the most difficult kind of persuasion because it involves asking people to switch from one attitude to another, to go from a neutral position to having a positive or negative attitude, to change behavior, or to adopt a new behavior. People are reluctant to change; thus, in order to convince them to do so, the persuader has to relate the change to something in which the persuadee already believes. This is called an "anchor" because it is already accepted by the persuadee and will be used to tie down new attitudes or behaviors. An anchor is a starting point for change because it represents something that is already widely accepted by the potential persuadees. Anchors can be beliefs, values, attitudes, behaviors, and group norms.

Beliefs

A belief is a perceived link between any two aspects of a person's world (Fishbein and Ajzen, 1975: 131). A belief expresses a relationship between two things ("I believe that a personal computer will help me get better grades") or a thing and a characteristic of that thing ("I believe that the world is round"). We have thousands of beliefs. In order for a persuader to change old beliefs or create new ones, he or she will have to build on beliefs that already exist in the minds of the audience. A persuader has to use anchors of belief to create new belief. The stronger the belief of a receiver, the more likely it is that it will influence the formation of a new belief.

Values

A value is a special kind of belief that endures and is not likely to change. A value is a belief that is prescriptive and is a guideline for a person's behavior. A value can be a means of behavior (honesty, sensitivity) or a desired end behavior (success, power). Values are concepts of right and wrong, good and bad, or desirable and undesirable. Most people regard their values as very personal and get quite upset when they are attacked; thus they make strong anchors.

Attitudes

An attitude is a readiness to respond to an idea, an object, or a course of action. It is expressed in a statement that evaluates the idea, object, or behavior. ("I like ballet" or "I disagree with communist ideology.") An attitude is a relatively enduring predisposition to respond; therefore, it already resides in the minds of the audience and can be used as an anchor.

Attitude change is often the desired response in persuasion; thus attitudes may be used as anchors or they may be used as persuasive end-states. People have thousands of attitudes, some of which are important, others inconsequential. A persuader can use strongly-held attitudes as anchors to promote related attitude change.

Behavior

Behavior can be used as an anchor not only because it is an overt expression of a way of being but also because behavioral patterns are fair predictors of future behaviors. When a behavior is recurrent, a script for behavior develops to the point that a great deal of consciousness is not necessary to continue the same behavior. References to successful behavior can be motivational. By reminding persuadees that their behavior has meant need-fulfillment in the past, a persuader can urge them to use the same or similar behavior in the future. Conversely, if certain behavior has negative consequences, the persuader can urge the persuadee to avoid the consequences by discontinuing the behavior.

Another successful motivational strategy is to show persuadees models of behavior. Modeling influences new behavior in persuadees because they offer new information about how to behave (Bandura, 1977).

Group Norms

Group norms are beliefs, values, attitudes, and behaviors that are derived from membership in groups. Group norms can be used as anchors because people have a tendency to conform to the norms of the groups to which they belong. Daryl Bem (1970: 75) says that the major influence on people is people. Peer pressure influences how people dress, talk, and behave. When they are uncertain about what position to take or what to do, people often adopt the attitudes and behaviors of their peers. They also succumb to peer pressure because it is easier to conform than to depart from the norms of their groups.

Resonance

A persuader who is well prepared knows the audience. Anchors can be discovered from knowledge of the audience's affiliation with groups as well as from insight into the audience's

beliefs, values, attitudes, and behaviors. Because these categories constitute important categories of the makeup of the audience, they can be used to motivate the audience to accept the
purpose of the persuader. Both persuasion and propaganda
tend to produce messages of resonance; that is, the recipients
do not perceive the themes of messages to be imposed upon
them from an outside authority to which they are required or
committed to defer. Rather the recipients perceive the anchors
upon which the message is based as coming from within.
Kecskemeti defines the propagandist's ideal role in relation to
the recipient of the message as that of an alter ego, "Someone
giving expression to the recipient's own concerns, tensions, aspi-
rations, and hopes. . . . Thus, propaganda, . . . denies all distance between the source and the audience: the propaganda
voices the propagandee's own feelings" (Pool et al., 1973: 264).
Likewise, in persuasion, identification must take place between
the persuader and persuadee. They share common sensations,
concepts, images, and ideas that make them feel as one. A persuader analyzes an audience in order to be able to express its
needs, desires, personal and social beliefs, attitudes, and values
as well as its attitudes and concerns about the social outcome
of the persuasive situation. The persuader is a voice from without speaking the language of the audiences' voices within. Yet
persuasive communication may be dialectic in nature and preclude homogeneity. Conversely, the propaganda message is
more often homogeneous because it is sent to a mass audience
rather than to one person in an interpersonal setting.

Persuasion Seeks Voluntary Change

In general, practitioners of persuasion assume that the audience has access to information about the other side of a
controversial issue as well as exposure to counterpersuasion. In
other words, there is a recognition that any change that occurs
within audience perceptions, cognitions, or behaviors will be
voluntary change. Both parties—persuader and persuadee—in
the interaction will perceive the change due to persuasion as
mutually beneficial.

Misleading and Manipulation

Of course, a persuader can mislead an audience regarding
his or her intent. Sometimes an audience is aware of this, which

gives an aura of voluntary compliance; that is, the audience can decide to consent to change while knowing quite well that the persuader has a hidden agenda. Sometimes an audience will believe a persuader regarding the spoken intent, and, consequently, it will be manipulated and used without knowing what is happening. This we regard as propaganda. More commonly, however, the propagandist may exploit an audience's beliefs or values or group norms in such a way as to fan the fires of prejudice or self-interest. When the audience goes along with such practices, mutual reciprocity occurs because both parties have needs fulfilled. The audience's needs—the reinforcement of prejudicial or self-serving attitudes—get fulfilled and spoken, but the persuader's needs—the attainment of a selfish end through the audience's compliance—get fulfilled but not spoken. No audience, no matter how perverse in its own needs, will put up with hearing that they are being manipulated and used to fulfill another's selfish needs. Thus the propagandist cannot reveal the true intent of the message.

RHETORICAL BACKGROUND AND THE
ETHICS OF PERSUASION

Since the beginnings of the study of rhetoric, which was what persuasion was considered to be until the early twentieth century, theorists have been concerned with ethics.

The form of government in ancient Greece encouraged public speaking. Men voiced their opinions openly and were encouraged to share in making political and judicial decisions. Because civic responsibility was presumed, there was strong encouragement to be honorable citizens and to acquire skill in public statement. The Athenian system disqualified any speaker who was "suspected of certain dishonorable acts . . . he could be prosecuted, not for the offense, but for continuing to speak in the assembly after committing the offense." (Bonner, 1933: 80) Men studied the art of rhetoric almost as an entire system of higher education if not a way of life. (Hunt, 1925: 3)

Plato opposed the place of rhetoric in Athenian life as well as whatever part rhetoric had in influencing public opinion. As Hunt (1925: 3) said, "He despised mere opinion almost as much as he did the public." He believed in a government ruled by philosopher-kings and not a government in which rhetoric was employed by those who did not possess true wisdom or knowledge. As a result, two of his writings, the *Gorgias* and the *Phaedrus*, attacked rhetoric as a system capable of making the worse appear the better reason. In the *Gorgias*, Plato criticized the study of rhetoric for misleading men into believing that by attempting through words to achieve what is good, that they can do good. Without insight and wisdom, a man who studied rhetoric was likely to become what we would call a propagandist. Plato, through his spokesman, Socrates, posed the questions:

"Do the rhetoricians appear to you always to speak with a view to what is best, aiming at this, that the citizens may be made as good as possible by their discourses? or do they, too, endeavour to gratify the citizens, and neglecting the public interest for the sake of their own private advantage, do they treat the people as children, trying only to gratify them, without being in the least concerned whether they shall become better or worse by these means?" (Cary, 1854: 125-126) In the *Phaedrus*, Plato admonishes the rhetorician to have high moral purpose and knowledge of truth or else not attempt rhetoric at all.

Aristotle, the great philosopher and social interpreter of fourth-century Greece, produced many classical works about the nature of ideas and people. The work that is seminal in the field of persuasion is *Rhetoric* (Cooper, 1932). Although Aristotle studied under Plato and embraced many of the ideas that Plato expressed in the *Phaedrus*, *Rhetoric* tends to be detached from issues of morality. Rather, it is an amoral and scientific analysis of rhetoric, defined as "the faculty of discovering in the particular case what are the available means of persuasion (Cooper, 1932: 7). Yet, it is in *Rhetoric* that Aristotle establishes the concept of credibility (*ethos*) as a form of proof and a mode of persuasion. Ethos, an artistic proof established within the discourse itself, provides the audience with insight into the persuader's character, integrity, and good will. Other forms of proof are emotional appeal (*pathos*) and the speech itself (*logos*), defined by Aristotle as "when we have proved a truth or an apparent truth from such means of persuasion as are appropriate to a particular subject" (Cooper, 1932: 9).

Central to the study of rhetoric is the audience, which Aristotle classifies and analyzes. Logic is established through audience participation in an interactive reasoning process. Known as the *enthymeme*, this practical device is like a syllogism with some part or parts missing. It requires the audience to mentally fill in the missing logical steps, thus stimulating involvement. Aristotle regarded the enthymeme as a way of guarding truth and justice against falsehood and wrong. He believed that audiences could not follow close and careful logical reasoning related to universal truths but could participate in reasoning related to probability in the sphere of human affairs. In his *Nicomachean Ethics*, Aristotle dealt with his expectations for high moral principles. With regard to persuasion, he indicated that a crafty person could artfully manipulate the instruments of rhetoric for either honest or dishonest ends. Depending upon which end is desired, the use of rhetorical devices is judged accordingly: "If . . . the aim be good, the cleverness is praiseworthy; but if it be bad, it becomes craft." (Browne, 1850: VI, xii,: 8) Mac-Cunn, (1906: 298) interprets this to mean that the Aristotelian thesis postulates that "cleverness and character must *strike alliance*." MacCunn also sees Aristotle's general point of view as judging the means according to the ends sought:

"He who would win the harper's skill must win by harping: he who would write, by writing; he who would heal the sick by healing them. In these, as indeed in all the arts, faculty is begotten of function, and definite proclivity comes of determinate acts" (MacCunn, 1906: 301).

Quintilian, the premier teacher of imperial rhetoric in Rome during the first century, A.D., wrote the *Institutes of Oratory*, in which he advocated that the Perfect Orator be the good man speaking well. This concept was reiterated by St. Augustine in his fifth-century work on Christian preaching and rhetoric, *On Christian Doctrine*. Insistence upon truth as the overall objective of public speaking is the cardinal tenet of this treatise. Augustine was concerned about using rhetorical techniques for false persuasion, but he felt that the way in which it was used did not reflect upon rhetoric itself:

"There are also rules for a more copious kind of argument, which is called eloquence, and these rules are not the less true that they can be used for persuading men of what is false; but as they can be used to enforce the truth as well, it is not the faculty itself that is to be blamed, but the perversity of those who put it to a bad use" (Shaw, 1873: IX, 5)

Classical concepts of rhetoric, especially that of the good man speaking well, were revitalized throughout the Middle Ages, the Renaissance, and the Reformation. Neoclassicism held forth in theoretical works on persuasion despite the appearance of despot princes and authoritarian rulers in the same countries in which the rhetorical works were published. In the same century that Machiavelli wrote *The Prince,* advocating the use of dishonest methods to gain and maintain power, rhetorical theorists such as Phillipp Melanchthon, the humanist educator and religious reformer of Germany, Leonard Cox, the first to write a treatise on rhetoric in the English language, and Thomas Wilson, whose *Arte of Rhetorique* was published eight times in thirty years from 1553 to 1583, were turning out works that echoed Cicero and Quintilian.

Even after the *Sacra Congregatio de Propaganda Fide* became an official organ of the Roman Catholic Church in 1622, no rhetorical theorist addressed its implications with regard to persuasion. The major rhetorical works of the seventeenth century were Francis Bacon's four treatises — adapting classical rhetoric to the needs of the scientist and affirming the value of ornamentation and imaginative coloring in rhetoric — and the early elocutionists, Robert Robinson and John Bulwer, whose works on delivery foreshadowed the rhetorical movement that placed major emphasis on delivery and pronunciation.

Rhetoric and Propaganda

The study of persuasion in the theories of rhetoric laid down throughout the centuries emphasized adherence to the truth in revealing the real intent of the persuader and a sincere concern for the welfare of the audience. These are the humanistic concerns of the classicists. There are no major rhetorical theories from nations whose governments have been totalitarian, thus the history of rhetoric hardly includes the study of propaganda except for allusions to misuse of rhetorical techniques for dishonest ends. The Bolsheviks had Eisenstein to describe and demonstrate the use of propaganda in film, and the Nazis had Hitler's *Mein Kampf* and Goebbels's diaries as guidelines for propaganda, but these have not been part of the history of rhetoric. The reason for this comes from the rhetorician's insistence upon a consideration of ethics in rhetoric. It was not until

Kenneth Burke, the American literary critic, wrote "The Rhetoric of Hitler's 'Battle'" in 1939 that a serious rhetorical critic tackled and analyzed propaganda while simultaneously contributing new ideas to rhetorical theory. Drawing upon what he called the Dramatistic Pentad—five interrelated motivational or causal points of view—Burke analyzed the Act (what took place in thought or deed), the Scene (the background of the Act, the situation in which it occurred, the Agent (the actor or person or institution who performed the Act), the Agency or Agencies (the means or instruments used by the Agent), and the Purpose (the motive or cause that lay behind the Act). Burke determined that in *Mein Kampf* the Act was the bastardization of religious thought; the Agent was Hitler; the Agencies were unity identification such as "one voice," the Reich, Munich, the army, German democracy, race, nation, Aryan, heroism, and so on versus Disunity identifications such as images, ideas, and so on of parliamentary wrangle of the Hapsburgs, Babel of opinion, Jewish cunning, together with spiritualization and materialization techniques; the Scene was discordant elements in a culture weakened progressively by capitalistic materialism; and the Purpose was the unification of the German people. Burke's description of Hitler's strategies to control the German people is a masterful criticism of propaganda, yet it also is heavily flavored with moralistic judgment. It warns the reader about "what to guard against if we are to forestall the concocting of similar medicine in America" (Burke, 1973: 191).

In the twentieth century the study of persuasion became an inquiry into behaviorism. This happened almost concurrently with the serious study of propaganda by social scientists. This development and synopsis of the resulting research is presented in Chapter 4. Now let us return to the model that differentiates propaganda from other forms of communication.

Propaganda as a Form of Communication

Propaganda may appear to be informative communication when ideas are shared, something is explained, or instruction takes place. Information communicated by the propagandist may appear to be indisputable and totally factual. The propagandist knows, however, that the purpose is not to promote mutual understanding but rather to promote his or her own objectives. Thus the propagandist will attempt to control information flow and manage a certain public's opinion by shaping perceptions through strategies of informative communication. A persuader, likewise, shares ideas, explains, or instructs within the purpose of promoting interactive dependency. In fact, a persuader skillfully uses evidence to teach potential persuadees rather than to persuade them. Evidence itself does not persuade, but it can enhance a persuader's credibility (McCroskey, 1969). Persuasion, however, does not try to appear as informative communication. An effective persuader makes the purpose as clear as possible if he or she hopes to bring about attitude change. The explicitly stated conclusion is twice as likely to get desired audience response compared to the suggested one (Biddle, 1966; Hovland and Mandell, 1952).

Concealed Purpose

The propagandist is very likely to appear as a persuader with a stated purpose that appears to promote interactive dependency. In reality, however, the propagandist wants to promote his or her own interests or those of an organization, sometimes at the expense of the recipients, sometimes not. The point is that the propagandist does not regard the well-being of the audience as a primary concern. The propagandist is likely to be detached from the recipients. Not only does the propagandist not care about the audience, he or she may not believe in the message that is being sent. In fact, concealment of purpose may not be the only deviousness. Often a propagandist does not want his or her or its identity known.

Concealed Indentity

Identity concealment is often necessary in order for the propagandist to achieve desired objectives and goals. The propagandist seeks to control the flow of information, manage public opinion, and manipulate behavior patterns. These are the kinds of objectives that might not be achieved if their true intent were known or if the real source were revealed.

Control of Information Flow

Control of information flow takes the form of withholding information, releasing information at predetermined times, releasing information in juxtaposition with other information that may influence public perception, manufacturing information, communicating information to selective audiences, and distorting information.

There are two major ways in which the propagandist tries to control information flow: (1) controlling the media as a source of information distribution and (2) presenting distorted information from what appears to be a credible source. Using journalists to infiltrate the media and spread disinformation is one way to present distorted information. Altheide and Johnson (1980) make a case for what they call "bureaucratic propaganda" in which organizations, ranging from the military to television networks to evangelical crusades, release official reports containing what appears to be scientifically gathered and objective information to influential groups with the purpose of maintaining the legitimacy of organizations and their activities. The information in the official reports is often contrived, distorted, or falsely interpreted. This information, according to Altheide and Johnson, may never be seen by the public but rather by a congressional committee or some citizens' group and may be used for some action or program.

The Management of Public Opinion

Propaganda is most often associated with the management of public opinion. Public opinion has been defined by Land and Sears (1964) as "an implicit verbal response or 'answer' that an individual gives in response to a particular stimulus situation in which some general 'question' is raised" (quoted in Mitchell, 1970: 62). Lippmann (1922) regarded public opinion as that which emanated from persons interested in public affairs rather than a fixed body of individuals. He believed that public opinion was effective only if those persons supported or opposed the "actors" in public affairs. Speier (1950) felt that public opinion exists when a unique "right" is granted to a significant portion of extragovernmental persons: "In its most attenuated form this right asserts itself as the expectation that the government will reveal and explain its decisions in order to enable people outside the government to think and talk about these decisions, or to put it in terms of democratic amenities, in order to assure 'the success' of the government's policy" (quoted in Altheide and Johnson, 1980: 7).

Mitchell gives four forms that public opinion usually takes: (1) popular opinion as generalized support for an institution, regime, or political system (as opposed to apathy, withdrawal, or alienation), (2) patterns of group loyalties and identifications, (3) public preferences for select leaders, and (4) intensely held opinions prevalent among a large public regarding public issues and current affairs (Mitchell, 1970: 60-61). Mitchell likens the propagandist's management of public opinion to "a burning glass which collects and focuses the diffused warmth of popular emotions, concentrating them upon a specific issue on which the warmth becomes heat and may reach the firing-point of revivals, risings, revolts, revolutions" (p. 111).

The Manipulation of Behavior

Ultimately, the goal of propaganda is to manipulate behavior and behavior patterns; external rather than internal public opinion is sought. Voting, buying products, selecting entertainment, joining organizations, fighting for a cause, and other forms of action responses are sought from the audiences who are addressed by the persuader and the propagandist. These are *overt* behaviors that can be observed as both verbal and nonverbal responses. There are other categories of behavior according to Triandis (1977): *attributive* behavior, that which is derived from the conclusions drawn about the internal states of others from observations of their behavior; and *affective* behavior, emotional reactions to people and events. An example of an attributive behavior would a manufacturer concluding, "Consumers buy our product regularly; therefore they must like it." Affective behaviors could be cheering and yelling for a political candidate or experiencing a burst of pride when the national anthem is sung. Triandis (1977: 9) points out that behaviors become habits or behavior patterns when they are performed repeatedly over a long period of time. Patterns in past behaviors or habits are fair predictors of future behaviors. In other words, they become "scripts" for behavior in similar situations. When a similar situation is encountered, it does not require a great deal of consciousness to carry out the same behavior (Roloff, in Roloff and Miller, 1980: 50). A propagandist or a persuader will have difficulty changing behavior if the audience already has habits to the contrary. This is especially true when a habitual behavior is triggered by emotion (Triandis, 1977: 25). The point is that behavior change is not easy to bring about. Both persuaders and propagandists are well aware of this and actively seek information regarding the variables related to behavior change and predictors of behavior.

OVERVIEW OF THE BOOK

The modern study of propaganda came about after World War I and, interestingly enough, led the way to the social scientific study of persuasion. At the same time, as Doob (1966) points out, the word "propaganda" became less used and was replaced by words such as "communication," "information," and "persuasion" because they imply no value judgment and tend to embrace the development of new communication technologies as well as the "intricate perplexities inherent in developing societies and international diplomacy." (Doob, 1966: vi).

The historical development of propaganda and the developing media and audiences are the subjects of Chapters 2 and 3. Chapter 4 reviews the social science research regarding persuasion and propaganda. Chapter 5 examines the use of propaganda in psychological warfare and the emerging fear of propaganda in mass society. The remainder of the book concentrates on modern propaganda: methods of analysis (Chapter 6), case studies (Chapter 7), and a process model that depicts how propaganda works in modern society (Chapter 8).

2

PROPAGANDA THROUGH
THE AGES

The use of propaganda has been an integral part of human history, and can be traced back to Ancient Greece for its philosophical and theoretical origins. Used effectively by the Roman Empire and the early Christians, propaganda became an essential activity in the religious conflicts of the Reformation. The invention of printing was quickly adopted by Martin Luther in his fight against the Catholic Church and provided the ideal medium for the widespread use of propagandistic materials. Each new medium of communication was quickly adopted for use by propagandists, especially during the American and French Revolutions, and later by Napoleon. By the end of the nineteenth century the improvement in the size and speed of the mass media had greatly increased the sophistication and effectiveness of propaganda.

The use of propaganda as a means of controlling information flow, managing public opinion, or manipulating behavior is as old as recorded history. The concept of persuasion is an integral part of human nature, and the use of specific techniques to bring about large-scale shifts in ideas can be traced back to the ancient world. Many of the artifacts from prehistory and from earliest civilizations provide us with evidence that attempts were being made to use the equivalent of modern-day propaganda techniques to communicate the purported majesty and supernatural powers of rulers and priests. Thus dazzling costumes, insignia, and monuments all contribute toward evoking a specific image of superiority and power that these early propagandists wished to convey to their audience.

In Western civilization we have the first systematic attempts at persuasion and counterpropaganda in the Greek city-states about 500 B.C. with the codification of "rhetoric." Both Plato and Aristotle wanted to immunize "good" citizens against the use of false logic and emotional terms by "bad" lawyers and demagogic politicians. The use of deliberate forms of speech carefully calculated to deliver a persuasive message can also be found in the writings of Confucius in his *Analects*, where he suggests that the use of the "good" rhetoric, together with the proper forms of speech and writing, could be used to persuade men to live meaningful lives. Bruce L. Smith (1966: 579-580) has pointed out that this Platonic admonition is echoed today by the leaders of Communist China, only it is called "brainwashing."

The history of propaganda is based upon three interweaving elements: First, the increasing need, with the growth of civilization and the rise of nation-states, to win what has been called "the battle for men's minds"; second, the increasing sophistication of the means of communication available to deliver propagandistic messages; and third, the increasing understanding of the psychology of propaganda and the commensurate application of such behavioral findings. Throughout history these three elements have combined in various ways to enhance and encourage the use of propaganda as a means of altering attitudes and for the creation of new ideas or perspectives. It is, however, only in comparatively modern times that scholars and scientists have begun to assess the role of such mass propaganda techniques as an aspect of the social process. The history of propaganda is not necessarily a linear progression, but there are certain significant benchmarks that are worth examining as illustrations of how propaganda has been utilized at different times. In each case, those wishing to control or manage others (the propagandists) have made maximum and intelligent use of the forms of communication (the media) available to them, while also accurately gauging the psychological susceptibility of their audiences so that their messages can be tailored to ensure the best possible reception. The successful propagandist is always able to discern the basic needs of the audience, and to play upon those.

IMPERIAL ROME

The Imperial Roman Empire between 50 B.C. and 50 A.D. applied systematic propaganda techniques that utilized all of the available forms of communication and symbology to create an extremely effective and extensive network of control. The resulting "image" of Imperial Rome remains strong even today, and has become an integral part of our popular culture as we can all identify with the trappings associated with this great empire. The Roman Emperors developed their propaganda strategies to meet a very real need. The geographic extent of far-flung conquests had created a difficult problem of control and necessitated the development of a strong, highly visible centralized government. The wealth and power that had come with the conquests were used to maximum advantage as vast sums of money were spent on symbolizing the might of Rome through architecture, art and literature, and even the coinage. Coordinated from Rome, the policy of the Caesars was to combine all of the symbols into a form of "corporate symbolism" reminiscent of modern-day advertising plans, which projected the image of an all-powerful, omnipresent entity.

Whereas the Greek City-states had already discovered that judicious use of sculpture, poetry, building, and music and theater could project the desired image of sophistication, one historian has noted that "the skill of the Caesars was in expanding and mass-producing this means of communication so that it was projected successfully over a long period to a very large area" (Thomson, 1977: 56). There were other factors that contributed to the success of the Romans, for they were able to exploit a political and spiritual vacuum that made their imperial subjects much more susceptible to the sophisticated offerings of their conquerors. The Roman Empire was able to offer more than military protection—they provided both a moral philosophy and cultural aesthetic that was adopted by the local peoples. In this way the art and architecture of Rome was as much a symbol of imperial power as were the garrisons of armored legions; and the cultural legacy remained much longer.

Julius Caesar (100-44 B.C.) was particularly adept at utilizing sophisticated propaganda techniques throughout his rise to power and during his move to assert totalitarian power. Initially he used stories of his military exploits abroad, combined with actual terror tactics at home to put fear into the populace. One of the prime communication channels for conveying these messages was the coin; they were widely used to boast of victories or to show the emperors in various guises such as warlord, god, or protector of the Empire. Coins were the one social document that the Romans were certain would be seen by the widest possible range of subjects under their control. Caesar also made maximum use of the spectacle, spending lavishly on massive triumphal processions—more than four in one month at one point—each representing a victory in the civil war, and each different from the other. The cumulative effect of all of this pomp and show of power helped to create an atmosphere that enhanced Julius Caesar's reputation and seemed to justify his careful hints that he was descended from the goddess Venus. It was no accident that he chose the phrase, "I came, I saw, I conquered," which in Latin is reduced to the alliterating and rhyming words "veni, vidi, vici" (Thomson, 1977: 58).

Julius Caesar was a master propagandist, equaled only by Napolean and Hitler in his understanding of meaningful symbols and in his ability to understand instinctively the psychological needs of his audience. He understood the need to use such symbols of power and sophistication as a means of converting subject populations to the Roman way of life. This was far less expensive than maintaining elaborate garrisons of legionnaires, and induced obedience to the new regime through cooperation and identification rather than subjugation. Significantly, subject peoples were often granted the right to become Roman citizens under certain circumstances, thus increasing personal identification with the conqueror.

Caesar created his own legends out of ordinary events, and by making himself seem supernatural, he was able to set in motion the psychological changes in the minds of the Roman people that would lead away from republicanism and toward the acceptance of monarchical rule and the imperial goals. It is not surprising that throughout history there have been repeated evocations of the Caesarist image by those who aspire to leave their mark on the world. Thus not only Charlamagne, Napolean, Mussolini, and Hitler have invested themselves in Caesarist trappings, but so has almost every parvenu monarchy in Europe. Whether it be the image of the eagle, the armored breastplate, the man-god on the white horse, or the powerful orator, the propagandistic legacy of the Roman Empire is still much in evidence in our own world.

THE RISE OF CHRISTIANITY

When considering the effect of long-range propaganda activities, there have been no more successful campaigns than those waged by the great proselytizing religions of Buddhism, Christianity, and Mohammedanism. Although each of these great religions has used different strategies to achieve its purpose, they have all relied upon the use of charismatic figures, heavy symbolism, a simple and incessant moral philosophy, and an understanding of their audience's needs. In each case the new religion had to find a way to replace the existing religious beliefs, and to win over the minds and hearts of the populace. To examine the propaganda tactics of a religion in no way demeans it; on the contrary, it provides a clear example that not all propaganda messages are negative, but are often aimed at some positive social or political purpose.

The example of the rise of Christianity demonstrates how by skill and understanding of the audience, a specific appeal was made that eventually altered the shape of our world. Christianity was aimed to a large extent at the defeated, the slaves, and the less successful part of the Roman Empire. It had to compete with literally hundreds of other similar religions for this audience at the time of the dissolution of the Roman Empire, and considering that Christ and his followers did not have control over the existing communications media at the time, the ultimate level of adoption of Christianity must be considered one of the great propaganda campaigns of all time.

When the strategy of Christian techniques is broken down, we find a masterful use of images and emotion. The legacy of the synagogue preacher was well established, but Christ and his followers took what were basically traditional messages and put them into a new form. The use of parables, dramatic gestures on the floor of the Temple, the graphic use of metaphor—the seeds on stony ground, the eye of the camel, the shepherd and his flock—and the personal factor of singling out individuals as human metaphors—Peter, the Rock—combined to provide a powerful, emotional, and easily understood message. The keynote was simplicity and a promise of humanity and dignity for those who had often been denied such treatment. The early organizers of the Christian religion also developed the concept of cellular proselytization, later to be adopted and developed by Lenin in the Russian revolution and other revolutionaries since then. This was exemplified by the choice of twelve disciples as the dedicated core who would carry the message to other groups, who in turn would spread the word through personal contact in a system resembling today's pyramidal marketing schemes. Each cell would have its own leaders, and the loyalty and faith of the cell members were solidified by the rituals of baptism and communion (Thomson, 1977: 65-66).

It was more than four centuries after the death of Christ that the cross became the symbol of Christianity, but during that time the use of the two curved intersecting lines symbolizing a fish was widely used.

Not only was this symbol easy to draw, it also had mystical overtones in that it derived from an acronym for the Greek words for "Jesus Christ, Son of God, saviour," *ichthus*, which means "fish." The theme of the fish was particularly suited to a religion that relied upon recruitment; and the metaphor of the apostles as "fishers of men," which many of them were in real life, was most appropriate. Initially used as a secret sign during the time when Christians were persecuted by the Roman authorities, the fish symbolized the mission of the group it represented, and did so simply and effectively; and as a result it was found scrawled on walls, trees, in the dust, and any place where Christians wished to leave their mark to communicate their increasing numbers and strength to others. Even graffiti has a powerful propaganda value (Dondis, 1981: 78).

The early Christians persevered against great odds, not only in the form of persecution and competition from other religions but also from dangerous internal schisms and heresies from dissident groups. One of the factors that eventually allowed Christianity to flower was the rejection of attempts made to absorb it into a universal world-religion (Gnosticism), or to restrict it to the select few (Montanism). From the outset, Christianity had asserted that it was catholic, or universal in its message and appeal long before it became Catholic in fact. What helped was that Christianity was syncretic; it absorbed and utilized aspects from both Greco-Roman classicism and the new Germanic culture, as well as elements from ancient Oriental religions. When combined with the dramatic gospel of a saviour who had died to save the entire world, and told in the common Greek or *Koine* that was the universal literary language of the Roman Empire, the religion thus possessed identity as well as universality for its increasingly wider audience.

After Constantine I adopted Christianity for a mixture of personal and political motives about 313 A.D., Christianity became for all intents and purposes the official religion of the Emperors and was eventually adopted by the Germanic tribes who inherited the remnants of the Empire. It took several hundred years for the full panoply of Christian symbolism to develop, but aided by the remarkable infrastructure and communications system of the Roman Empire, the religion spread remarkably quickly. Its theme of universal love and a promise that the humble and meek would inherit the earth, was a dramatic reversal of the established order, but it found a sympathetic ear and gained audience empathy. In succeeding centuries the full symbolism of Christianity would be adopted—the cross, the lion and the lamb, the virgin and child, and even the horned and tailed figure (surely taken from pagan symbols) of the devil. These symbols have endured for nearly 1500 years, and today Christianity is practiced by several billion people. The success of Christianity is a testament to the creative use of propaganda techniques.

THE REFORMATION AND COUNTERREFORMATION

In the history of propaganda Christianity figures prominently, as both the proponents and adversaries of the various denominations have utilized every conceivable technique to maintain their power and spread their ideas. Development of the movable type printing press in the middle of the fifteenth century created a totally new form of communication that was almost immediately put to use as a major channel of propaganda in the titanic struggle for power between the Catholic Church and Martin Luther.

An explanation of the causes of the struggle between the Church and the "reformists" is beyond the scope of this book, but it essentially involved disagreements with increasingly corrupt practices in the established Church—such as the sale of indulgences for vast sums of money—and a desire to establish direct contact with God without having to go through the priests. This latter desire ultimately manifested itself in a call for the establishment of a simplified liturgy and Bible in the vernacular German language rather than in Latin, which prevented full participation by the congregation. Martin Luther provided the first vernacular liturgies in 1526 (the *Deutsche Messe*), and his major literary achievement, the German language Bible, was first printed in complete form in 1534. (A translation of the New Testament had appeared earlier in 1522). It was the printed Bible—which went through many editions in Luther's lifetime—that was the highest achievement of the Reformation, and was the direct result of the application of a new technology to the furthering of a specific cause. As noted Reformation historian A. G. Dickens (1968: 51) has pointed out,

> Between 1517 and 1520, Luther's thirty publications probably sold well over 300,000 copies. . . . Altogether in relation to the spread of religious ideas it seems difficult to exaggerate the significance of the Press, without which a revolution of this magnitude could scarcely have been consummated . . . For the first time in human history a great reading public judged the validity of revolutionary ideas through a mass-medium which used the vernacular languages together with the arts of the journalist and the cartoonist.

The development of the printing press was a quantum leap in the speed of communication, and in the sixteenth century printing speeds increased from about 20 sheets per hour to over 200; although this was slow in comparison to modern printing presses, it was nevertheless an important step toward the evolution of true mass media. Luther's works were widely circulated

by printers using aggressive sales tactics, but then their appeal
for the increasingly literate population was enhanced by his vigorous, entertaining style as well as the use of woodcut illustrations by leading artists of the time such as Cranach. These early
cartoons were able to convey in a simplified manner Luther's
attack on the Papacy and Catholicism, and greatly increased
the effectiveness of his message.

As a study in propaganda, the Reformation, particularly the
role played by Martin Luther and his followers, is a perfect example of how the channeling of the message, couched in an em-
pathetic emotional context and provided with an effective
means of delivery can bring about mass changes in attitudes.
Luther used plain German language laced with the common idi-
omatic expression of Northern Germany and Austria, and based
his sermons on metaphor and folk wisdom, which allowed effective communication over a wide area and with a heterogeneous audience of Germans of all social classes. Basing his
operations in the small town of Wittenberg, he distributed his
stirring pamphlets all over Northern Europe, taking advantage
of the lack of effective censorship in the divided German states.

Using a novel and entertaining "dialogue" style in his printed
sermons, he was able to attack precisely those aspects of the
established Church practices, such as the sale of indulgences,
the buying and selling of church offices, the open hypocrisy of
clerical celibacy, and papal corruption, all of which had already received wide attention among the general public. Luther
used the basic strategy of widely disseminating and emphasizing information that had previously been a part of what can be
called the "general public paranoia," thus confirming the public's fears and increasing the potential for attitude change on a
mass scale. But he was also able to offer a positive message of
hope as a counter to this aggressive negativity; now the people
could control their own religious destinies, and using a language they understood they could now participate more mean-
ingfully in the religious ceremony. What Luther encouraged in
essence was the concept that individuals could communicate
directly with God without the intervention of the Church. Comparing the hold of the Catholic Church over the German population to that of the Hebrews held in captivity in Babylon, he
struck a very sympathetic chord with his audience.

Luther made sure that his religious activities were supported on the political front, once again demonstrating a masterful grasp of the elements of a successful propaganda campaign. Immediately after he had been condemned by the Papacy in 1520, he penned a manifesto entitled *An Appeal to the Christian Nobility of the German Nation* that was addressed to the rulers of Germany, the princes, the knights, and cities, which under the young Emperor Charles V had a series of grievances against Rome. Although the emperor was himself a devoted Catholic, for political reasons (the Turkish menace was a constant problem) he seemed powerless to act against Luther, and Luther suddenly found himself swept along with the tide of national resentment against Rome. Luther was thus able to exploit the political disorganization in Germany at this time to serve his own purposes, pitting the German nobility, Protestant and Catholic, against each other.

Luther did not limit his propaganda strategies to the sermon or the pamphlet but used a range of other techniques. The dramatic public gesture of nailing his 95 theses to the church door in Wittenberg on the eve of All Saint's Day in 1517 was a major propagandistic gesture. Had it not been for the printing press, only a few copies of this protest may have circulated among the people of Wittenberg; but with the new technology this gesture was turned overnight into a manifesto that swiftly circulated throughout Germany, attracting an ever-widening audience, and eventually becoming the precipitating factor in the greatest crisis in the history of the Western Church.

Luther also used the emotional power of music in the form of the vernacular hymn, as well as the poetic version of Lutheran doctrine put to verse by Hans Sachs, the most prolific German poet and dramatist of his age. It was the work of artist and engraver Lucas Cranach (1472-1553) that was of most assistance to Luther's propagandistic efforts. His portraits of the reformers and the Protestant princes were widely circulated, thus giving them greater personal identification with the audience and turning them into visual embodiments of heroic proportion; however, it was Cranach's engraved caricatures satirizing the pope or depicting the Catholic Church as the Babylonian woman of the Revelation that had the greatest propaganda value. These were easily identifiable and provided a measure of entertainment as well as underscoring political and religious tensions. From all accounts these caricatures and portraits sold extremely well in the Protestant sections of Germany.

The Reformation spawned a number of other master propagandists besides Luther; on the side of the reformers was John Knox in Scotland who utilized both the pulpit and his writing skill to achieve broad popular appeal; on the counter-Reformation side, we cannot ignore the important figure of Ignatius Loyola, the founder of the Jesuits, who developed his own highly effective and instinctual propaganda techniques. The "Society of Jesus," which was the official name of the Jesuits, was organized into a cellular structure, and Loyola created in his followers a highly emotional, almost mystical fanaticism. He understood the significant power of education as a means of altering and then fixing attitudes in the young, and he insisted on total obedience from those in his order.

The Jesuits became the major force in the Church's attempt to counter the Lutheran reformation, and under Loyola they achieved some remarkable successes. Austria was restored completely to the Catholic position, and the Polish peasantry were converted to Catholicism in the face of strong opposition from the reformers (Thomson, 1977: 79). Later, it was through the use of Jesuits that the Catholic Church began to expand its missionary efforts in other continents, most notably South America and China. For his efforts, Ignatius Loyola was made a saint by Pope Gregory XV in 1622. The Society of Jesus continues as one of the major teaching arms of the Catholic Church today — a fitting tribute to the power of propaganda.

It was also in 1622 that Pope Gregory XV, after examining the state of the Church in Europe, decided to establish on June 22 of that year the *Sacra Congregatio Christiano Nomini Propaganda*, or as it was more commonly known, the *Sacra Congregatio de Propaganda Fide* (**Congregation for the Propagation of the Faith**), which was charged with carrying the faith to the New World and with reviving and strengthening it in Europe as a means of countering the Protestant Revolution. This unified and centralized Catholic Church missionary activities, and within a few years, in 1627, Pope Urban VIII founded the *Collegium Urbanum*, the seminary that served as the training ground for the *Propaganda*.

It is interesting that the methods to be used by the mission-
aries of the Propaganda were left to the discretion of those in
the field. The object was to bring men to a voluntary acceptance of the Church's doctrines, not through coercion. It was
Gregory's plan that laid the foundation for modern propaganda
techniques in that it stressed the control of opinions, and
through them the actions of people in the mass; and it also provided a convenient term for the description of the practice of
public opinion control. At first the word *propaganda* was applied to any organization that set out to propagate a doctrine;
then it was used to describe the doctrine itself, and finally it
came to mean the techniques employed to change opinions and
spread the doctrine. Thus was born the modern day usage of
"propaganda" (Qualter, 1962: 4).

In his study of propaganda, Qualter (1962: 4-5) points out that
the Catholic origins of the word gave it a sinister connotation in
the northern Protestant countries that it does not have in Southern Catholic countries. He cites an English encyclopedist of the
mid-nineteenth century, W. T. Brande, as saying of Gregory's organization: "Derived from this celebrated society the name
propaganda is applied in modern political language as a term of
reproach to secret associations for the spread of opinions and
principles which are viewed by most governments with horror
and aversion." This concept, as we have seen in the first chapter,
continues to cloud the discussion of propaganda.

After the development of the printing press, and the examples of its judicious use in the Reformation, the adoption of
propaganda techniques became a normal part of the strategies
devised by those seeking to control or manipulate others. Now
all major conflicts in society, whether they were religious or territorial, provided an opportunity for the contesting forces to utilize whatever techniques they could find for disseminating
propagandistic information. As an example, both sides in the
Thirty Years' War (1618-1648), that titanic struggle waged all
over Germany by competing religious forces, turned out massive quantities of leaflets, pamphlets, and line drawings, including vicious caricatures of the religious and secular leaders. A
new development of some importance in this conflict was the
printing of posters from copper plates, which made possible a
much wider distribution than was possible from woodcuts. Both

sides engaged in writing about the atrocities that the other had committed (a technique widely used even today), while the roving bands of uncontrolled soldiers produced printed materials warning towns of starvation if they resisted and promising booty to those who joined with them. Historians have noted about the Thirty Years' War that in spite of the low level of literacy, all classes of the population were reached by one or more of the various propaganda techniques (Thomson, 1977: 81; Davison, 1971: 2).

THE EMERGENCE OF PROPAGANDA

The eighteenth century was a century of revolution, and much of the increasing political agitation as subject populations sought to march toward a greater degree of political freedom was fueled by the developments in printing and improved transportation. As the century progressed, so did the technology of printing and paper making, and with improved efficiency and speed in transportation, it was now possible to disseminate messages to increasingly wide audiences. The availability of printed materials provided an impetus for the increase in the rates of literacy among the general population of most countries, and written propaganda appeals became quite sophisticated in their appeal to the reader.

It is also interesting to note that the path to literacy has not always been a smooth progression, for at various times there have been political, economic, or social reasons for discouraging literacy in a society. Those in power may wish to prevent literacy as a means of controlling the flow of information; or there may be no real economic incentive to devote the time to acquiring literate skills; while the internal values of the society itself may not encourage the need to read and write in the majority of the population. As an example of the danger of generalizing about literacy, in certain countries women were not encouraged to become literate, whereas in others there were far more literate women than men (Graff, 1981).

The use of political cartoons and other visual material that established direct communication with the audience became quite common, and satirical prints were a staple part of most eighteenth-century propaganda campaigns. This was the age of

the great English graphic satirists and propagandists William
Hogarth (1697-1764), James Gillray (1757-1815), and Thomas
Rowlandson (1756-1827), whose drawings were sold to bolster
rival political activities or to make telling moral points for
their eager audiences. It was Gillray who became the most
obvious propagandist, devoting his entire output to creations of
social or political satire, many of which were circulated widely
throughout Europe and even in North America. King George
III— "Farmer George"—and his family suffered widely at
Gillray's hands; and after Gillray's conversion to conserva-
tism as a result of his dismay at the French Revolution, he
launched a long series of political attacks ridiculing Napolean
and the French, while glorifying John Bull and the common
Englishman.

Gillray's work was very influential on nineteenth-century political satirists such as the American Thomas Nast (1840-1902).
Nast was most famous for his crusade against the political machine of William Marcy Tweed in New York City. Tweed was reported to have said, "Stop them damn pictures. I don't care so
much about what the papers write about me. My constituents
can't read. But, damn it, they can see pictures" (Hess and
Kaplan, 1975: 13). This propaganda campaign has now become
a historical legend, and constitutes the most dramatic instance
of deliberate propagandistic cartooning in American politics.
However, Nast was only one of several American cartoonists
whose work was influential in shaping political opinions in an
age when journalism was not required to be objective, and politically biased reporting was normal.

THE AMERICAN REVOLUTION

Historians agree that the philosophical underpinnings of the
revolution of the American colonists against their British rulers
can be found in a variety of sources, most notably the series of
political writings beginning during the seventeenth century, including the work of John Locke (1632-1704)—especially his
Treatises on Government (1690), in which he refuted the divine
right of kings, and the absolutist theory of government. Written
in defense of the coming to the British throne of King William III, in the place of the deposed and beheaded James II,

these documents had a significant effect on subsequent political action in the American colonies. Essentially Locke suggested that the people are the ultimate sovereign, and that they always have the right to withdraw their support and overthrow the government if it fails to fulfill its trust. Such ideas had a profound influence on the writers and pamphleteers whose propagandistic work was so instrumental in helping to foment and sustain the energy of the American Revolution.

Bernard Bailyn (1967: vi-vii), in his important book *The Ideological Origins of the American Revolution*, notes,

> the American Revolution was above all else an ideological, constitutional, political struggle and not primarily a controversy between social groups undertaken to force changes in the organization of the society or the economy ... intellectual developments in the decade before Independence led to a radical idealization and conceptualization of the previous century and a half of American experience, and it was this intimate relationship between Revolutionary thought and the circumstances of life in Eighteenth-century America that endowed the Revolution with its peculiar force and made it so profoundly a transforming event.

The American colonists were remarkably literate and well informed on political matters; therefore the spread of ideas through the printed word was a major factor in the development of a revolutionary ideology. In particular, the ideas contained in Richard Price's *On Civil Liberty* (1776), which sold 60,000 copies in hardback and 120,000 unbound, and Thomas Paine's *Rights of Man* and *Common Sense*, which sold nearly as well, were widely distributed throughout the colonies (Wish, 1950: 193). Thomas Paine (1737-1809) can be considered to be the first great propagandist of the American Revolution, and George Washington claimed that *Common Sense*, an emotional pamphlet that contained persuasive arguments for independence from England, had been a powerful influence on the minds of many men. The son of a Quaker corset maker from Norfolk, England, Paine came to America in 1774 and worked for Benjamin Franklin editing the *Pennsylvania Journal*. Paine used a simple, forthright writing style, not unlike Luther's, and shocked his readers by his boldness, while also using wit and satire to bring opposing ideas into sharp ridicule. His appeals were equally balanced between the head and the heart, and he noted that his aim was to "fit the powers of thinking and the turn of the language to the subject, so as to bring out a clear conclusion that shall hit the point in question and nothing else."

The newspaper provided the major vehicle for the dissemination of propagandistic information, and there had been a steady development of these after 1740 despite various attempts to tax such periodicals by the British. No sooner did a newspaper close down than it would reappear under another name, and precisely because of this newspaper editors were willing to print inflammatory material, knowing that they could restart anytime they wished. Also, printing attacks on the colonial powers was sure to increase circulation among an audience primed to accept such information.

A classic example of newspaper propaganda was the so-called Boston Massacre, which took place in 1770. British troops had been quartered in Boston for a year and a half, against the wishes of the citizens, and they were forced to face continuous harassment, a situation that was not helped by the historical aloofness of British troops toward the colonists. On March 5, 1770, a crowd looking for trouble started pelting snowballs, sticks of wood, and oyster shells at ten soldiers outside the Boston customshouse, daring the soldiers to fire. Eventually they did fire, and eleven of the unarmed rioters were injured, four of them fatally (a fifth died later). This event provided the impetus for numerous propaganda attacks on the British in which the facts of the event were totally blown out of proportion or exaggerated to emphasize British tyranny. The most famous of these attacks was Paul Revere's engraving, which, masquerading as a realistic picture of the event, was in fact a political cartoon deliberately created as propaganda for the anti-British element. Revere's engraving included a sign "Butcher's Hall" above the British customshouse, and interestingly he also changed the race of one of the victims, Crispus Attacks, who was, in reality, a towering black man. The cartoon was considered to be so inflammatory that when the soldiers were brought to trial, their lawyer warned the jury to not be swayed by drawings that add "wings to fancy" (Hess and Kaplan, 1968: 55). This cartoon was widely reprinted in the colonial press, and was followed by other Revere efforts including an engraving of four coffins, above which were the initials of the American dead.

The political cartoon proved to be a potent propaganda weapon throughout the Revolutionary period. As early as 1754, Benjamin Franklin had drawn his famous snake, severed into eight pieces to symbolize the separate colonies, with the legend "Join, or Die." This was the first cartoon to appear in an American newspaper. Published first on May 9, within a month it had been reprinted by virtually every newspaper on the continent. Although the snake was ridiculed by those loyal to the British side, the serpent won out in the end, and in his equally famous cartoon James Gillray showed the defeated British camp completely surrounded by a large rattlesnake.

There was a macabre fascination with the symbology of death in American political cartoons, as we have noted with Paul Revere's work. The most obvious example took place on October 31, 1765, when eight newspapers being shut down as a result of the imposition of the notorious Stamp Act, used black mourning border and symbols from tombstones on their front pages to symbolize their death. William Bradford's *Pennsylvania Journal* included the masthead motto, "EXPIRING: In hopes of a Resurrection to Life again." The association of death with the lack of freedom was a simple one for the colonials to grasp, and as individual freedoms were restricted by the British powers these were symbolized as "deaths." The restriction of the freedom of the press was a particularly galling one for the Americans, as this was the chief means of dissemination of both political and commercial information.

Samuel Adams was considered to be the chief architect of the anti-British propaganda activities, and he based all of his plans on the achievement of five main objectives: The aims of the revolution needed to be justified; the advantages of the victory needed to be advertised; the masses needed to be aroused to action by creating hatred for the enemy; logical arguments from the opposition needed to be neutralized; and all issues needed to be stated in clear black and white terms to ensure that even the common laborer could understand (Emery and Emery, 1984: 68-69). Adams devoted his life to the Revolutionary cause and became known as the "master of the puppets" because of his ability to orchestrate and manipulate others. Nor was he the most scrupulous individual, and many of his numerous attacks on the British, printed under a variety of names, painted the actions of governors, customs men, and judges in the darkest possible colors.

Adams was also a master of organization, helping to elect men who were sympathetic to his cause, and procuring the passage of resolutions that he favored. Operating from his base as a journalist with the *Boston Gazette*, Adams put together his Committee of Correspondence in 1772, and this group became the propaganda organization for the Revolution. He had his agents cover every important meeting and gathering to collect "news" that was immediately relayed back to Adams's central committee, where the information was processed and disseminated to the appropriate areas.

Perhaps his greatest individual propaganda coup was the organization of the Boston Tea Party, which symbolized the opposition to the Tea Act of 1773, although he took no personal part in the dumping of the tea into Boston Harbor. The incident was a classic example of provocation, which was turned into a major item of propaganda when the British predictably retaliated, as Adams knew they would, by the passing of the Boston Port Bill which closed the harbor and ruined trade. This just served to increase the hostility of the colonists, particularly after more troops were dispatched to the city; the stage for open revolt was being carefully set. Eventually it would come at Concord in 1775, when the British troops sent to confiscate weapons and ammunition stored by the skeleton colonial army engaged in a skirmish that eventually led to a full-scale war. It was also this incident that served as the background to another great American legend—Paul Revere's famous ride to warn the inhabitants of Concord, "The British are coming! The British are coming!"

During the Revolutionary War itself incidents such as the skirmish in Lexington were turned into major victories, and events such as Paul Revere's ride took on an almost supernatural stature. Adams, Benjamin Franklin, Thomas Jefferson, and even George Washington were skilled propagandists who tried to instill into the colonists a belief that not only was their cause right, but that their "native" skills were more than a match for the trained soldiers and mercenaries of the British army. Wash-

ington had Tom Paine's *American Crisis* read to his troops; words
written on a drumhead that have survived through the centuries
as inspiration in the darkest times in a nation's history:

> These are the times that try men's souls. The summer soldier and
> the sunshine patriot will, in this crisis, shrink from the service of
> his country. . . . Tyranny, like hell, is not easily conquered; yet we
> have this consolation with us, that the harder the conflict the
> more glorious the triumph. What we obtain too cheap, we es-
> teem too lightly [Emery and Emery, 1984: 82].

Written on December 19, 1776, these words were broadcast
widely during the difficult period in the early days of World War
II. It is also to Washington's and Paine's credit that a week after
hearing those inspirational words, the frozen and tattered colonial forces won a solid victory in Trenton.

Jefferson was a master propaganda strategist, with his draft
of the *Declaration of Independence* one of the great propaganda statements in all of history. Based upon a combination of
the ancient Greek and Roman philosophy of the rationalist
"laws of nature" earlier expounded by Locke, and the modern
philosophy of a secular natural law derived from Isaac New-
ton's scientific work, Jefferson was able to write a document in
which he emphatically declared, "We hold these truths to be
self-evident, that all men are created equal." Dropping all pretense at the fiction that a good king had been misled by evil advisors, Jefferson listed a long series of charges against King
George III, and suggested that because all appeals for redress
had been rebuffed, there was now no alternative but to "alter or
abolish" a government destructive of the principles of freedom.
The *Declaration* thus became the legal and philosophical
justification for the Revolution sought by Adams as one of his
objectives.

Benjamin Franklin also proved to be an instinctual master of
propaganda, using his talents as journalist, scientist, and diplomat to great advantage. In his role as diplomat he was assigned
to the French Court to plead the colonist's case. Dressing in a fur
hat and openly wearing spectacles, he became a living symbol
of the unsophisticated nobility of the New World seeking to free
itself from its feudal masters. His portrait began to appear on a
wide range of popular culture objects, from snuff boxes to

chamber pots, and his company was eagerly sought by scientists, politicians, and fashionable ladies whose company he revelled in. Going out of his way to promote his new status as a cult figure, he used these contacts to enormous advantage, pleading for both financial and military assistance in the fight against the British, and he was so successful that his personal popularity endured in France for many generations.

In his role as a journalist, Franklin had of course many years of experience both as an editor and as what we would today call a "publicist," having promoted a wide variety of schemes and ideas during his lifetime. He was particularly famous for his series of *Poor Richard Almanacs*, which contained a collection of maxims and proverbs culled from throughout the world's literature and given a pragmatic American flavor—"Early to bed, early to rise, makes a man healthy, wealthy and wise!" He became a master of both white and black propaganda during the Revolutionary War. He published *The Sale of the Hessians*, which dealt with the British press gangs in Germany forcibly recruiting mercenaries, and later was responsible for a fake issue of the *Boston Independent* in which the British appeared to be boasting of scalp-hunting. (Thompson, 1977: 87). In many respects, Franklin was a man ahead of his time, including his grasp of the rudiments of the psychology of modern propaganda techniques.

Once the Revolutionary War was over, the young nation was faced with developing its own propaganda campaigns to endure its commercial and political survival in the face of a skeptical world. All the trappings of rampant patriotic nationalism were required to give the newcomer a clear identity of its own, separate from the mother country, and thus were created the military uniforms, the flags, the patriotic songs and slogans, and the diplomatic stances such as the Monroe Doctrine, which proclaimed the United States sphere of interest in the New World. The development and international publicity attendant upon the framing of the "democratic" Constitution was perhaps the greatest propaganda vehicle of all for gaining the attention of the rest of the world. Eventually the "image" of the United States would be most successfully propagandized through its industrial and commercial achievements, together with the enormous output of material from its developing mass communication industries.

THE FRENCH REVOLUTION AND NAPOLEON

The French Revolution was a complex political event that has had wide political and philosophical implications for the course of modern Western history. Taking their inspiration from the American patriots' revolution against their colonial masters, the French overthrew their despotic monarchy in an attempt to establish an entirely new form of government. Such action meant denying the concept of the "divine right of kings" and overturning the "natural order," and required a major shift in the philosophical underpinnings of French society. In order to accomplish this change the leaders of the revolution resorted to a massive propaganda campaign, the purpose of which was to "sell" these new ideas and the resulting alterations in the structure of French society and culture.

By 1788 there was a well-developed newspaper readership in France, and pamphlets were appearing at the rate of 25 a week; this reached a climax of information in 1789 when more than sixty new newspapers were started. Although much of the information offered was contradictory, the tone was becoming steadily more radical and critical of the monarchy and government. Many of the critics were the skilled propagandists known as the *Encyclopedists*, who had worked on Diderot's famous compendium of human knowledge. The key events of the eventual revolution were themselves all carefully orchestrated pageants of propaganda. The storming of the Bastille—the dreaded symbol of oppression full of tortured prisoners—has remained with us until today as an archetypical image when, in fact, the prison was almost empty, containing only seven individuals. Further, the destruction of the building (which took place two days after the "storming") has assumed mythical proportions. Total demolition was still incomplete in 1792. However, the destruction of the physical edifice was symbolic of the overthrow of the old regime.

The adoption of specific forms of dress was a major propaganda device during the ebb and flow of the course of the French Revolution, as were other symbolic devices. The national colors of red, white and blue were seen everywhere, as was the Phrygian stocking cap and the tricolor sash. Crowds were manipulated by fireworks displays, the burning of effigies of hated politicians and aristocrats, and especially patriotic music, where the great theme of the *Marseillaise* remains even today a stirring tribute to the power of musical propaganda. The Revolution even had its own official propagandist artist, the great Jacques Louis David (1748-1825), whose works had been an incitement to revolution before 1789 and who served in this capacity through the reign of Napoleon. David was far more than a painter, directing the artistic affairs of the new Republic, until he too fell out of favor at the time of the downfall of Robespierre in 1794. He was later restored to his former glory by Napoleon for whom he created a very specific "imperial" image. David's style utilized a sense of realism that sought to create art for the middle classes, and was entirely appropriate to the revolutionary context of the times. His work continues to serve as an inspiration to later political regimes seeking to glorify their exploits through works of art.

The French revolutionaries used a wide variety of media to export their doctrines throughout the world at the end of the eighteenth century. W. Phillips Davison (1971: 2) points out that even their style of dress was worn by revolutionary sympathizers throughout Europe. This form of symbolic propaganda was countered when "a conservative German prince, the Langraf of Kassel, seeking to combat these subversive styles, ordered that all prisoners be dressed in them and sent out to sweep the streets." This provides an excellent example of counterpropaganda. Despite small victories of this sort, the French Revolution was so devastating to the existing social and political structure of Europe that entirely new forms emerged, and these required that new myths and heroes be created to provide the necessary social and cultural cohesion.

It was out of the chaos of the destruction of the old French society that the "man on the white horse" emerged—Napoleon Bonaparte, who must be considered one of the great masters of the use of propaganda in history. He recognized the power of manipulation of symbols early in his career as an army officer, and throughout his life he learned to glory in his victories while placing the blame for his failures at the feet of others. Like Caesar before him, he wrote self-congratulatory accounts of his military exploits, and created for himself a swashbuckling image of the dashing commander. Napoleon was among the first of the modern propagandists to understand the need to convince the population that the rights of the individual were less important than the willingness to sacrifice one's life for emperor and nation. In this way he was able to gather large, populist armies even in the worst of times.

The visual image of the romantic hero was created with the assistance of David, who helped design the clothes, hairstyle, and other accoutrements that have come down to us today as an unmistakable symbol of the diminutive French leader. His portrait appeared everywhere, accompanied by his ubiquitous eagles, and he took the lead in designing a specific form of imperial architecture that was a mixture of Roman, Etruscan, and Egyptian styles—all great empires of the past. Triumphal arches and massive victory columns were erected, again evoking images of the Roman Caesars.

It was at his coronation at Notre Dame Cathedral on December 2, 1804, that Napoleon achieved one of his great propaganda triumphs—when he took the imperial crown from the hands of Pope Pius VII, and placed it on his own head, symbolizing that he owed allegiance to no one, and that he was a self-made emperor. The imperial regime that followed his coronation had its own symbols, with the Roman eagle figuring prominently above the tricolor flag, and the use of princely titles was brought back for members of Napoleon's family.

Napoleon quickly learned to exploit the power of the press to his advantage as a political weapon, devising new propaganda techniques that caught his opponents by surprise. Like most European governments of the time, he maintained domestic censorship, but he went out of his way to plant pro-French items in foreign language newspapers on the continent. Several papers were even founded by the French in occupied German territories, while in Paris there appeared a newspaper called *The Argus of London*, which was allegedly edited by an Englishman, but was, in actuality, produced by the French Foreign Office. Supposedly written from an English viewpoint, the newspaper attacked the "war mongering journals" back in London, and was widely distributed throughout the West Indies and to British prisoners of war in places such as Verdun (Thomson, 1977: 97). Napoleon also made wide use of leaflets distributed before his invading armies; he projected a promise of French "liberty" to countries such as Italy where oppression had been the normal political way of life, and a hint of freedom was bound to create widespread excitement. Even the Napoleonic Code, an easily translated one-volume of law, was an impressive demonstration of revolutionary imperial power that could be readily transported to other European countries.

One of his major internal propaganda weapons was the use of the plebiscite, in which the population were asked to vote on an issue, the outcome of which was already clearly decided, and then publicizing the results as an unequivocal indication of his popularity. As an example, in May 1802, the French people were asked to vote on the following question: "Shall Napoleon Bonaparte be consul for life?" The result was an overwhelming majority of 3,500,000 votes in favor against less than 10,000 opposed. Two years later he became emperor when another plebiscite approved the change. The use of such predetermined plebiscites has been a favorite technique of modern dictators and political regimes such as Hitler and the current South African government, who are eager to give international recognition to the apparent popularity of their internal programs.

So successful were Napoleon's propaganda techniques in creating his imperial image that his legend became even stronger after his death in 1821. Hundreds of books appeared, some attacking, but most praising him, and finally in December 1840 his body was returned from the remote island of St. Helena to a magnificent funeral in Paris. Nearly a million people watched as his remains were conveyed through the Arc de Triomphe to his specially built tomb in the Place de l'Etoile. He left behind an enormous legacy of important institutions, such as his legal Code, the French internal administrative system, the national banking system, the military academies and universities, and, most important of all, a dramatic symbol of French might and glory so deeply ingrained into Western popular culture that it continues to have useful propaganda value even today.

PROPAGANDA IN THE NINETEENTH CENTURY

The main development in propaganda techniques during the nineteenth century was the increase in the speed in which messages could be conveyed to increasingly urban-based audiences. The importance of printing, especially after the introduction of steam and later electricity, created new opportunities for refining propaganda as a political and economic weapon. As each new form of mass communication found an audience, it was immediately seized upon as a vehicle for conveying propaganda. Thus newspapers, then magazines, and later motion pictures were each used by propagandists in their attempts to capture the public's attention.

The development of democratic political institutions was the single most important impetus to the growth of the use of propaganda in the nineteenth and twentieth centuries. As Qualter (1962: 33) so eloquently states it,

> Even those whose attitude toward the role of public opinion in politics did not change found that of necessity they had to learn the mechanics of peaceful persuasion by propaganda. With an extended franchise and an increasing population it was becoming too expensive to do anything else. Where at one time voters could be bought, they now had to be persuaded. Politicians had, therefore, to become interested in propaganda.

It was the combination of the demands created by democratic political institutions and the increasing sophistication of propaganda techniques used in warfare that marked the emergence of an awareness of propaganda as a ubiquitous force in the late nineteenth and early twentieth centuries. We must also not overlook the increasing importance of advertising as an integral part of economic development and the emergence of consumerism, for many of the techniques developed to persuade customers to purchase products were later adopted by other propagandists. One significant aspect of twentieth-century propaganda is the symbiotic relationship between advertising and other forms of propaganda, particularly as techniques for reaching audiences become more sophisticated and reliable. Propaganda began to emerge as a modern force in the nineteenth century; it has become an integral part of the social, political, and economic life of the twentieth century.

3

PROPAGANDA INSTITUTIONALIZED

The late nineteenth and early twentieth centuries were periods of great expansion of propaganda activities. The growth of the mass media and improvements in transportation led to the development of mass audiences for propaganda, increasing its use and effectiveness. Each of the mass media — print, the movies, radio, and then television — contributed its unique qualities to new techniques of propaganda. Radio, in particular brought into existence the possibility of continuous international propaganda, whereas television has increased the problem of "cultural imperialism," where one nation's culture is imposed upon another nation's. This has led to a call for a New World Information Order by many Third World Countries.

The nineteenth and twentieth centuries saw an unprecedented explosion in the field of communication and transportation. Initially, the limitation on both the speed of communication and the difficulties experienced in transportation in an age of rough roads and horse-drawn traffic severely restricted the flow of information between geographically separated points. Even within the growing urban centers, which were now a common manifestation of the push toward industrialization, there were problems in circulating and controlling information to a large number of people within a short period of time. The newspapers and commercial newssheets of the early nineteenth century did not have wide circulations, and despite the increase in the literacy rate among the middle classes, books were not yet as widely available for the general population as they would be later in the century. Public oratory, though important, also had inherent handicaps of size of audience and irreproducibility. The result was that rumor and gossip continued to be an important means of maintaining communication links between groups and individuals wishing to circulate specific messages.

The major problem with rumor as a means of communication is that it lacks the necessary control to ensure that the message content is not distorted. As Shibutani (1966: 9) explains, "Rumor content is not viewed as an object to be transmitted but as something that is shaped, reshaped, and reinforced in a succession of communicative acts. . . . In this sense a rumor may be regarded as something that is constantly being constructed; when the communicative activity ceases, the rumor no longer exists." Clearly this is not a useful means of disseminating propaganda; it may work splendidly if the rumor continues to take the direction intended, but rumors have a life of their own, and they could just as easily turn on the propagandist. (We have recently witnessed the difficulties that one of the world's largest manufacturers of household products, the Procter and Gamble Company, has had fighting a rumor that their trademark of the moon and stars is not meant to be a satanic symbol, despite the enormous sum of money they spend on advertising trying to create a specific public image. Ultimately, because of their failure to halt the economic damage caused by the continuance of this rumor, the company has decided to change its trademark.) Before the practice of propaganda on the mass scale could proceed, new forms of communication, which provided a greater degree of message control and targeting of audiences, had to emerge. This is exactly what did happen in the nineteenth and twentieth centuries, and propaganda became increasingly more sophisticated, widely practiced, and accepted as part of modern society.

Plate 1: Benjamin Franklin's famous cartoon in support of a "Plan of Union" for the colonies. It first appeared in the *Pennsylvania Journal* of May 9, 1754, and was based on the superstition that a snake that had been severed would come back to life if the pieces were put together before sunset. Each segment represents one colony. This cartoon was revived at the time of the Stamp Act Crisis in 1765, and again at the start of the American Revolution in 1774. (p. 53).

Plate 2: Although Franklin's cartoon had been ridiculed and parodied, in October 1776, when General Cornwallis surrendered at Yorktown, an English cartoon by James Gillray, who opposed British policies in the American colonies, showed the defeated British camp completely encircled by a rattlesnake. (p. 53).

Plate 3: A facsimile of the front page of *The Pennsylvania Journal* of October 31, 1765, showing the black mourning border and other emblems of death symbolizing the death of freedom of the press as a result of the imposition of the Stamp Act. (p. 53).

Plate 4: Paul Revere's famous engraving, named "Boston Massacre," from March 5, 1770. While masquerading as a depiction of the actual events, this was in reality a propagandistic cartoon. The words "Butcher's Hall" have been added above the British House. (p. 54). (Photo courtesy: Metropolitan Museum of Art.)

Plate 5: "A Group of Vultures Waiting for the Storm to 'Blow Over'"—"Let Us Prey." It was Thomas Nast's cartoons such as these which caused Boss Tweed so much anguish, and eventually resulted in his downfall. First published in *Harper's Weekly*, September 23, 1971. (p. 50).

REMEMBER · THE LUSITANIA!

One mother lost all her three young children, one six years, one aged four, and the third a babe in arms, six months old. She herself lives, and held up the three of them in the water, all the time shrieking for help. When rescued by a boat party the two eldest were dead. Their room was required on the boat, and the mother was brave enough to realise it. "Give them to me," she cried. "Give them to me, my bonnie wee things. I will bury them. They are mine to bury as they were mine to keep."

With her hair streaming down her back and her form shaking with sorrow, she took hold of each little one from the rescuers and reverently placed it into the water again, and the people in the boat wept with her as she murmured a little sobbing prayer to the great God above.

But her cup of sorrow was not yet completed. For just as they were landing, her third and only child died in her arms.

BERLIN, MAY 8.

Hundreds of telegrams have been sent to Admiral von Tirpitz congratulating him.

* * *

ARTICLE IN COLOGNE GAZETTE.

The news will be received by the German people with unanimous satisfaction, since it proves to England and the whole world that Germany is quite in earnest in regard to her submarine warfare.

* * *

ARTICLE IN KOLNISCHE VOLKSZEITUNG.

With joyful pride we contemplate the latest deed of our Navy and it will not be the last.

* * *

NEW YORK, MAY 8.

Riotous scenes of jubilation took place last evening amongst Germans in the German clubs and restaurants. Many Germans got drunk as the result of toasting "Der Tag."

ENLIST TO-DAY.

Plate 6: A poster which appeared a week after the passenger liner Lusitania was sunk by a German U-boat on May 7, 1915 with a loss of 1,198 lives, 128 of them American.

RED CROSS OR IRON CROSS?

WOUNDED AND A PRISONER
OUR SOLDIER CRIES FOR WATER.

THE GERMAN "SISTER"
POURS IT ON THE GROUND BEFORE HIS EYES.

THERE IS NO WOMAN IN BRITAIN
WHO WOULD DO IT.

THERE IS NO WOMAN IN BRITAIN
WHO WILL FORGET IT.

Plate 7: An anti-German poster showing a supposed atrocity. Note that the Kaiser is depicted approving of the nurse's actions, thus linking him directly with German atrocities. (pp. 129-130).

Plate 8: A highly emotional and exaggerated poster published in the period after the First World War. It was propaganda such as this which antagonized many Britons and made them suspicious of later attempts to describe the atrocities of the Nazis. (pp. 129-130).

Plate 9: "We Can, We Must, and We Will!" A cartoon by Charles H. Sykes which first appeared in the Philadelphia *Evening Public Ledger* in June, 1918. This cartoon aimed at mobilizing the American labor force was circulated by the National Committee of Patriotic Societies as part of its work to enlist cartoonists for the war effort. (pp. 127-128).

Plate 10: A poster for *The Eternal Jew* exhibition held in the German Museum on Munich in late 1937. This is an archetypal caricature of a Jew showing off shekels in the right hand, and a map of the Soviet Union and a whip in the left. It did not seem to concern the German propagandists that these were contradictory symbols. A vicious film based upon this exhibition was released by the Nazis in 1940. (pp. 139-141).

Plate 11: This safe conduct pass, deliberately printed in an official and formal manner to appeal to German soldiers even in the midst of chaos and defeat, was widely used by surrendering troops on the Western Front in 1944-45. It is signed by Supreme Commander General Dwight D. Eisenhower, and was scrupulously honored by the allied forces. (p. 142).

Plate 12: After the Japanese executed captured American airmen who had bombed Tokyo on April 18, 1942, President Roosevelt referred to the "barbarous execution by the Japanese government." This cartoon by Sy Moyer portrays the enemy as an ape-like barbarian, a familiar device used by both sides. (p. 119).

THE NEW AUDIENCE

The introduction of new forms of communication also created a new historical phenomenon — the mass audience. For the first time in history, the means now existed to disseminate information to large, heterogeneous groups of people within a relatively short period of time. With the introduction of the *New York Sun* in 1833, the era of the "penny press" was begun; and the entire shape of news was altered. Whereas the earlier commercial press had disdained much interest in everyday events, the penny press deliberately sought to cultivate the audience's interest in local events and everyday occurrences. Also, as Schudson (1978: 30) notes, "The new journalism of the penny press . . . ushered in a new order, a shared social universe in which 'public' and 'private' would be redefined. . . . With the growth of cities and of commerce, everyday life acquired a density and a fascination quite new."

The formation of these new mass publics came about at the same time as democracy as a political process was gradually being introduced into many countries; and although the United States had been founded on entirely democratic principles, the young nation was still struggling to internalize exactly how this rather novel experiment of "government by the people" would work in practice. Historians have often labeled the 1830s the era of "Jacksonian Democracy" because of the emergence of a clear populist sentiment at this time. It is against this historical-political background that we must view the introduction of the mass press. Schudson (1978: 12-60) after examining this important historical event suggests that the penny press was a response to what he calls the emergence of "democratic market society," created by the growth of mass democracy, a marketplace ideology, and an urban society. He notes, "The penny press expressed and built the culture of a democratic market society, a culture which had no place for social or intellectual deference. This was the groundwork on which a belief in facts and a distrust of the reality, or objectivity, of 'values' could thrive" (Schudson, 1978: 60).

As the newspaper assumed a larger and more consistent role in the dissemination of information, the public came to depend upon such daily information to a much greater degree than ever before. There were several reasons for this. First, there were, as yet, few competing voices besides the remaining commercial newsletters and the occasional book. Second, even those competing news sources could not match the newspaper for timeliness and consistency. Third, newspapers made no pretense at being politically neutral in this early period, and therefore they appealed directly to the biases of their readers. Fourth, the demands of a democratic political system required that the electorate have a continuous knowledge of the workings of the political system, and only newspapers were able to provide this continuity. Fifth, the average working-class or middle-class citizen did not have the time nor the organization at his or her disposal to keep up with political or economic developments, and therefore was forced to rely upon the newsgathering abilities of the newspaper. Last, the newspaper provided more than just political and economic information; it also offered entertainment and local news that created a sense of social cohesion in an increasingly fragmented world. The reader was made aware that he or she was part of a wider world sharing and reacting to the news.

It was the existence of this shared experience that made it possible for propaganda to work, for propaganda can only be successful when it is targeted toward specific groups, without having to diffuse the message through a variety of channels. The gradual increase in importance of the mass media throughout the nineteenth and into the twentieth century not only brought into existence viable and reachable publics, but the media themselves began to assume the mantle of "expertness." This proved to be a potent combination, for now the media were both collectors and disseminators of information, and this placed them in a powerful position to act as the channel for all types of persuasive messages, from advertising to the most blatant forms of propaganda.

THE EMERGENCE OF MASS SOCIETY

What was more important than the real power of these new media was their perceived power, for politicians and others reacted to what they assumed this power to be. This was an age when very little was known about the psychology of communication, and it was naturally assumed that the audience would react in a homogeneous manner to whatever stimulus was exposed to them. Much of the concern for the power of the media stemmed from the growing body of sociological literature in the nineteenth century that suggested that the shift from a rural society to an urbanized, industrial society was creating something known as "mass society." Leon Bramson (1961: 27-44) notes that European sociological pessimism on the subject of mass society stems from the nineteenth-century notion of the breakdown of the traditional community. Thus European sociology of this period had a preoccupation with "social disorganization" and "social disintegration" caused by the emergence of an industrialized and urbanized, large-scale society. The end result is that

this perspective of 19th century sociology is recapitulated in the 20th century theory of mass society, particularly in its view of the past. By contrast with the anarchic individualism of life in the cities, the impersonality of social relationships, the peculiar mental qualities fostered by urban life with its emphasis on money and abstraction, theorists of mass society idealized the social aspects of the traditional society of the later middle ages [Bramson, 1961: 32].

The role of the emerging mass media in this shift from the traditional type to the modern type of society was seen as crucial, for it was through the popular media that the public was acquiring new ideas. It was further suggested that the media encouraged a cultural blandness that satisfied public tastes at the lowest possible level, and thereby severely hampered attempts to elevate humankind to its full potential. Further, from the perspective of the socialist and communist thinkers whose ideas were beginning to gain some credence at the turn of the century, the mass media were seen as the handmaidens of the capitalist system, lulling the populace into a political lethargy that prevented them from realizing their true plight as victims of the system. The dominance of the negative concept of mass society in intellectual circles in the first part of the twentieth century was a salient factor in shaping the attitudes and subsequent attempts to control the perceived power of the mass media. It is in this intellectual context that subsequent developments in propaganda must be examined, for early propaganda efforts seemed to justify all the fears and doubts surrounding these new channels of information, and their potentially dangerous ability to manipulate their audiences.

One of the major concerns that emerged at the end of the nineteenth century was for the future of the democratic process itself in the face of the possibilities of manipulation of the voter's mind through propaganda. The potential for such manipulation led many theorists to even reject democracy as a viable political system. Qualter (1962: 50-51) cites the case of the English philosopher Graham Wallas, who in his book *Human Nature in Politics* (1908) suggested that men were not entirely governed by reason, but often acted on "affection and instinct" and that these could be deliberately aroused and directed in a way that would eventually lead to some course of action desired by the manipulator. Qualter (1962: 51) notes of Wallas,

> Given a greatly expanded franchise, with its corollary of the need to base authority on the support of public opinion, political society invited the attention of the professional controller of public opinion. When to the demand for new methods of publicity there were added revolutionary advances in the techniques of communication, and the latest discoveries in social psychology, mankind had to fear more than ever "the cold-blooded manipulation of popular impulse and thought by professional politicians."

Graham Wallas was but one of many concerned with the future of democracy in a world in which propagandistic manipulation seemed to be increasing. Others such as Walter Lippmann (1922), Karl Mannheim (1929-1931), and Harold D. Lasswell (1927; 1939) have each taken the position that manipulation of the masses is possible because individuals tend to react to emotional impulses rather than sober analytic statements. As the various forms of mass communication emerged into their full institutional structures, such views would increase, particularly after their apparent spectacular success in World War I.

THE NEW MEDIA

Each of the major forms of mass communication that emerged in the nineteenth and twentieth centuries have their own peculiar set of strengths and weaknesses. What they had in common was their ability to establish direct contact with the public in such a manner as to bypass the traditional socializing institutions such as the church, the school, the family, and the political system. Because of this historically unique and very significant ability, the media were feared by those concerned with the moral welfare of society, but welcomed by those who sought to use this "direct contact" in order to present their own cases to the mass audience, whether it be an advertiser trying to convince the public to purchase a new product or a politician "selling" policies.

The Print Media

We have already noted earlier in this chapter how significant the penny press was in the early part of the nineteenth century in the creation of the first modern media publics. Throughout the rest of the century and into the twentieth, the mass press continued to grow both in size and in significance as a purveyor of information and as a shaper of ideas. During the fight for abolition of slavery and the American Civil War, newspapers on both sides played significant roles as propaganda agents, and in the postwar years the newspaper business grew spectacularly. As Emery and Emery (1984: 231) note,

Between 1870 and 1900, the United States doubled its population and tripled the number of its urban residents. During the same 30 years the number of daily newspapers quadrupled and the number of copies sold each day increased almost sixfold. . . . The number of English-language, general-circulation dailies increased from 489 in 1870 to 1967 in 1900. Circulation totals for all daily publications rose from 2.6 million copies in 1870 to 15 million in 1900.

Another feature of the last half of the nineteenth century was the spectacular rise of magazines as important sources of information. Spurred on by cheap postal rates established by Congress in 1879, magazines such as *Ladies' Home Journal* and *Saturday Evening Post* soon had circulations that exceeded half a million. Smaller "literary" publications, such as *Harper's Weekly* (1857), *Atlantic Monthly* (1857), and *The Nation*, although limited in circulation, nevertheless had a profound influence on public opinion. There were many other magazines of political and social opinion that also contributed to the shaping of the public agenda on issues such as poverty, immigration, business corruption, and public health. Magazines were and continue to be a very personalized medium, creating strong reader identification and association with the editorial tone and content. It was in magazines that most of the political and social "muckraking" took place.

By the beginning of the twentieth century the major daily newspapers in the United States had clearly established themselves as leaders and shapers of public opinion on a wide range of issues. This was the era of "yellow journalism" in which the major New York dailies, Joseph Pulitizer's *World* and William Randolph Hearst's *Journal*, competed with each other for the coveted circulation by seeing who could cover or create the most spectacular news. One famous example of the increasing potential of the press to create propaganda in this period was the battleship Maine incident. As a result of their direct intervention in a series of incidents fomenting the Cuban insurrection (1895-1898) the major daily newspapers in America have been accused of having created an extreme war psychosis in the minds of the American people, leading up to the mysterious sinking of the battleship Maine in Havana harbor in 1898, and the subsequent Spanish-American War of the same year. There has never been a satisfactory answer as to why the Maine sunk, but this did not stop Hearst's New York *Journal* from offering a $50,000 reward for information leading to the arrest of the alleged criminals, while the paper's headlines screamed for war (Wilkerson, 1932; Wisan, 1934). Once war had been declared, the newspapers spent enormous sums of money covering it, with the *Journal* proclaiming, "How do you like the *Journal's* war?" (Emery and Emery, 1984: 295).

Although newspapers have declined in readership in the twentieth century, they continue to provide a continuous source of propaganda in our society. During both World Wars, newspapers were the major source of information for the general public, and as such were used for propaganda purposes rather extensively. Despite the significant inroads made by broadcast journalism, newspapers are still read for in-depth information and perspectives on news and events, and, as such, under the guise of both straight newsreporting and editorializing, they do carry propaganda messages. There is nothing in the Constitution of the United States that forces a newspaper publisher to be totally neutral and objective in reporting the news, and thus whether it be in clearly labeled editorial opinion, or the particular slant of an "innocent" newsreport, or in paid advertising, newspapers are a prime source of propaganda in our society. This is equally true for the large newsmagazines such as *Time* and *Newsweek* in which both the selection of the specific stories to be featured and the manner in which those stories are treated can be considered to be propaganda. Even an apparently harmless publication such as the *Reader's Digest* can, in fact, be carefully constructed to be a propaganda vehicle for the values and politics of the owner (Schreiner, 1977).

In 1979, more than $6 billion worth of books were sold in the United States (Coser et al., 1980: 59). Although books are still an important source of propaganda, they are somewhat limited in their circulation, and seldom have a mass audience. Nevertheless, they can and do have an impact far beyond their primary readership circle, as the opportunity to develop specific ideas in-depth makes the book a particularly potent source of propagandistic information. Throughout history books have played a very pivotal role in the shaping of ideas and attitudes on a large scale—certainly beyond their actual primary readership. The Bible, even for those who do not read it, continues to provide the source of social and cultural values that shapes a great portion of our lives, whereas books such as Charles Darwin's *Origin of the Species* (1859) or Harriet Beecher Stowe's *Uncle Tom's Cabin* (1852) were the sources of major conflicts in our society. Even closer to our present day, Rachel L. Carson's *Silent Spring* (1962) was really instrumental in gaining public attention for the damage done to the environment by pollution.

Although not deliberately propaganda, we cannot ignore the work of Sigmund Freud as an important factor in shaping twentieth-century thought about the nature of human beings. Unfortunately, one of the most significant propagandistic books in this century was largely ignored when it was first published. In fact, had the world taken Adolf Hitler's *Mein Kampf* (*My Struggle*) seriously in 1926, when it appeared in Germany, rather than waiting until the first English edition in 1939, the international diplomatic approach to Hitler's conquests throughout the 1930s might have been quite different.

The Movies

It is rather surprising that despite the enormous inherent appeal of the motion picture, this medium has never become the powerful propaganda vehicle that its critics feared it would be. In fact, it might be precisely because of its popularity as one of the world's great entertainment forms, rather than as a medium of conscious information dissemination, that it has failed to fulfill its initial promise as both an educator and as a channel for the propagandist. Of all the mass media, the motion picture has the greatest potential for emotional appeal to its audience, offering a deeper level of identification with the characters and action on the screen than found elsewhere in popular culture. The motion picture can also make audiences laugh, cry, sing, shout out loud, create sexual arousal, or fall asleep—in short, they have the ability to evoke an immediate emotional response seldom found in the other mass media. Yet systematic attempts by governments or other groups to use the motion picture as a channel for the delivery of propagandistic messages have not, on the whole, been very successful.

On the other hand, the motion picture has been extremely successful in influencing its audience in such areas as courting behavior, clothing styles, furniture and architectural design, speech mannerisms, and eating and drinking habits (Jowett, 1982). In these and other areas the motion picture has proven itself to be an excellent shaper of subtle psychological attitudes and can under the right circumstances be a potent source of social and cultural information. In his famous study of *Movies and Conduct* social psychologist Herbert Blumer (1933: 196-197), after examining hundreds of diaries kept by young moviegoers, noted,

> For many the pictures are authentic potrayals of life, from which they draw patterns of behavior, stimulation to overt conduct, content for a vigorous life of imagination, and ideas of reality. They are not merely a device for surcease; they are a form of stimulation . . . motion pictures are a genuine educational institution . . . in the truer sense of actually introducing him [the stu-

dent] to and acquainting him with a type of life which has immediate, practical and momentous significance.

Immediately after projected motion pictures were introduced in 1896, they were used for propaganda purposes in a variety of ways. Raymond Fielding (1972: 8) in his history of the newsreel recounts fake news films of the Dreyfus affair in France in 1896, while actual political events were also the subjects of early films, including fake footage of the charge up San Juan Hill, and the sinking of the Spanish Fleet in Santiago Bay in the Spanish-American War. The pure visual power of the motion picture can be seen in one of the first films to be made after the declaration of war against the Spanish. Made by Vitagraph studios, it was entitled *Tearing Down the Spanish Flag*, and simply showed a flagpole from which a Spanish flag was flying. The flag was abruptly torn down, and in its place an American flag was raised. In the words of Albert E. Smith, one of the founders of the Vitagraph Company, "Projected on a thirty-foot screen, the effect on audiences was sensational and sent us searching for similar subjects. . . . The people were on fire and eager for every line of news. . . . With nationalistic feeling at a fever pitch we set out to photograph what people wanted to see" (Fielding, 1972: 29-30).

The fear of the motion picture's power both to communicate and educate resulted in early and consistent attacks on it from all those institutions and individuals who had the most to lose from its inherent appeal. Thus throughout the world the clergy, social workers, educators, and politicians were all involved in trying to make the motion picture more responsive to their call for social control of this obtrusive new form of information (Jowett, 1976). In the United States the Supreme Court refused to allow the motion picture the right of free speech granted by the First Amendment to the Constitution. In the landmark case of *Mutual vs. Ohio* (1915), Justice McKenna, speaking for the unanimous court, noted that motion pictures were

> not to be regarded, nor intended to be regarded as part of the press of the country or as organs of public opinion. They are mere representations of events, of ideas and sentiments published or known; vivid, useful and entertaining, no doubt, but . . . capable of evil, having power for it, the greater because

of their attractiveness and manner of exhibition. (Jowett, 1976: 120).

Thus of all the various forms of mass communication that have been introduced into the United States, only the motion picture has been subjected to systematic legalized prior-censorship. This situation continued until the mid-1970s, at which time the Supreme Court began to strike down the various censorship restrictions against the medium (Randall, 1968).

During World War I there were crude attempts made to utilize the motion picture as a propaganda device, including such films as *The Kaiser, The Beast of Berlin*, and *My Four Years in Germany*, but the most important of these propaganda efforts, aimed at moulding public opinion in favor of the United States entering the war, was *Battle Cry of Peace* (1915) produced by J. Stuart Blackton (whose hand had earlier ripped down the Spanish flag in 1898). This film showed the Germans attacking New York by sea, and reducing the city to ruins, but it also had a reverse effect, in that the pacifist movement used the film to expose the war profiteers and armament manufacturers who would benefit from American entry into the war. Before 1916, most American films were decidedly pacifist in tone, reflecting the mood of the American people; as an example in *War Brides* (1916) the peace-loving heroine committed suicide rather than give birth to a future soldier. (Furhammer and Isaksson, 1971: 10). Once America declared war in 1917, encouraged by public sentiment there was a flurry of anti-German films.

All of the Allied countries made propaganda films, the British government going so far as to import the great American director D. W. Griffith to direct *Hearts of the World* (1918), featuring the Gish sisters in a plot that was set against authentic war-shattered backgrounds from the Western front. In the United States, the Committee on Public Information (CPI), formed by the government to become the propaganda agency for the war effort, worked with the film industry in making films with patriotic content, including offering suggestions for stories and military expertise and props as required by the studios. In Germany in 1917, Chief of Staff General Ludendorff sent a letter to the Imperial Ministry of war, in which he noted,

The war has demonstrated the superiority of the photograph and the film as means of information and persuasion. Unfortunately our enemies have used their advantage over us in this field so thoroughly that they have inflicted a great deal of damage. . . . For this reason it is of the utmost importance for a successful conclusion to the war that films should be made to work with the greatest possible effect wherever any German persuasion might still have any effect [Furhammer and Isaksson, 1971: 11].

By the time the German government got around to setting up its film propaganda arm the war was nearly over; but this same organization, Universium Film Aktiengesellschaft—UFA—would survive and thrive to become a major propaganda agency for the Nazis during the 1930s and through World War II.

The period between the two world wars was known as the "golden age" of the commercial cinema, as the medium achieved heights of popularity that had not been thought possible for a medium that had started out in cheap storefront nickelodeons. The Hollywood product dominated world screens as the European film studios were still recovering from their devastation from the war. Audiences were so used to seeing commercial escapist material that it was extremely difficult to get them to view anything that appeared to be educational. The only propaganda films that were ever seen in the commercial theaters were the often innocuous newsreels and the occasional documentary such as *Nanook of the North* (1926), which was a surprising commercial success despite the fact that it had originally been made as a propaganda film for a fur company. If audiences were being propagandized, then it was under the guise of entertainment, and they numbered in the hundreds of millions every week.

In 1928, the Motion Picture Research Council was given $200,000 by the philanthropic Payne Fund to conduct the most extensive research into the influence of the movies on American life ever undertaken. This research was conducted by a distinguished group of social scientists on a nationwide basis, and was aimed at determining the degrees of influence and effect of films upon children and adolescents. The research was carried out over a four-year period, 1929-1933, and was eventually published in ten volumes. The research itself became the center of a propaganda campaign when a popularized version of some of the research findings was published in the book entitled *Our Movie-Made Children* by journalist Henry James Forman in 1933.

Forman had been employed to simplify and in some cases distort the research so as to arouse public concern in favor of the establishment of a national film censorship commission. While this ploy did not work in the end, the Payne Fund Studies (usually as interpreted by Forman) were widely quoted in all types of media and formed the platform for the launching of many critical essays on the state of the motion picture industry (Jowett, 1976: 220-229).

It was in the Soviet Union that films were controlled more firmly by the political authorities than anywhere else in the world. The theme of revolution was fundamental to almost all Soviet films, with Lenin as the central figure. In order to achieve the maximum emotional impact, Soviet filmmakers developed a visual technique called "montage," in which the various film images were juxtaposed to create a specific response from the viewer. The idea was that the skill of the director could create a reality from the different pieces of film that would almost assault the visual sensibilities of the audience and achieve the desired psychological effect. The great Russian propaganda films such as Sergei Eisensteins's *Battleship Potemkin* (1925), Vsevolod Pudovkin's *Storm Over Asia* (1928), and Alexander Dovzhenko's *Earth* (1930) all used montage as a central technique for eliciting the proper audience response.

But even in the Soviet Union, despite the achievements of the filmmakers of the early revolutionary period, the authorities were not satisfied with the medium's role, and with the coming to power of Josef Stalin in the late 1920s the Soviet cinema began to concentrate on socialist realism. This meant that "all films were to be comprehensible to and appreciated by the millions, and their one aim was to be the glorification of the emerging Soviet state" (Isaksson and Furhammer, 1971: 20). As a result of this edict, Soviet films were drained of their vitality, and they only regained their original powers of propaganda in the mid-1930s after Hitler had come to power and several successful antifascist films were produced. These included Eisensteins's *Alexander Nevsky* (1938), which used the theme of a thirteenth-century battle as an obvious prophesy of what was to come. After the war, the Soviet film industry turned its attention to making blatant anti-American propaganda films up until the death of Stalin, at which time there was a change in tone. The

Soviet cinema continues to be a mixture of politics and art, and there is little pretense about the propagandistic goals. The enormous Hollywood film industry has never lent itself to overt propaganda on any grand scale, but there have been times when even the commercial filmmakers have used their entertainment medium for putting forward a specific idea. As an example, after several years of conspicuous silence, motivated no doubt by international marketing considerations and not wishing to alienate the important German market, Hollywood finally produced its first anti-Nazi film in 1939, more than seven years after Hitler had come to power. This film, *Confessions of a Nazi Spy,* was based upon the exploits of a former FBI agent who had cracked a spy ring inside the German-American Bund. Once war broke out in Europe in 1939, Hollywood countered with films such as *Devil Dogs of the Air, Here comes the Navy,* and *Miss Pacific Fleet,* which were deliberate recruiting films for the still neutral U.S. armed services. These became known as the "preparedness films" and they immediately aroused the suspicion and anger of those who did not wish to see the United States become involved in a European war.

In 1941 the isolationist senator from North Dakota, Gerald P. Nye, recognized the potential power of the movies in a famous radio speech when he criticized the Hollywood studios for their role in bringing America "to the verge of war" (Nye, 1941: 722). He was perceptive in his assessment of the movies' potential for successful propagandizing when he noted,

> But when you go to the movies, you go there to be entertained. You are not figuring on listening to a debate about the war. You settle yourself in your seat with your mind wide open. And then the picture starts—goes to work on you, all done by trained actors, full of drama, cunningly devised, and soft passionate music underscoring it. Before you know where you are you have actually listened to a speech designed to make you believe that Hitler is going to get you if you don't watch out . . . the truth is that in 20,000 theaters in the United States tonight they are holding war mass meetings, and the people lay down the money at the box office before they get in.

Once the United States did enter World War II in December 1941, the industry did contribute toward the total war effort, but not only by making war films, for less than one-third of all the films released in the United States in the period 1942 to 1944 actually dealt with the war (Jowett, 1976: 318). What the Hollywood industry did so well was to provide morale-building films for consumption on the home-front and overseas, for during the war, entertainment was not a luxury but an emotional necessity. American films managed to develop a most potent combination of being able to entertain and propagandize at the same time, thus "getting the message across" while also attracting the large audiences that obvious propaganda and documentary films were seldom able to do.

In November 1941 a prominent and articulate Hollywood producer, Walter Wanger, noted that motion pictures should be used in the upcoming conflict "to clarify, to inspire and to entertain." He continued, "The determination of what ought to be said is a problem for our national leaders and our social scientists. The movies will make significant contributions to national morale only when the people have reached some degree of agreement about the central and irrefutable ideas of a nation caught in the riptide of war" (Wanger, 1941: 381). What Wanger was saying is that the movies were merely a medium of entertainment, albeit a very popular one and therefore with a powerful potential, but that the content of its propaganda messages should be based upon national interests and not left up to the heads of the studios. Once the war did begin for the Americans in 1941, that is precisely the dictum that was followed.

Film was an important medium for propaganda during World War II, but seldom in the manner in which the official propagandists intended. In many cases audiences were far more sophisticated than expected, and the result was a rejection of obvious, blatant efforts to bring about changes in existing opinions. When film propaganda was most successful it was usually based upon a skillful exploitation of prexisting public emotions, eliciting an audience response that closely matched public sentiment. Thus when the Nazi film *Baptism of Fire*, which showed the supposed invincibility of the German armed forces as they battered the Polish army out of existence under three weeks, was screened in those countries that expected to be invaded, the film had a definite effect. American films were most successful when they stressed positive themes, particularly as they depicted normal life on the homefront, or the inner strength of the ordinary fighting men — usually carefully balanced to show the various ethnic origins of Americans such as Irish, Italians, Jews, and so on. In fact, the most successful American films during the war did not concern themselves with the fighting at all.

In a 1945 study of the contribution made by movies to the war effort, Dorothy Jones of the Office of War Information (OWI) found that between 1942-1945, only about 30% of Hollywood films actually dealt with the war itself. Although she was critical of the movie industry for "lacking a real understanding of the war" she ignored the established fact that by 1943, having grown tired of war films, not only the homefront audience but also the combat forces preferred to see the spate of musicals, comedies, and escapist romances that the movie industry was only too happy to turn out. This blend of war films and escapist material, which still tended to emphasize the positive aspects of the "American way of life," combined to be a potent propaganda source for morale building during this difficult period in American history. Of equal significance was the appeal that these "domestic" films had among both America's allies and conquered enemies, where their popularity was exceeded only by the demand for American food. Recognizing this fact, at the end of the war some efforts were made to make available to the occupied countries only those films that tended to show America and democratic institutions in a favorable light.

Since the end of World War II, there has been little systematic use of film for propaganda purposes on a large scale. There are occasional commercial films that "propagandize" in the sense that they espouse a particular point of view about a controversial subject (*The China Syndrome* — about the dangers of nuclear power; *Missing* — dealing with American complicity in the overthrow of the Chilean government), but these are not part of an organized campaign on behalf of a recognized propaganda agency. This was not always so, for in the Cold War period (roughly 1947-1965) the American film industry was actively solicited by the U.S. government to make commercial films that pointed out the dangers of Communism. This contrasted wildly with the pro-Russian films that Hollywood had turned out once Hitler had marched into Russia in 1942, and the American public had to be convinced that we were all now allies. Previously exposed to films such as *The North Star* (1942), *Mission to Moscow* (1943), and *Song of Russia* (1944), the American film audience was now treated to *The Iron Curtain* (1948), which confusingly starred Dana Andrews, who only a few years before had been featured in a sympathetic role in *The North Star* as a Russian partisan; *The Red Menace*, which cataloged the methods of Communist subversion in the United States; *Whip Hand* (1951), which dealt with Communists running a prison camp in a small town in the United States to test biological weapons; *I was a Communist for the FBI* (1951), which later became the basis of a television series, and *Big Jim McLain* (1952), which featured John Wayne hunting Communists in Hawaii. (It was no coincidence that the name McLain was used to identify the hero closely with noted anti-Communist Senator Joseph McCarthy).

It was also no coincidence that much of the focus of the House Un-American Activities Committee on Communist subversion in the United States in the period after 1947 was on ferreting out potential Communists in the Hollywood community. Not only did the Committee gain national attention by questioning entertainment personalities who were widely recognized public figures (who cared about anonymous government employees?), but there was a genuine fear that because the film industry was very powerful, it would be dangerous to allow Communist sympathizers to use it as a propaganda tool. Much the same could be said for the attention given to both radio and television, for the commercial media were considered to be potent sources of propaganda disguised as entertainment, as Senator Nye had pointed out in 1941.

Since the breakup of the large Hollywood studios and the emergence of largely independent producers, there has been little attempt to use the motion picture industry for organized propagandizing. On the other hand, show business personalities are increasingly using their media-obtained popularity to espouse political causes. The majority of the public seems clearly able to distinguish the on-screen persona of the actor from the off-screen political causes with which he or she might be identified. As an example, there was and continues to be considerable hostility toward Jane Fonda for her activities during the Vietnam War, and subsequent support of liberal causes, but she still has an enormous number of fans who are willing to ignore her political stances and pay money at the box office to see her in such films as *"Nine to Five."* (It is interesting to note that this film was a political film, dealing with significant issues of feminism; however, audiences did not really perceive it as such). The propaganda value of such personalities lies mainly in their ability to gain media attention for their favorite causes; however the public seldom sees them as credible sources. Jane Fonda can create public interest in the issues of Vietnam, but she was not considered an expert in foreign policy.

When Hollywood attempted to make so-called message films in the period after World War II, it quickly became obvious that most people do not go to the movies to have their consciences disturbed. Subsequent research has clearly demonstrated that movies, like other mass media, rarely bring about a major change of opinion; however, we also know that consistent exposure to a specific point of view when the audience has none of its own stands a good chance of making some impact. Thus the cumulative effect of filmic propaganda is greater than any individual film. Foreign audiences, often knowing little about the United States, will after years of exposure to American films develop very specific attitudes about the American way of life. On the other hand, no single film can change an individual's racial attitudes ingrained after years of socialization.

The motion picture is still a highly effective form of information dissemination, but its use as a propaganda vehicle is severely restricted by several factors. First, audiences worldwide have become used to large budget films with high quality production values, and this works against the use of low-budget productions. Second, the concept of the fictional story complete with acknowledged stars as the basic attraction in commercial films is so well established that it is very difficult to generate a mass audience for anything else. Third, the distribution system for commercial films is tightly organized and extremely difficult to break into for those outside of the mainstream filmmaking community. Last, filmmaking technology has been superceded by new video technologies that offer greater opportunities for dissemination of propaganda messages without the need for a large audience base to justify cost. Thus the motion picture's effectiveness as a propaganda medium is now totally limited to the values and ideologies that are an integral part of the plot structure. Such content, although subtle, is in its own right an extremely potent source of modern propaganda, and is certainly more powerful in the long run than the deliberate and often clumsy attempts in the past.

Radio

The invention of radio in the late nineteenth century totally altered for all time the practice of propaganda, making it possible for messages to be sent across borders and over long distances without the need for a physical presence. Ultimately radio has become the major medium of full-scale international "white" propaganda, where the source of the message is clear and the audience knows and often eagerly expects to hear different political viewpoints. Despite the inroads made by television viewing on leisure time activities in most industrialized countries, there is no indication of any decline in the use of radio for propaganda purposes, and large sums of money are currently spent on the worldwide dissemination of information from a variety of political ideologies.

The first known use of radio for international broadcasting was in 1915 when Germany provided a daily news report of war activities, which was widely used by both the domestic and foreign press that was starved for up-to-date news. Although these broadcasts were in Morse code, and therefore not available to all, they served their purpose. Radio was used dramatically by the Soviets in 1917, when under the call sign "To all . . . to all . . . to all . . ." the Council of the People's Commissars' Radio put out the historic message of Lenin announcing the start of a new age on October 30 (Hale, 1975: 16). The message stated,

> The All-Russian Congress of Soviets has formed a new Soviet Government. The Government of Kerensky has been overthrown and arrested. . . . All official institutions are in the hands of the Soviet Government.

This was an international call to all revolutionary groups throughout Europe as well as those inside of Russia, and later broadcasts would be aimed specifically at foreign workers to "be on the watch and not to relax the pressure on your rulers." Soviet radio was quickly placed under the control of the government, for Lenin noted that radio was a "newspaper without paper . . . and without boundaries," and a potentially important medium for communicating his Communist ideas to the dispersed workers and peasants in both Russia and the rest of Europe, and, ultimately, the world. By 1922 Moscow had the most powerful radio station in existence, followed in 1925 by a powerful shortwave transmitter, which soon began broadcasting in English.

The interest in radio grew rapidly during the 1920s, and turning the radio dial in the hope of picking up foreign stations became the pastime of millions of listeners in many countries. In the United States much of the pioneering credit can be given to station KDKA in Pittsburgh, which started the first regularly scheduled radio service in 1920. By the end of 1923 the station had successfully transmitted a special holiday program to Great Britain, which was picked up and rebroadcast from a Manchester station; and later in 1924 and 1925 it broadcast programs to South Africa and Australia, respectively. These early broadcasts set the scene for a regular exchange of radio programs between countries during the late 1920s and early 1930s and shortwave radio listening became a fascinating hobby for enthusiastic radio fans. It was the Dutch who inaugurated the first regular shortwave broadcasts in 1927, sponsored by the giant electrical engineering company Phillips; by 1930 this station was broadcasting to most parts of the world in more than twenty languages.

Radio Moscow started broadcasting in French in 1929, and this action caused an outcry from the French Press, which questioned the right of the Soviets to broadcast in a language other than their own, and The League of Nations was asked to consider the matter. Within a year the French had seen the light and began their own international broadcasts. In 1930, the English language broadcasts from Moscow had caused sufficient concern to warrant the British Post Office to monitor these on a regular basis. The success of these foreign broadcasts were not lost on the BBC, which in 1929 proposed to the Imperial Conference (where all parts of the British Empire were represented) that a worldwide service be established to maintain the links of the Empire. In proposing this service, the BBC submission noted that in presenting national cultures to other parts of the world, "The boundary between cultural and tendentious propaganda is in practice very indefinite" (Bumpus and Skelt, 1985: 13). The Empire Service was begun in 1932, in English only. One week after it opened, King George V delivered a Christmas message to his subjects throughout the world, and the New York Times ran a banner headline, "Distant Lands Thrill to his God Bless You!" The BBC gained enormous publicity and prestige from this broadcast.

In 1929, Germany also started broadcasting to its nationals abroad from a shortwave transmitter outside of Berlin, and Italy set up its service in 1930, broadcasting at first only Italian domestic programs. By 1932 even the League of Nations had its own station broadcasting new bulletins in three languages: English, French, and Spanish. Only in the United States did the government steer well clear of any involvement with international broadcasting, preferring to leave this to the large commercial networks then being established. These stations, of course, broadcast in English only, and therefore did not have the same direct propaganda value in foreign countries.

With the coming to power of the National Socialist Government in Germany in 1933, the role of international broadcasting was dramatically elevated to major prominence. (The use of radio by the Nazi regime will be discussed in more detail in Chapter 5.) Both Hitler and his Propaganda Minister Josef Goebbels had been impressed with the Soviet Union's German language service and the development inside Germany of widespread and powerful listener groups for these propaganda broadcasts. By August 1934 the Nazi administration had reorganized German broadcasting, and programs were now being beamed to Asia, Africa, South America, and North America. The Germans pioneered in the use of music as a means of attracting listeners, and by all accounts the quality of the music was superb, with news bulletins and special programs interspersed. One German radio expert was quoted as saying, "Music must first bring the listener to the loudspeaker and relax him" (Grandin, 1939: 46). The 1936 Olympic Games in Berlin provided the impetus to construct the world's largest shortwave radio transmitter facilities, and by the end of 1938 the Germans were broadcasting more than 5,000 hours a week in more than 25 languages. The Nazis also introduced medium-wave broadcasts for the neighboring

European countries, especially those with pockets of German-speaking minorities.

Italy followed Germany's lead, increasing foreign and Italian broadcasts to both Europe and the Americas, including the provision of Italian language lessons that cleverly used many passages from Mussolini's speeches as texts. Listeners were asked to send their translations to Rome for correction, and by 1939 more than 35,000 people had done so (Grandin, 1939: 30). Japan also began its own foreign language radio service in June 1935 as a means of informing the large number of Japanese living on the Pacific rim about activities in the home country. This soon changed, for after Japan found itself internationally isolated following its invasion of Manchuria in 1936, Radio Tokyo was used as a propaganda medium for putting across the Japanese government's position on Japan's role in creating a new Asian alliance. Broadcasts were aimed at the United States and Europe, but the quality of these broadcasts was hampered by a lack of personnel trained in foreign languages. Interestingly, the Japanese government did all that it could to discourage the ownership of shortwave radio sets to diminish the impact of broadcasts from outside.

By the beginning of World War II in the summer of 1939, there were approximately 25 countries that were broadcasting internationally in foreign languages. The outbreak of war once again brought about an enormous expansion of international radio services. In particular, the BBC was charged with becoming a major arm of the Allied propaganda effort, so that by the end of 1940, 23 languages had been added and more than 78 separate news bulletins were being offered everyday, with special attention given to Germany and Italy. Governments in exile in London were also given the opportunity to broadcast to their home countries. By the end of the war the BBC was the largest international broadcaster by far, programming in more than 43 languages, and because of its earned reputation for total accuracy, even the German troops were tuning in to find out what was happening.

In the United States at the time of the attack on Pearl Harbor, there were only 12 shortwave transmitters in action, all owned by private broadcasters. Under the guidance of the Office of War Information, these stations became collectively known as

the Voice of America. Eventually the U.S. government rented
the stations and all programs were prepared by the foreign operations unit of the OWI, under the control of playwright Robert
Sherwood. By 1943 the number of transmitters had risen to 36,
and the VOA was broadcasting in 46 languages for some 50
hours a day. There was some uncertainty about the future role
of VOA once the war was over, for there has always been a ner-
vousness in the U.S. Congress about propaganda activities,
whether domestic or foreign. (This fear stems largely from the
concern that the Administration in power will eventually utilize
such activities to serve its own domestic ends.) Immediately after the war ended, VOA was severely cut back, but with the start
of the "cold war" Congress, feeling that American response to
increasing Soviet propaganda actions was inadequate, voted in
1948 to create a permanent role for VOA as part of the information activities of the State Department.

It was in the decades following World War II that the unprecedented expansion of international broadcasting activities took
place. Immediately after the war the main thrust of such broadcasts were toward Europe, but gradually during the 1950s,
1960s, and 1970s more attention was given to India, the Arab
countries, Africa, Latin America, and Asia. As the dynamics of
world politics were being played out, international radio broadcasts became a prominent weapon in the arsenal of propaganda. With the Communist takeover in China in 1949 a new
major world and radio power appeared, while the Soviet Union,
threatened with defections in the Soviet Bloc, steadily expanded its broadcasts in an increasing number of languages.
The non-Communist countries retaliated, with West Germany
expanding its facilities, as did all three of the United States operations. (Radio Free Europe had begun in 1951; Radio Liberation started broadcasting in 1953.) By the end of the 1970s, the
use of radio as a major medium for international propaganda
was greater than it had ever been.

Current International Radio Propaganda

There are several distinct kinds of international broadcasting
systems that can be said to be clearly propagandistic. The most
important by far are the national broadcasting organizations
that are usually state funded, or supported by a group of politi-

cally or religiously active citizens eager to reach a specific audience, usually in other countries. More than 80 nations are currently involved in this type of activity, some operating more than one such service (Bumpus and Skelt, 1985). The United States has the Voice of America, which is the main international service, Radio Free Europe, which transmits to 5 countries in Central and Eastern Europe, Radio Liberty (formerly Radio Liberation), broadcasting to the USSR, and has recently added Radio Marti as a special service aimed at Cuba and other Caribbean countries. The USSR has two main stations, Radio Moscow, the national service, and Radio Station Peace and Progress, as well as many regional outlets. The Federal Republic of Germany also has two, Deutsche Welle and Deutschlandfunk; and although the United Kingdom has only one official station, the British Broadcasting Corporation's External Services, it has an extensive rebroadcasting network throughout the world.

It is not really the number of stations that is important, for these national organizations have access to extremely high-powered transmitters that ensure a wide reception, and there is constant technological improvement. Of greater significance is the number of languages in which these international services are offered. The USSR broadcasts nearly 2,100 hours a week in more than 80 languages. (The number of hours differs for each language.) The Chinese People's Republic Radio Peking broadcasts more than 1,400 hours in 45 languages; the combined American services broadcast more than 2,000 hours in 43 languages, the German stations broadcast more than 780 in 39 languages, and the BBC broadcasts more than 720 hours in 37 languages. Even such minor world powers as North Korea (593 hours), Albania (581 hours), Nigeria (322 hours), and South Africa (205 hours) all transmit their messages over the world's airwaves.

There are other kinds of international broadcasters, but their impact as direct propaganda media is far less. First are the commercial stations, which garner large audiences by targeting their broadcasts to specific listening groups attracted to popular commercial programming. The use of pop music (in a variety of languages) forms the staple content for such stations as Radio Luxembourg, Radio Monte Carlo, and Sri Lanka's All Asia Service. These stations perform a subtle but valuable propaganda role in the international transmission of popular culture. The United States has found that its popular music broadcasts, particularly jazz, have wide appeal throughout the world, especially in the Soviet Bloc countries.

In recent years a third kind of international broadcaster has begun to make a significant impact on the propaganda scene: the religious broadcaster. Broadcasting more than 1,000 hours a week in a variety of languages, these stations seek to promulgate their own brand of religion to as wide an audience as their transmitters will allow. Usually financed by subscriptions, much of it raised in the United States, they have brought a new type of propaganda to the international scene. Listening to these broadcasts it is often difficult to separate out the political content from the religious. Vatican Radio began its worldwide service in 1931, the first of the international religious services, and this number has grown to more than 40 (Hale, 1975: 124). In the United States there are seven worldwide religious operations, including Adventist World Radio, World Radio Gospel Hour, and the Voice of the Andes. One of Radio Cairo's channels was given over entirely to Islamic teaching—The Voice of the Holy Koran—which used to break off for one hour a day to broadcast the Palestine Liberation Organization's propaganda program. (This service has since been discontinued—a further example of the changes in propaganda priorities brought about by shifting political alliances.) Even the BBC uses the powerful lure of Islamic devotion to attract listeners in Arabic countries by broadcasting readings from the Koran in its Arabic service.

Who is listening to all of this international flow of propaganda information, and what effect is it having? Here we must be careful to examine the effects of international broadcasting in the specific historical, social, and cultural context within which it takes place. There are over 600 million radios in the world outside of the United States, two-thirds of which can receive shortwave broadcasts. In the United States there are over 300 million sets, of which only 3 million can tune into the shortwave band. The transistor revolution and subsequent development of printed circuits have made it possible for radios to be made available in the smallest and poorest villages in the most remote parts of the world. From the rural areas of Latin America to the outback of Siberia and Australia, radio is the major source of outside communication and information. We must also keep in mind that much of the radio received in these areas is of the domestic variety; however, there is still a great deal of international broadcasting that can clearly be labeled "propaganda" attracting audiences.

The main attraction for audiences listening to foreign language broadcasts is to get something they cannot get from their domestic radio services. The most important of these "alternatives" seems to be the desire for timely, accurate, objective information that the domestic media of many of these countries fail to provide. Often internal control of communications for political reasons forces the population to seek outside sources of information, such as occurred in Brazil after censorship was imposed in 1968. At that time, the VOA and the BBC became the most reliable source of news on events in Brazil itself (Ronalds, 78). The BBC in particular has earned a reputation for being fair and unbiased in its reporting of events, so much so that during the recent British-Argentinian conflict British Prime Minister Thatcher became angry because the service reported the truth about casualties and other information that she considered to be harmful to British domestic morale.

In August 1985, members of the news service of the BBC went on strike to protest government interference in the showing of a television documentary on terrorism, which included an interview with a reputed leader of the Irish Republican Army. The government called the interview "dangerous propaganda"; the television news team called it "pertinent information." This strike gained worldwide attention because of the BBC's vaunted reputation for being unbiased. This reputation, earned during World War II, has continued to make the BBC a major international information source for hundreds of millions of listeners who have come to rely upon its daily news reports. The VOA also has a reputation for objectivity, and this accounts for the strong reaction whenever presidents attempt to interject their personal political philosophies into the operations of the VOA, as was recently the case. Only by maintaining an unblemished history of fairness do these stations carry any weight with their listeners.

In the United States, where there is an enormous variety of available news sources, all of which is unrestricted by government censorship, there is no clearly perceived need to listen to outside news broadcasts. For this reason there has never been a history of massive shortwave listening, and shortwave radio receivers are not normally found on domestic radio sets. Those who do listen on a regular basis do so more out of curiosity and as a hobby than to seek out alternative news sources. Thus international radio propaganda is essentially ineffective when aimed at the U.S. population, but such propaganda broadcasts are nevertheless routinely monitored by the government because they can, with careful analysis, reveal the strategies and political maneuvering of the originating countries.

International radio propaganda covers a wide spectrum: on one end there is the osmotic effect of the BBC, which has with patience and professionalism carved a very special niche for itself as a reliable source of information, and all the other nonaggressive national news and cultural services; somewhere in between we find the more propagandistic broadcasts of the VOA, Radio Free Europe, Radio Moscow, Radio Peking, and other nationalistic services deliberately aimed at promoting a specific political perspective to audiences in other countries; at the far end are the aggressive, sometimes vitriolic broadcasts found on Arab language stations in the Middle East, certain African countries, Radio Moscow at times, and wherever there is a need to proclaim "a struggle for freedom."

It is difficult to measure the exact impact of all of this international propaganda broadcasting. Clearly some of it is very effective, particularly when the domestic population is denied access to a variety of alternative news sources, and they turn to outside channels of information. By all accounts most listeners to international broadcasts are sophisticated enough to be wary of blatant propagandizing, although here again the emotional circumstances providing the content of such broadcasts must be taken into consideration. If the message is too much at odds with what the audience believes or suspects to be true, then the end result is less effective than it would have been had it concentrated on a modicum of reality. As Brown (1963: 309) pointed out, "The main lesson to be drawn . . . is how very resistant people are to messages that fail to fit into their own picture of the world and their own objective circumstances, how they deliberately (if unconsciously) seek out only those views which agree with them."

However, despite the caution in claiming success for international propaganda broadcasts, the fact is that many governments are concerned enough about the provision of alternative news sources to resort to highly costly jamming of signals. Although the jamming of signals has been around since the beginning of radio itself, in recent years the techniques have been greatly improved, although it remains an expensive and largely wasteful exercise, and is not always successful, especially in trying to cover large geographic areas. Thus the USSR, despite its most strenuous efforts, cannot prevent some of the signals of the VOA, Radio Free Europe, and Radio Liberty from reaching target audiences. The United States has never had to resort to jamming signals because, as indicated above, the domestic audience for such broadcasts is not very large or likely to be negatively influenced.

International radio broadcasts have at times been a potent force in shaping the world of propaganda in this century, and it is likely to remain so in the foreseeable future. The total number of listeners to foreign radio stations is rising, partly as a result of the increase in radio sets, but also because of larger populations and the increasing frustration with the inadequacy of the local media in many Third World countries (Hale, 1975: 171). Future technological developments such as Direct Broadcasting Satellites (DBS), which will enable both listeners and viewers to receive signals directly into their homes from satellite dishes parked in space, pose additional problems that have already been the subject of international rancor. (For a detailed discussion of this issue see Nordenstreng and Schiller, 1979: 115-165.) Increased international tensions, and the aggressive tactics employed in the "battle for men's minds," will ensure that radio propaganda continues to be a feature of modern life in a large section of the world.

Television

Because television is essentially a domestic medium, it has not been extensively used as a means of direct international propaganda. This may change with the introduction of the DBS

technology indicated above, but it is unlikely that many countries would allow the cultural disruptions caused by such daily
doses of foreign propaganda. Of far greater current danger is
the immense amount of indirect propaganda presented under
the guise of entertainment that forms the basis of the worldwide
trade in television programming. Much like the motion picture
industry has done, the giant television industries of the United
States, Great Britain, and Germany have dominated the international market for television programs. Most Third World countries are unable to produce sufficient programming to meet
their own needs, and the voracious appetite for television entertainment is met by importing programs from elsewhere. The
United States alone sells more than 150,000 hours of television
programs annually. (This problem is analyzed in some detail in
Lee, 1980.)

The content of these programs clearly carries ideological
messages, and often they create what is called "the frustration
of rising expectations" in viewers from less developed countries
by presenting an attractive lifestyle that is beyond their economic means. Ultimately, it is theorized, constant exposure to
such a divergence in living conditions will bring about hostility
toward the originating country. Schiller (1970: 114) notes, "To
foster consumerism in the poor world sets the stage for frustration on a massive scale, to say nothing of the fact that there is a
powerful body of opinion there which questions sharply the desirability of pursuing the Western pattern of development." In
more sanguine times, it was often thought that the worldwide
exchange of television programs would lead to greater international understanding and tolerance, but this has not proved to
be the case. Today we have the anomalous situation in which
American television programs (such as *Dallas*) are followed with
almost religious devotion, while there is intense political hostility toward the United States as a symbol of capitalist oppression expressed by those same audiences.

Where television does have a major propaganda function is
in the area of news reporting. There have always been complaints about misrepresentation in the reporting of international (as well as domestic) news, but this issue has recently
received an unprecedented amount of attention as a result of
complaints from Third World countries that their images are be-

ing distorted in the Western press. The issue of the imbalance in the "free flow" of information between the industrialized and developing countries became a major topic at international meetings, and a significant issue on the agenda of the fundamental political and economic issues in contemporary society. In particular, UNESCO has been the arena of many ardent discussions on the necessity to develop what has been called the *New World Information Order* (NWIO). At the General Conference of UNESCO in Nairobi in 1976, it was decided to undertake a major study of the problem of international communication flows. Known as the McBride Commission (Irish statesman Sean McBride was the president of the Commission), the subsequent report *Many Voices, One World* (1980) detailed the extent of the difficulties in reconciling widely differing philosophies on the issue of what constitutes a "free flow" of information. As the Commission report noted, "It has been frequently stated . . . that due to the fact that the content of information is largely produced by the main developing countries, the image of the developing countries is frequently false and distorted. More serious still, according to some vigorous critics, it is this false image, harmful to their inner balance, which is presented to the developing countries themselves" (McBride, 1980: 36).

Predictably, the response in the United States to a call for government involvement to ensure a more balanced flow of communication was negative, and was based upon the historical notion of "freedom of the press" from all government interference. The issues are complex and easily open to misinterpretation depending on one's political philosophy (see Nordenstreng, 1982, for a discussion of this issue). Ultimately, the concept of developing a new world information order, which would provide more balanced coverage to news from developing countries, has not had wide acceptance in the West, and images of famine, corruption, and conflicts still predominate on our nightly news broadcasts. It is in this way that the powerful visual images are presented to television viewers — in broadcasts that seldom have enough time to develop the stories to provide adequate explanations. The "shorthand" nature of television news lends itself to such distortion, thus creating a form of indirect propaganda affecting our perceptions and shaping our attitudes toward a wide variety of issues. We learn to rely on the news media for information, and repeated frequently enough, these images become fixed beliefs, shaping our understanding of the world around us.

There is no clear-cut solution to this problem of distortion; it is an inherent part of a free media system in which market forces dictate the content of the media. The difficulties in reconciling this free market media system — in which the commercial mass media allow audience preferences to shape content — with the understandable desire by countries and individuals to present their "best" images are almost insurmountable. Clearly everyone would like to use the media to propagandize favorably on their behalf, but if the news agencies and television networks in the West feel that their audiences are more interested in learning about political coups, wars, and corruption in Third World countries rather than increases in food production, educational advances, and stable political regimes, then that is what will be featured on the news. This type of indirect and unconscious propaganda is a major product of modern media systems.

Television by its visual nature is vulnerable to misuse as a propaganda medium because it places a premium on finding material with great visual interest to broadcast. The use of "talking heads" is only relied upon as a last resort when there is little visual support. Thus in the recent TWA/Beruit hostage crisis, the American television networks were forced to rely upon visual material largely generated by the Lebanese hijackers, almost all of which was aimed at presenting the case for the Shiite Moslems in a favorable light. The networks therefore served as unwitting propagandizers, caught by their desperate need to present whatever visual material they could find and in their desire to compete with each other for the viewing audience. The American public, as we have noted before, is not always receptive to such blatant propaganda messages, and the networks were constantly apologizing for presenting them. Here again we witness the differences in conditions favoring successful propaganda in two cultures; for the Moslems, in a heightened emotional state of conflict and influenced by years of propaganda for their cause, were naive to think that American television viewers would uncritically accept the images emanating from Beruit.

It is difficult to predict exactly how much of a role television will play in direct international propaganda in the future. It is doubtful that the use of DBS will be allowed in the same fashion as international radio broadcasting, and the methods of technological control (going so far as to destroy offending satellites), are much easier. It is very likely that we will see a continuation of the argument surrounding the misrepresentation of countries and groups in those countries where the media are not too tightly controlled by the government. On the other hand, where governments do have control of the media systems, television will continue to play a major role in propagandizing activities, as much through the ideological perspectives of so-called entertainment as through the management of the images presented in the news. Television's potential as a propaganda medium has yet to be fully realized in modern society.

4

PROPAGANDA AND PERSUASION EXAMINED

A seventy-year history of social science research has yielded much valuable insight into propaganda and persuasion. Researchers began to investigate propaganda after World War I, and by World War II major studies were being conducted in attitude research. Recent research has been in the study of behavior and attempts to predict behavior change. It is believed that effects are determined according to individual differences and the context in which propaganda and persuasion take place.

THE MODERN STUDY OF PROPAGANDA AND PERSUASION

Studies of propaganda in the early part of the twentieth century were antecedents to the social scientific study of persuasion. Somewhere along the way, researchers stopped referring to their subject of study as "propaganda" and started investigating various constructs of "persuasion." Today, there are relatively few research studies concerning propaganda, but persuasion has become a highly developed subject in communication. Although many books date the modern study of propaganda and persuasion in the 1930s and 1940s with the beginnings of the scientific study of persuasion, interest in the use of propaganda in World War I prompted earlier investigation.

Propaganda in World War I

The period during World War I was the first time that the populations of entire nations were actively involved in a global struggle. The citizens of Europe and America were asked to forego their own pleasures for the sake of the war effort. Money had to be collected; material comforts had to be sacrificed. All-out public cooperation was essential. To accomplish these ends, attempts were made to arouse hatred and fear of the enemy and to bolster the morale of the people. Mass media were used in ways they had never been used before to propagandize entire populations to new heights of patriotism, commitment to the war effort, and hatred of the enemy. Carefully designed propaganda messages were communicated through news stories, films, phonograph records, speeches, books, sermons, posters, rumors, billboard advertisements, and handbills to the general public. "Wireless" radio transmission was considered to be the new medium for shaping public attitudes. It was believed that radio propaganda could weld the masses into an amalgamation of "hate and will and hope" (Lasswell, 1927: 221).

Nationwide industrial efforts were mounted with great haste, and the support of civilians who worked in industry was enlisted. Propaganda was developed and used to bring about cooperation between the industrialized society and the fighting armed forces. Posters depicting workers and soldiers arm in arm were plastered over walls in factories throughout America. The Committee on Public Information (CPI), under the direction of George Creel was commissioned to "sell the war to America." Creel established a division of labor publications with former labor organizer Robert Maisel as its head. Maisel's task was to produce and distribute literature to American workers. Another organization, the American Alliance for Labor and Democracy, was formed under the leadership of Samuel Gompers of the American Federation of Labor (AFL) to maintain peace and harmony in the unions in connection with the war effort.

The CPI sponsored a national speakers bureau on behalf of Liberty Bond sales drives and distributed more than 100 million posters and pamphlets. Wartime propaganda in America and abroad turned out to be very skillful, highly coordinated, and was considered by its audiences to be quite powerful.

Although much of the propaganda was factual and accurate, some of it was deceptive and exaggerated. Both the Allies and the Germans circulated false atrocity stories. The Allies told the story of Germans boiling down corpses of their soldiers to be used for fats. The story's inventors deliberately mistranslated "kadaver" as "corpse" instead of "animal" and circulated the story of a "corpse factory" worldwide in an effort to destroy pro-German sentiments. They knew that the German word "kadaver," which literally means "a corpse," is used in German to refer only to the body of an animal and never to that of a human body, but the non-German-speaking audience did not know this. The story was invented in 1917 and was not exposed as false until 1925 during a debate in the British House of Commons (Qualter, 1962: 66). Atrocity stories along with other more tasteful propaganda efforts were considered to be quite effective.

Aftermath of World War I
and the Growing Concern about Propaganda

After the armistice, in the early 1920s, the experts who were involved in the development of wartime propaganda began to have second thoughts about their manipulation of the public. Some of them experienced guilt over the lies and deceptions that they had helped to spread.

George Creel recounted his experiences with the CPI in *How We Advertised America: The First Telling of the Amazing Story of the Committee on Public Information, 1917-1919*, published in 1920. In his book, Creel tells of the congressional attempt to suppress his report of the CPI's propaganda activities. Creel, who was proud of his activities, discussed in detail the history of the CPI's domestic and foreign activities.

There was widespread concern about the power of the developing forms of mass media and a generalized belief that the mass media had extensive, direct, and powerful effects on attitude and behavior change. The belief that the media could sway public opinion and the masses toward almost any point of view was stated by Harold Lasswell (1927: 220-221) in grandiose language:

> But when all allowances have been made, and all extravagant estimates pared to the bone, the fact remains that propaganda is one of the most powerful instrumentalities in the modern world. It has arisen to its present eminence in response to a complex of changed circumstances which have altered the nature of society.... A newer and subtler instrument must weld thousands and even millions of human beings into one amalgamated mass of hate and will and hope. A new flame must burn out the canker of dissent and temper the steel of bellicose enthusiasm. The name of this new hammer and anvil of social solidarity is propaganda.

Lasswell's awe of propaganda was expressed in his pioneer work, *Propaganda Technique in the World War*, published in 1927. He noted that the people had been duped and degraded by propaganda during the war. Works such as Lasswell's and Creel's expressed a fear of propaganda. Others saw the need to analyze propaganda and its effects.

The Social Sciences and the Study of Propaganda

It was also after World War I that social psychology began to flourish. In 1918, Thomas and Znaniecki defined social psychology as the study of attitudes. Other social sciences such as sociology and psychology were also stimulated by the need to understand the phenomena of propaganda, public opinion, attitude change, and communication. Learning theories and theories of operant conditioning based on stimulus-response research in behavioristic psychology influenced the development of a theory of mass communication known as the "Magic Bullet" or "Hypodermic Needle Theory" of communication effects.

At this time in the development of psychology, it was believed that people's behavior was determined to a large extent by genetic biological mechanisms that operated between a stimulus and a response. It was thought that human responses were rather uniform because people had inherited the same sets of built-in biological mechanisms that caused them to respond to stimuli in certain ways. The combination of the psychologist's view of a uniform human response system and the political view that the mass media were powerful produced the idea that mass media messages were received in the same way by all people in an audience and, furthermore, that the responses to such messages were immediate and direct. As E. D. Martin said, "Propaganda offers ready-made opinions for the unthinking herd" (in Choukas, 1965: 15). Later, research concerning important intervening variables—for example, demographic background of the audience, selective perception, and other social and mental states of receivers—weakened the idea of direct influence in the Magic Bullet theory. This eventually led to "Limited Effects" models that explained the impact of media as a function of the social environment in which they operate. Effects came to be understood as activating and reinforcing preexisting conditions in the audience. It was not, however, until the end of the 1920s that human individual modifiability and variability began to be demonstrable through research.

Marketing research also began to be developed in the 1920s. Surveys of consumers to analyze buying habits and effectiveness of advertising were refined by sampling techniques in the 1930s and were used to poll political as well as consumer preferences.

Public opinion research also began to develop. Walter Lippmann's (1922) *Public Opinion* voiced a concern that people were influenced by modern media, especially by the newspapers. In 1937, *Public Opinion Quarterly* began to be published. The Editorial Foreword in the first issue proclaimed, "For the first time in history, we are confronted nearly everywhere by mass opinion as the final determinant of political and economic action. . . . Scholarship is developing new possibilities of scientific approach as a means of verifying hypotheses and of introducing greater precision of thought and treatment" (1937: 3).

The Payne Fund studies, discussed in the previous chapter, assessed the effects of films on children and adolescents in the 1930s with respect to individual differences such as economic background, education, home life, neighborhood, gender, and age.

In 1933, the President's Research Committee on Recent Social Trends called the fields of research in propaganda analysis, public opinion analysis, social psychology, and marketing research "agencies of mass impression" (Czitrom, 1982: 126). Mass media, then, was considered to be a common denominator from which questions of behavioral and attitudinal change were to be studied. The media industries provided funding for research along with easily quantifiable data to be analyzed. Applied research also became the by-product of industrial and government institutions and centers, institutes, and universities. A substantial body of behavioral and social scientists turned their attention to communication studies.

RESEARCH IN PERSUASION:
THE STUDY OF ATTITUDES

Although the flurry of research following the end of World War I was related to evaluating propaganda messages, much of the subsequent research had to do with persuasion, specifically the study of attitudes. During the 1920s and 1930s, research in persuasion was attitude research. Emphasis was placed on conceptually defining attitudes and operationally measuring them. Gordon Allport's (1935: 784) definition of attitude was one of the most important: "An attitude is a mental and neural state of readiness organized through experience, and exerting a directive influence upon the individual's response to all objects and situations with which it is related." The concept of attitudes was so central to research that Allport said, "Attitude is probably the most distinctive and indispensable concept in contemporary American social psychology" (p. 784).

Bogardus (1925), Thurstone (1929), and Likert (1932) developed three measures of attitudes. The Likert scale has been one of the most widely used attitude-measurement techniques and is still being used. It is a scale consisting of categories indicating attitude strength with a "strongly approve" answer graduating down to a "strongly disapprove" response on a five-point linear scale. The Thurstone scales, which weighted a series of attitudinal statements at equal intervals, were used in some of the Payne Fund studies. A representative study that used attitude-

measuring scales to determine propaganda effects was done by
Rosenthal (1934), who found that Russian silent propaganda
films changed socioeconomic attitudes of American students.
He also found that stereotypes were easier to arouse than to
eradicate.

The study of attitude and attitude change received more attention than any other topic in social psychology or communication, yet scholars are still far from achieving conclusive links
between attitudes and behavior. One of the early studies of behavior and attitudes was done by Richard Lapiere in 1934 who
toured the United States with a Chinese couple. They stayed at
hotels and ate at restaurants, keeping records of how they were
treated. After the trip, Lapiere wrote to all of the places they had
visited and asked if they accepted or served Chinese persons as
guests. A great majority wrote back and said that they did not.
From this, Lapiere concluded that the social attitudes of the hotel
and restaurant managements had little correspondence with
their behavior.

World War II and Research
in Communication

When the World War II broke out in Europe, researchers
turned their attention to studies of propaganda, counterpropaganda, attitudes, and persuasion. The studies conducted during
and after the war were primarily undertaken by social psychologists and psychologists who used careful controls to measure
effects. The war caused intense concern about the persuasive
powers of the mass media and their potential for directly altering attitudes and behavior. Wartime research was conducted by
the American government which was greatly concerned with the
nature of German propaganda, the British communication system in wartime, and the means by which the United States Office
of War Information bolstered civilian morale as well as how to
make commercial media fare more relevant to the military
struggle (Lazarsfeld and Stanton, 1944).

Paul Lazarsfeld, Professor of Sociology at Columbia University and Head of the Bureau of Applied Social Research, along
with other behavioral scientists produced "Research in Communication" in 1940. This memorandum was a review of the "state
of the art" of research at that time. He reduced the subject of

communication research to four categories: (1) who (2) said what (3) to whom and (4) with what effect. Lazarsfeld regarded the last category as the most crucial one.

The four-question scheme ("who said what to whom with what effect?") became the dominant paradigm defining the scope and problems of American communication research. It restricted communication to a narrow model of persuasion that guided research into the postwar era.

Some of the wartime research could not measure effects. A study by Speier and Otis, reported in Lazarsfeld and Stanton's (1944: 208-247) *Radio Research, 1942-43*, is representative of the content analyses of newscasts to determine the functions of such newscasts. Speier and Otis (1944) content-analyzed German radio propaganda to France during the Battle of France. They found that the function of propaganda to the enemy in total war is "to realize the aim of war—which is victory—without acts of physical violence, or with less expenditure of physical violence than would otherwise be necessary" (Lazarsfeld and Stanton, 1944: 210). They also found that when actual fighting had not yet begun, the propagandist used propaganda as a substitute for physical violence, whereas, when actual fighting was going on, propaganda changed into a supplement to physical violence. For example, before fighting began in France, the Germans attempted to terrorize with words, threatening physical violence in order to get France to negotiate rather than fight. Once fighting actually began, the Germans changed their tactics and chronicled their acts and victories over the radio.

Merton and Lazarsfeld summarized the nature of effect studies in "Studies in Radio and Film Propaganda" (in Merton, 1968: 563-582). These studies used content analysis and response analysis of pamphlets, films, and radio programs. Response analysis was derived through the "focused interview" and a Program Analyzer, a device that enabled the listener of a radio program to press a button to indicate what he or she liked or disliked. Responses recorded on tape synchronized with the radio program, registering approval, disapproval, or neutrality, and were plotted into a statistical curve of response. Through response analysis, the researchers were able to determine (1) the effect aspects of the propaganda to which the audience had responded, (2) the many-sided nature of responses, (3) whether the expected responses had occurred, and (4) unanticipated responses. For example, a radio program designed to bolster American morale shortly after Pearl Harbor contained two dominant themes: the first stressed the power and potentiality of the United States in order to combat defeatism; the second emphasized the strength of the enemy in order to combat complacency and overconfidence. Response analysis revealed that the emphasis on the strength of the United States reinforced complacency of those who were already complacent, and, correlatively, references to enemy strength supported defeatism of those who were already defeatist (Merton, 1968: 573-574).

The benchmark for the initiation of sociobehavioral experiments in the area of attitude change, communication, and the acquisition of factual knowledge from instructional media came from studies conducted by a group of distinguished social and behavioral scientists who had been enlisted into service by the U.S. Army. Working within the Information and Educational Division of the War Department, the Research Branch assisted the Army with a variety of problems involving psychological measurement and evaluation of programs. Some of their experiments were among the first to determine how specific content affected particular audiences. The best known of these experiments was the research that tested the effects of the army orientation films, a series called Why We Fight.

Frank Capra, the well-known Hollywood director, had been commissioned by the Army to make a series of training films for recruits. He produced seven films that traced the history of World War II from 1931 to Pearl Harbor and America's mobilization for war. As they trained to fight in the war, hundreds of thousands of Americans saw these films. The Army wanted to find out whether the films did an effective job of teaching the recruits factual knowledge about the war and whether the factual knowledge shaped interpretations and opinions in ways necessary to developing an acceptance of military roles and related sacrifices.

The main team that conducted the studies consisted of Frances J. Anderson, John L. Finan, Carl I. Hovland, Irving L. Janis, Arthur A. Lumsdaine, Nathan Macoby, Fred D. Sheffield, and M. Brewster Smith. The results were published by Hovland, Lumsdaine, and Sheffield in 1949 in a work entitled *Experiments* on *Mass Communication,* which also included other experiments on communication issues. This work touched off considerable interest in the experimental study of persuasion during the postwar years.

Four of the seven *Why We Fight* films were included in the study. Several research procedures were used, including sampling, control groups, matching, pretesting, and measurement. The results showed that the films were not effective in achieving the goal of motivating the recruits to serve and fight in the war. The films were also not effective in influencing attitudes related to the Army's orientation objectives, for example, deepening resentment toward the enemy, giving greater support to the British, and demanding unconditional surrender. They were, however, somewhat effective in shaping a few attitudes related to the interpretation of the content of the films, for example, that the failure of Germany to invade England during the Battle of Britain was a Nazi defeat. On the other hand, the films were markedly effective in teaching the subjects factual knowledge about the war. In fact, the majority of the recruits tested retained the same, correct answers when retested one week later. Although the films failed to influence attitudes and motivation of the recruits, they were most successful in presenting information to enhance learning.

Other research on the *Why We Fight* films tested the subjects' attitudes toward the films themselves. Results showed that the recruits liked the films, accepted the information in them as accurate, and did not perceive them as untruthful propaganda (Lowery and DeFleur, 1983: 128-137). Several characteristics of the audience were tested including intellectual ability and how it related to learning from the films.

There were other studies to determine if a one-sided argument was more effective than a two-sided argument. After the German surrender, soldiers in training camps listened to radio speeches that attempted to persuade them to continue the war against Japan. Results indicated that the two-sided message produced greater attitude change than the one-sided message, especially among those who initially opposed prolonging the war. In contrast, the one-sided message brought about greater attitude change among those who initially supported prolonging the war. In addition, it was found that the better educated respondents were more favorably affected by the two-sided message, whereas the less well-educated were more responsive to the one-sided message.

The results of the research conducted by the Information and Education Division during the war was very important to the development of communication research. No longer were the media considered to be an all-powerful shaper of attitudes because the effects of films and radio broadcasts were clearly *limited*. Now the effects of mass communication were understood to be strongly influenced by individual differences in the audience.

Another research breakthrough occurred during the same era along with the development of new survey techniques for studying the interrelationship between the media and persuasion in natural settings over time. Lazarsfeld and his associates conducted a panel study during the presidential election of 1940 to determine whether mass media influenced political attitudes. What they found instead, as the interviews progressed from month to month, was that people were receiving information and influence from other people. Face-to-face discussions were a more important source of political influence than the media. The finding was a serendipitous one that had not been anticipated.

When they discovered what was happening, the researchers revised their plans and gathered as much data as they could about interpersonal communication during the campaign. They discovered that people were actually being influenced by opinion leaders who had received their information from the media. From this they developed the "Two-Step Flow" model of communication effects: information flows from the mass media to certain opinion leaders in the community who facilitate communication effects through discussion with their peers (Lazarsfeld et al., 1948). This model was later revised to become a "Multi-Step Flow" model that has people obtaining ideas and information from the media, but seeking out opinion leaders for confirmation of their ideas and forming their attitudes. Recent research indicates that a highly variable number of relays can exist between the media, the message receivers, and attitude formation (Rogers and Shoemaker, 1971).

Lazarsfeld and his associates also found that when the political campaign persuaded at all, it served more to activate and reinforce voter predispositions than to change attitudes. Lazarsfeld (1948: 166) concluded, "Exposure is always selective; in other words, a positive relationship exists between people's opinions and what they choose to listen to or read."

The Yale Studies

After the war, Carl Hovland returned to Yale University, gathered a group of thirty colleagues, and developed what has since become known as the "Yale approach" to persuasion. The Yale group examined attitude change in a variety of experimental contexts. Working from a learning theory perspective that was based on stimulus-response, they investigated effects of many variables in persuasion. They were among the first researchers to examine the effects of source credibility on information processing. They found that source credibility had no effect on immediate comprehension, but it had substantial effect upon attitude change, although it was a short-lived effect. Kelman and Hovland (1953) found that because people tend to disassociate source and content over time, the effects of source credibility were not as pervasive as they thought. Kelman and Hovland called this a "sleeper effect." After people have forgotten the name and qualifications of a persuader, the influence of source credibility in changing their attitude disappears, leaving the people with the message content that provided the basis for their attitudes. Contemporary researchers call this a "dissociation hypothesis" rather than a true sleeper effect, which would be the case when a persuasive message results in little initial change followed by a delayed increase in impact on attitude or behavior change (Pratkanis and Greenwald, 1985: 158-160).

Other variables that the Yale group investigated were personality traits and susceptibility to persuasion, the ordering of arguments (primacy-recency), explicit versus implicit conclusions (see ch. 1: 33), and fear appeals. The results on fear appeals were surprising to the researchers and of great interest to anyone studying propaganda because weak fear appeals turned out to have more influence on subjects than moderate and strong fear appeals did (Hovland et al., 1953: 80). Over the next thirty years, researchers continued to study the impact of fear appeals on audiences with paradoxical results. In some instances, strong fear appeals were found to be persuasive; in others they were not. Boster and Mongeau (1984) did a review of fear-arousing messages since 1953, ir.cluding a meta-analysis of 25 studies on fear appeals and attitude change. They concluded that a positive correlation between fear-arousing messages and attitude change might exist when certain potentially intervening variables are taken into account. These are as follows: age, certain personality traits, and whether the individual voluntarily has exposed him- or herself to the message.

The Yale group had wanted to discover governing laws of persuasion in laboratory settings. Many of the "laws" did not hold up over time, but their work led to a greater understanding of persuasion and stimulated subsequent research in persuasion for years to come.

Cognitive Dissonance

In 1957, Leon Festinger published his *Theory of Cognitive Dissonance,* which generated a great deal of research, speculation, and argument over the long term. Festinger said that once a person has made an important decision, he or she is in a committed state. If alternatives are presented, the person is susceptible to cognitive dissonance or psychological discomfort. This is based on the need to have consistency among one's cognitive elements. For example, if a person was committed to working for a large corporation and was forced to make a negative speech about it, that person would be put into a state of cognitive dissonance because of the inconsistency. Dissonance can be alleviated in a number of ways including rationalization, avoidance, and seeking new support. The person could say that "it's only a job," or not think about the speech after it is given, or look for stronger reasons to support the commitment to the company. If there is a high discrepancy between the commitment and the inconsistent act, change will occur. Festinger would say, in the case of wide discrepancy, that the person would change the commitment to the corporation after making a negative speech about it to bring attitude in line with behavior. This theory accounts for the practice of forced behavior producing attitude change. This influenced Daryl Bem's (1970) Theory of Self Perception, which states that an individual relies on external cues to infer internal states. Bem uses the example of the question, "Why do you like brown bread?" with its response "Because I eat it." This is an example of a self-attribution theory that will be discussed later in this chapter.

Resistance to Persuasion

Most of the research of the 1950s and 1960s was based on attempts of a persuader attempting to change attitudes in an audience, but William J. McGuire (1964) investigated factors that induced resistance to persuasion, producing work that changed the focus of persuasion research. Using some novel techniques to involve people in creating their own defenses against persuasion, McGuire developed "Inocuation Theory," which focused on a strategy analogous to physical immunization against disease. He used what he called "cultural truisms," that is, beliefs one holds that are so ingrained within the cultural milieu that they had never been attacked. First, a cultural truism would be mildly attacked. Because the subject had never dealt with such an attack, he or she needed help in developing a defense against it. Pretreatment in the form of supportive statements and refutational arguments was given by an instructor. If the pretreatment were assimilated, the subject could then provide counterarguments and defenses against subsequent attacks.

McGuire's Model of Persuasion

McGuire (1969) also developed a model for persuasion that emphasized its processes: attention, comprehension, yielding, retention, and action. Attention and comprehension were considered to be receptivity factors and yielding was acceptance of the message purpose or attitude change. Most laboratory studies up to this point stopped there. McGuire extended the idea that persuasion stopped with attitude change by recognizing that to achieve persuadee action at a later time, retention of the message was necessary. Also, in testing receptivity, McGuire found that receivers with high self-esteem were receptive to persuasive messages because they have confidence in their initial positions. Yet they were resistant to yielding because they were satisfied with their existing attitudes. He also found that receivers with high intelligence were receptive to a message because they have longer attention spans and are better able to comprehend arguments. Yet they, too, resisted change due to confidence in existing attitudes. This demonstrated opposite effects on receptivity and yielding in a curvilinear relationship between the variables. This also led him to conclude that receivers with moderate levels of self-esteem and intelligence will be more affected by persuasive messages.

Diffusion of Innovations

Another development in the late 1960s was the Diffusion of Innovations developed by Rogers and Shoemaker (1971). They related diffusion of innovations to the process of social change. Innovations were any new ideas in a social system. The diffusion process occurred through a combination of mass and interpersonal communication, and often took years until an idea had spread. It is a complex process that begins with the people involved who exist within a system. Their variables, including personality, social characteristics, and needs, are examined. Next, the social system itself has to be looked at in terms of its variables. Third, the characteristics of the innovation are analyzed. The adoption of the innovation itself may vary from optional decision, collective decision, or authority decision. All of this occurs in networks where change takes place. Mass communication channels may stimulate change, but interpersonal networks are crucial to the process. Innovation occurs as the result of interaction along the links of a network. Individuals can modify innovations as part of the adoption of them. This theory is of particular importance to those who are interested in attitudinal and behavioral change in a natural setting such as in a developing nation or an organization.

Research on Persuasion and Behavior

In the 1970s, experimental research on attitudes waned and more emphasis was placed on behavior and media influence. Studies that attempted to link attitude to behavior change have not been very successful, and there has been disenchantment with the utility of attitudes for understanding human activity. A new development has been to measure attitudes toward behavior and intentions to carry out a behavior (see discussion in O'Donnell and Kable, 1982: chs. 3, 4). Researchers are attempting to determine what can enable them to predict behavior. Fishbein and Ajzen (1975) have measured the strength of intentions to perform behaviors with strong predictive results. Another predictor of behavior is the goal of the person who enacts the behavior. Bandura (1979: 161) found that explicitly defined goals create incentive to carry them out.

Bandura's (1977) Social Learning Theory links behavior and behavior change to modeling that people observe in their homes, among their peers, and in the mass media. According to this theory, modeling influences produce new behaviors because they give people new information about how to behave. Through observation, people acquire symbolic representation of modeled activities that serve as guidelines for their own behavior. There are four processes necessary to acquire new behavior: (1) attentional processes, (2) retention processes, (3) motor-reproduction processes, and (4) motivational processes. The first process is that of attending to a modeled behavior, then subsequently relating to it. How people relate to other's behavior is determined by perception, motivation, needs, and goals. Also, if the person doing the modeling is considered attractive or a friend, more attention will be given to observing that person. Second, what has been observed has to be retained in the memory. Bandura says the modeled behavior has to be stored in some symbolic form. His studies found that subjects who expressed modeled behaviors in concise terms or vivid imagery remembered them better.

Third, motor-reproduction processes have to be activated, for they convert symbolic forms into appropriate action. This requires initiation of responses, monitoring, and refinement on the basis of feedback. Fourth and most important, the actual performance of the modeled behavior requires motivation to do so. The primary motivation is the observation of positive consequences associated with the new behavior. Repeated observation of desirable consequences associated with a behavior provides a strong motivation to perform a behavior. Reinforcement is important to modeling behavior when it is used as an antecedent to the behavior. According to Bandura (1977: 37), the anticipation of positive reinforcement can effectively influence what is observed and the degree of attention paid to the observation of a given behavior. In other words, learning new behaviors through observation can be more successful if those observing the behavior are told ahead of time that they will benefit from performing the behavior.

The whole notion of consequences of behaviors is still under consideration. Edwards (1954) developed a model known as SEA: Subjective Expected Utility Model. This model suggests that when faced with behavioral choices, people tend to choose the alternative that has the highest expected utility. Gerald Miller, in the afterword to a recent work on message-attitude-behavior relationships (Cushman and McPhee, 1980: 326), suggests that people have expectations related to their behaviors and that they may influence reception of related messages. Further, Miller indicates that people may behave according to perceived rewards and punishment for carrying out the behavior. People may not have supportive attitudes but will behave according to consequences. Marwell and Schmitt (1967) developed a list of strategies for persuasion that focus on persuadee outcome rather than on the content of the messages used in their study. They developed sixteen "compliance-gaining" strategies with both positive and negative consequences, including reward, punishment, debts, altruism, and conformity.

Another aspect of research into behavior has been self-attribution research. When subjects believe that the cause of a given behavior is derived from an attitude, they will consequently adopt that attitude. Valins (1966) conducted an experiment in which he showed male subjects slides of scantily clothed women. He told them that their physical reactions to the pictures were being measured. The men could hear a heartbeat each time they saw a slide, and each man was told that it was his own heartbeat. The supposed heartbeat was manipulated by increasing or decreasing the rapidity of the beats. The men were asked to rate the slides. Predictably, they chose as the best pictures those that were accompanied by rapid heartbeats. Attribution Theory seems also to be on the wane, probably because of the disenchantment of studying attitudes in the 1980s.

THE INFLUENCE OF THE MEDIA

After the turbulent 1960s, researchers turned their attention to investigations of media influence, especially in relation to violent behavior. In 1968, President Lyndon B. Johnson created the National Commission on the Causes and Prevention of Violence. There were seven task forces and five investigative teams who produced fifteen volumes of reports. One of these reports, *Violence and the Media,* has become a landmark study in the question of media influence. Through content analysis of television entertainment programming and survey research on actual violence in America, the researchers concluded that not only was violence a predominant characteristic on television but that it was way out of proportion in comparison to actual violence in the real world. Furthermore, they concluded that the extent and intensity of media violence, especially on television, was capable of creating a view of the world as "totally violent" (Lowery and DeFleur, 1983: 319). This was followed in 1969 by the Surgeon General's Advisory Committee on Television and Social Behavior, which produced several volumes of studies conducted prior to and during the committee's duration. The general conclusion of the studies was that viewing of violent entertainment increases the likelihood of subsequent aggressive behavior, but it should be noted that the evidence was derived from laboratory settings and from surveys.

Some of the studies cited were conducted by Bandura, others by Leonard Berkowitz, both of whom had been testing children, adolescents, and young adults in laboratory settings for more than a decade. Their conclusions were somewhat more tempered. Both Berkowitz and Bandura and their colleagues were very careful to state that they made no claim to any situation outside of the laboratory. They did find, however, that television violence could incite violent behavior in viewers. Berkowitz said it was possible for subjects to behave aggressively in later situations if the fantasy situation on film or television seemed justified. He also indicated that repeated exposure to violence increased the probability of subsequent aggressive acts for some members of an audience, but other factors also determine what may happen — how aggressive the subject is, how hostile the media make him or her, how much the subject associates the story in film or television with situations in which he or she learned hostile behavior, and the intensity of the guilt and/or aggression anxiety aroused by exposure to the film. Bandura also found that children under certain conditions were apt to reproduce aggressive action after observing adults exhibit novel and aggressive action on the screen. A review (O'Donnell and Kable, 1982: 210-211) of their extensive research concludes that sometimes media violence may be persuasively effective with the attitude changes consisting more often of modifications than of conversions. With respect to behavior changes, it can be generalized that some types of depicted violence will be found to have some types of effects on the aggression levels of some types of children, adolescents, and young adults under some types of conditions.

One of the most interesting aspects of the experimental evidence concerning the relationship between the media and behavior change is that subjects tend to be influenced by film and television characters that they perceive to be similar to themselves. Berkowitz, McGuire, and others have found that viewer identification is the central concept in the interpretation of film and television effects. The extent to which viewers rated themselves as similar to particular characters influenced their reactions to aggressors in the media.

Watching violence on television seems to have caused large numbers of Americans to be fearful, insecure, and dependent upon authority, according to George Gerbner and his associates (1979). The most significant and recurring conclusion of their long-range study of heavy television viewers was that "one correlate of television viewing is a heightened and unequal sense of danger and risk in a mean and selfish world" (Gerbner et al., 1979: 194). The researchers felt that this would lead people to demand protection and even welcome repression in the name of security. A recent study of students in junior and senior high schools revealed that those who were heavy viewers of crime shows were more likely to have anti-civil libertarian attitudes (Carlson, 1983). These studies indicate that television influences political learning and, in the case of televised violence, may produce an increasing dependence on the exercise of authoritarian power in society. Comstock (1980) views television as a reinforcer of the status quo in society. He believes that television portrayals, particularly violent ones, assign roles of authority, power, success, failure, dependence, and vulnerability in a manner that matches the real-life social hierarchy. Other researchers have found that some television programming creates the learning of prosocial behaviors. Liebert and his associates (1973) found that children learned altruism, self-control, and generosity from television viewing. Stein and Friedrich (cited in Greenberg, 1980: 105) demonstrated that children learned prosocial behaviors such as cooperation, nurturing, and expressing feelings after watching television programs such as *Mr. Rogers*.

Recent research on the effects of filmed pornography (Donnerstein and Malamuth, 1984) has suggested a possible link between pornography and violence against women. It was found that after exposure to aggressive pornography some men showed less sensitivity toward rape victims, an increase in the willingness to say they would commit rape if not caught, an increase in the acceptance of certain myths about rape, and increased aggressive behavior against women in a laboratory experiment. The overall link between media violence against women and real violence against women is as yet inconclusive, but researchers are actively exploring it in both laboratory and field studies.

The multitude of studies on the effects of television on human behavior has restated society's concerns with effects. It is generally accepted that media does influence individuals but does so among and through a nexus of mediating factors and influences. Mass media is viewed as a contributory agent but not the sole cause in the process of reinforcing existing conditions or in bringing about change.

Research on the effects of mass media continues to thrive, but it has not become a unified behavioral science envisioned by its pioneers. Lazarsfeld referred to communication research as "administrative research" in 1941 and suggested that research be carried on in the service of some kind of administrative agency. Although government-sponsored research has been important with regard to examining the effects of violence in the media, it has not been as prevalent as marketing and advertising research. The broadcasting industry puts research in a central position for decision making. Meanwhile, other forms of research are taking hold. There is criticism of empirical and experimental research that research questions are limited by laboratory methods and laboratory settings. Questions related to the functions of cultural communication within the total process of society are being asked. Books such as Katz and Szecsko (1981) examine how culture reproduces and articulates existing social structures and how media maintains industrial capitalist societies. New journals such as *Critical Studies in Mass Communication* examine rhetorical, ideological, economic, and cultural questions. The nature of research in propaganda and persuasion is and always has been interdisciplinary.

SUMMARY

Research on the nature and effects of propaganda flourished during the World War II years. After the war, research generated into persuasion and communication studies. Research questions were concerned with the variables of communication interaction, especially with regard to attitudes and attitude change. Later, attempts were made to predict behavior and behavior change. With regard to the focus of the book, it would be useful to have a catalogue of practices relevant to propaganda that produce effects, but it is not possible to develop such a catalogue. The Limited Effects Model prevails. The most pertinent conclusion that one can draw after such a review of more than sixty years of research is that individual differences and contexts determine the nature of effects.

Generalizations about Propaganda
and Persuasion Effects

There are a few generalizations that can be made regarding the effects of both propaganda and persuasion. First, it seems safe to say that communication effects are the greatest where the message is in line with the existing opinions, beliefs, and dispositions of the receivers. Selectivity in the perception of messages is generally guided by preexisting interests and behavior patterns of the receivers. The result is that most messages are more likely to be supportive of, than discrepant from, existing views. Furthermore, mass communication effects tend to take the form of reinforcement rather than change. Second, when change does occur, it does so as the result of a multitude of factors including mass media, socially contextual conditions, group interaction, the presence and influence of opinion leaders, and the perceived credibility of the source or sources of the message. Topics that are most likely to be influential are on unfamiliar, lightly felt, peripheral issues that do not matter much or are not tied to audience predispositions. Issues that are deeply rooted and based on values and past behavior patterns are not likely to change. Ideas related to political loyalty, race, and religion tend to remain stable over time and resistant to influence. It is as John Naisbitt (1982: 191) said in *Megatrends:* "When people really care about an issue, it doesn't matter how much is spent to influence their vote; they will go with their beliefs. When an issue is inconsequential to the voters, buying their vote is a snap."

Third, there is an economical aspect in the way we maintain consistency of attitudes and behaviors that gives a propagandist the advantage. As Karlins and Abelson (1970) point out, a propagandist does not have to win people over on every issue in order to get their support. If the propagandist can get people to agree with him or her on one or two issues, then their opinion toward him or her may become favorable. Once that has happened, and the mention of the person's name evokes a favorable response in the people, they may find themselves inventing reasons for agreeing with other issues advocated by him or her (Karlins and Abelson, 1970: 157).

Fourth, people can appear to accept an idea publically without private acceptance. Behavior can be guided by a system of rewards and punishments that do not require attitude change. Furthermore, public compliance will continue under conditions of surveillance by authority but not necessarily under conditions of nonsurveillance.

Finally, the greater the monopoly of the communication source over the receivers, the greater is the effect in the direction favored by the source. Wherever there is a dominant definition of the situation accompanied by a consistent, repetitious, and unchallenged message, the greater the influence of the message.

5

PROPAGANDA AND PSYCHOLOGICAL WARFARE

Propaganda is an essential element in warfare, going back to the pre-Biblical period. It was, however, during World War I that sophisticated techniques of propaganda were utilized that eventually created negative attitudes in the twentieth century toward both propaganda and the potential dangers of mass media influence. In the interwar period radio broadcasting became important, and was increasingly used by the European nations in the political conflicts leading up to World War II. Propaganda played a significant role in the rise of both Communism and Fascism, and reached a new level of scientific sophistication during the war. In the period after 1945, propaganda has become a major weapon in the ideological struggle between East and West. In modern society, advertising is now considered the most pervasive form of propaganda.

The use of propaganda as an integral part of waging war has been a basic part of human history. War itself can be considered to be a violent means of attaining a specific objective, but there has always been a continuous flow of carefully directed propaganda messages that seek to bring about much the same result, but in a nonviolent manner. In a book devoted to the subject,

/aul M. A. Linebarger (1954: 40) defined psychological warfare as "comprising the use of propaganda against an enemy, together with such other operational measures of a military, economic, or political nature as may be required to supplement propaganda." Harold D. Lasswell, one of the pioneers in propaganda studies, has pointed out that psychological warfare is a recent name for an old idea about how to wage successful war. "The basic idea is that the best success in war is achieved by the destruction of the enemy's will to resist, and with a minimum annihilation of fighting capacity" (Lerner, 1951: 261).

By its very nature, the use of propaganda for such directed purposes commences long before actual hostilities break out or war is declared. It also continues long after peace treaties have been signed, and soldiers have gone back to their homes. It is a continuous process, shifting in emphasis as required. It is not hindered by the usual constraints of war such as terrain, arms, or specific battles, but is free to float as only human minds can. The success or failure of these campaigns cannot always be immediately measured, and the results are often known only years later.

It is interesting to note that the term "psychological warfare" is distinctively an American one; the British, with greater candor refer to these activities as "political warfare." Daniel Lerner (1951: xiii) has noted that what we are talking about when we speak of "psychological warfare" is the use of symbols to promote policies, that is, *politics*. Propaganda is, after all, a manipulation of the symbolic environment, and although it can be carried out independently of the physical environment, it can also under certain circumstances be shaped by that environment. Thus the development of new technologies of communication has altered the way in which propaganda is disseminated, but it would be wrong to suggest that old methods are automatically discarded in favor of the new. There continues to be a considerable overlap of media usage, and total propaganda campaigns will encompass all available form of communication, from the very effective oral tradition still widely used to the most sophisticated modern electronic systems.

It is true to say that where there is a communication channel, there also exists a potential propaganda medium. An excellent example would be the increased use in the last twenty years of the technology of Xerography to photocopy large quantities of information for easy distribution. In the United States photocopy machines are widely available to all who would wish to use them; in the Soviet Union, however, all (official) photocopy machines are under the control of the state, and their use is thus limited. This does not stop Soviet dissidents from producing their material on such machines, but the policies of information control makes the (for us) common photocopy machine an exotic and much valued propaganda tool in the Soviet Union.

The public seems most familiar (and comfortable) with the use of propaganda as a wartime activity, a notion that has contributed to the generally negative connotations associated with the term. It is true that it is in times of political conflict that propaganda becomes most visible, as groups use directed persuasion to achieve their goals. Propaganda of this sort must be viewed in its specific historical context, for without this context such symbolic manipulation can later appear to be gross distortions of reality, racist, naive, and essentially silly. "Who would have believed that?" we exclaim looking at wartime posters showing the Japanese soldier as a barbaric, ape-like subhuman. The fact is that within its historical context, such impressions were readily accepted as part of the mythology created by the reality of the conflict (the Japanese did, after all, initiate a sneak attack on Pearl Harbor), and the collective public mentality that develops is eager to believe such stereotypes.

It is often strange to look back with nostalgia on historical artifacts of propaganda, such as wartime posters, leaflets, and especially motion pictures made during the conflict, for they dramatically reveal how context-bound certain types of propaganda can be. We no longer think of the Germans or the Japanese as brutal, rapacious enemies, but these anachronistic artifacts remain. The West German government has been particularly concerned with the showing of old war movies on American television, claiming that this practice continues to provide new generations of Americans with a distorted view of the present German character. There is a certain justification to this claim.

Throughout history there were recorded instances of psychological warfare. One of the best known is the biblical story of

Gideon, who created panic in the numerically superior Midianite camp by equipping 300 of his men with a torch and trumpet each. Conventional warfare of the period called for one such equipped soldier for every 100 men, and Gideon was therefore able to create the illusion of an army of more than 30,000. These three hundred were strategically placed around the Midianite camp in the dead of night, and upon command they each revealed their torches while blowing on their trumpets. Thinking themselves under attack by a superior force, the enemy became confused, and even attacked each other. Eventually the Midianites gave up and fled the battlefield with the Israelites in hot pursuit. (Book of Judges, Chapter 7).

There are many other examples of successful employment of psychological techniques used in warfare, such as Cortez's use of horses as instruments of terror, as well as the exploitation of the indian legends concerning the "Fair God" in his conquest of Mexico; the ancient Chinese use of rockets, not as weapons but to intimidate their enemies; the Boers' use of commando units to attack the British far behind their lines in South Africa during the Boer War, and their anti-British appeal for sympathy on a world-wide scale; and the widespread use of a variety of propaganda appeals from both sides during the American Revolution. The American colonists particularly delighted in pointing out the class distinctions between the British officers and their enlisted men. Even in so-called primitive cultures, the use of drums before battle, or the conjuring up of magic spells all serve to unnerve the enemy. Thus the use of psychological techniques of persuasion for war propaganda purposes is not really new, but the emergence of new forms of information dissemination and the increased sophistication in the understanding of human behavior greatly increased its application and intensity in the twentieth century.

WORLD WAR I AND THE FEAR OF PROPAGANDA

In the foreword to a book on the history of propaganda in World War I, Harold Laswell (1938: v) noted the following:

There is little exaggeration in saying that the World War led to the discovery of propaganda by both the man in the street and the man in the study. The discovery was far more startling to the former than to the latter, because the man in the study had predecessors who had laid firm foundations for his efforts to understand propaganda. The layman had previously lived in a world where there was no common name for the deliberate forming of attitudes by the manipulation of words (and word substitutes). The scholar had a scientific inheritance which included the recognition of the place of propaganda in society.

At the end of World War I even the scholars were surprised by the apparent power that propaganda had exhibited as the conflict raged over almost the entire globe, for nothing in previous historical experience had prepared them for the potent combination of the perfect social, political, and economic conditions with the newly established power of the mass media. By 1914, the nations involved in the war had made the mass media an important part of their social infrastructure and this allowed propaganda activities to assume a role of greater significance than ever before.

Each nation, with the exception of the Soviet Union (which is a special case that will be examined later), was now able to call upon established systems of communication, such as the press or motion pictures, as well as skills developed during peacetime, to aid in the propaganda effort. By 1914 advertising had developed into a highly sophisticated form of persuasion, as was the skill of press agentry, and both were put to good use in creating propaganda messages or obtaining press coverage of specific events such as warbond rallies. Linebarger (1954: 62-63) has pointed out that the character of the indigenous communication systems dictated the way in which each nation approached the use of propaganda. Thus the British, who had one of the world's finest international newsgathering and distribution systems in 1914, backed by a sophisticated domestic "free" press and extensive experience in international communication for technical and commercial purposes through their ownership of undersea cables, turned this background to excellent advantage. The Germans, on the other hand, had a more regimented press system and a much more limited network of international telecommunications connections. The Americans, who only entered the war in late 1917, nevertheless used every available form of communication at hand. This included not only the enormous power of the most extensive mass media system in the world but also the churches, the YMCA and Chatauqua groups, and the large number of private clubs and organizations found in such a polyglot society. The French, on whose ground the battles were being fought, used their professional skills at diplomacy to ensure that messages emanating from Paris received a very sympathetic hearing.

The result of all of this utilization of existing skills was a barrage of propaganda messages that assaulted the ears of civilians and soldiers at every turn. In no previous conflict had "words" been so important, reflecting as it did the fundamental change in the nature of war in an age of mass communication and mass production—the first global conflict of the emerging mass society. For no longer did single battles decide wars; now whole nations were pitted against other nations, requiring the cooperation of entire populations, both militarily and psychologically. (One reason that the Russian army did not play a decisive role in World War I was the confusion and subsequent low morale of the population, which eventually became one of the direct causes of the Russian Revolution in 1918.)

British Propaganda

The British took the lead in propaganda activities because they were forced to think seriously about it earlier than any of the other belligerent powers. This was because at the outbreak of war in August 1914, only in Britain was there an internal disagreement about entering the conflict. Unlike the other major powers on the continent, Britain did not have universal conscription into the army, and thus the decision to mobilize its armed forces was more of a political one than in France or Germany. In Britain, the Liberal Party that had been in power since 1905 was predominantly anti-war, as was the opposition Labour Party, and there was a widespread pressure to remain neutral in what was seen as primarily an Austro-Hungarian dispute in southeastern Europe. The Germans unwittingly settled this internal dissension when they decided to invade Belgium while marching to attack France, for Belgium's neutrality had been specifically guaranteed by the Great Powers, including Germany. The Germans miscalculated that the British would not go to war over a "mere scrap of paper," but when Belgium actually resisted the "dreaded Huns" the British became united in their resolve to defend "brave little Belgium." By September 1915, more than 2,250,000 volunteers had enlisted in the British army (Roetter, 1974: 30-31). The circulation of atrocity stories coming out of Belgium signaled the first major propaganda salvo, and had an immediate impact on British public sympathies.

The chief agency for developing this successful patriotic campaign in England was a private organization, the Central Committee for National Patriotic Associations, which was formed in late August 1914, immediately after the war started, with Prime Minister Asquith as the honorary president. This group organized lectures, patriotic clubs, and rallies in cities and counties, and also extended its influence into the far reaches of the British Empire to ensure that there was no opposition to the war among the subjects of the king. (In Canada, as an example, many French Canadians had long opposed the British Crown, and they saw no reason to fight what was essentially a British war.) Of special interest was the Neutral Countries Subcommittee, which used the direct personal approach to enlist sympathy and support from countries not in the war. Distinguished Britons lent their names to this enterprise, and as a result acquaintances, colleagues, fellow workers, or business associates in neutral countries received a flood of propaganda materials. More than 250,000 pamphlets, booklets, and other publications were distributed in this manner between August 1914 and September 1915 (Bruntz, 1938: 19). Another important organization that was eventually appointed to coordinate all British propaganda activities after March 1918 was the War Aims Committee, founded in June 1917 and initially formed to combat pacifism in Britain. (There were still enough Britons against all forms of armed conflict to warrant such an organization.)

The first official propaganda organization in Britain was the War Propaganda Bureau, which concerned itself initially with the distribution of printed materials inside neutral countries, and eventually inside Germany itself, which it did through sympathizers using the mails from Holland and Switzerland. When Lloyd George became Prime Minister in 1916, dissatisfied with British propaganda efforts and in an attempt to avoid what had become a very confused and decentralized situation, he reorganized the War Propaganda Bureau and created the Department of Information. This agency concentrated on enemy civilian psychological warfare outside of Britain whereas the National War Aims Committee dealt with internal propaganda efforts. The concept of mobilizing such a massive propaganda effort was so new that it had taken the relatively experienced British nearly five years to devise a workable system of propaganda management suitable for a great power at war. In the end the British became quite adept at coordinating their efforts at external political warfare aimed at the enemy with the internal, morale-building efforts of news-propaganda. By the time of World War II in 1939, these lessons had been thoroughly learned.

German Propaganda

The Germans, on the other hand, were never able to gain the same degree of control over their propaganda activities, and in the end they had only limited success in making their political ambitions clear to important neutral countries such as the United States. Long after the war there were many in Germany who attributed their loss to the superiority of British propaganda; foremost among these was Adolf Hitler, who in *Mein Kampf* praised the British efforts and noted that the British had understood that propaganda was so important that it had to be handled by professionals. This belief that Allied (American efforts were also lauded) propaganda had been a major contributor to Germany's defeat became a part of the mythology of the Nazis, which held that the German army could not be defeated on the field, and that only a "stab in the back" had betrayed the German people in 1918. Thus the enemy's successful use of propaganda itself was used as a form of propaganda to make the German people wary of becoming complacent and therefore susceptible to information from outside sources. The importance of propaganda as an extension of modern warfare was not lost on the fascist German leaders during the interwar period, as we shall examine later in this chapter.

Initial German international propaganda efforts were amateurish, consisting mainly of using enlisted writers and scholars to explain why the Allies were responsible for starting the war.

Unfortunately, all they succeeded in doing was to create antagonism in the targeted countries with their arrogance in the face of
the atrocity stories coming out of Belgium and France. The
stodginess of the German military communiques also failed to
garner any worldwide sympathy. Essentially German propaganda lacked both organization and moral drive, and they did
not receive the cooperation from the international press for
which they had hoped. The British Royal Navy dealt the German efforts a serious blow when on August 15, 1914, they cut
the undersea cable linking Germany and the United States. This
deprived the Germans of the means to communicate and effectively shut off attempts to make their position on the war clear
to the neutral American population. Before trans-Atlantic radio
service could be established, the European Allies had already
created the propaganda agenda for the American public, and
stories of German atrocities in Belgium and elsewhere were being widely circulated.

For once the vaunted German efficiency failed to operate,
and there was never any real coordination of the various German propaganda efforts throughout the war. Even the German
Foreign Office seemed to be unaware of the importance of trying to establish goodwill and support for the German cause.
Roetter (1974: 38-39) suggests that most of the German diplo-
mats were so convinced of the "rightness" of Germany's cause
that they felt no need to justify it, and in any case, it was always
arrogantly stated that "the War would be over by Christmas"
(Roetter, 1974: 38-39). Eventually the Foreign Office did establish a special department to deal with overseas propaganda, but
there was virtually no cooperation from the armed services. (At
the outbreak of the war, the army had only one officer who was
in contact with the press.) One of the most serious problems was
the enormous amount of conflicting information that was sent
out by the various civilian and military authorities, and this conflict became a major source of the internal struggle for political
control of Germany as the war continued on. As the military in-
variably won these arguments, it tended to underscore for both
the German people and those overseas that Germany was essentially a military state. It was very difficult for most of the
neutral countries to understand the German military argument

that it had been forced to defend the decaying Hapsburg Empire by invading poor Belgium.

The biggest philosophical difference was that whereas German propaganda efforts were only able to convey the fact that the war was being fought to avenge the country's honor, the British were able to make the war appear to be, as H. G. Wells put, "the war to end all wars"—that is, the war that would defend humanity everywhere. Germany was never able to claim a moral position to compete with this platitude. What the Germans failed to learn in World War I, they studied and applied with a vengeance in World War II. Hitler did not really care what the rest of the world thought about his policies; he was mainly concerned with domestic propaganda success.

American Propaganda

American propaganda, which the Germans admired so much, was the work of two agencies. The civilian agency was the Committee on Public Information (CPI), which became known as the "Creel Committee" because of its chairman, George Creel, who had been a newspaper editor. (The Committee also had as members the secretary of state, and the secretaries for the Army and the Navy.) The military agency was the Propaganda Section (or Psychologic Section) of the American Expeditionary Forces, under Captain Heber Blakenhorn, also known as G-2D. The CPI had the advantage of a leader who had the confidence of President Wilson, and George Creel was therefore able to force a coordination of propaganda efforts with other civilian and military agencies.

Creel (1920: 3), in his fascinating book about his wartime work, *How We Advertised America*, saw the conflict as "the fight for the *minds* of men, for the 'conquest of their convictions,' and the battle-line ran through every home in every country." His approach to the problem was to use a technique that he thought Americans knew best—sales. He noted, "In all things, from first to last, without halt or change, it was a plain publicity proposition, a vast enterprise in salesmanship, the world's greatest adventure in advertising" (Creel, 1920: 4). Operating with a wide mandate, and with a relatively loose organizational structure, the CPI used every available means of communicating with the American public with an intensity never before devoted to a single issue in the United States. Creel (1920: 5) congratulated himself on the fact that

> there was no part of the great war machinery that we did not touch, no medium of appeal that we did not employ. The printed word, the spoken word, the motion picture, the telegraph, the cable, the wireless, the poster, the sign-board—all these were used in our campaign to make our own people and other peoples understand the causes that compelled America to take arms. All that was fine and ardent in the civilian population came at our call until more than one hundred and fifty thousand men and women were devoting highly specialized abilities to the work of the Committee, as faithful and devoted in their service as though they wore the khaki.

The output of the CPI was intended mainly for domestic consumption, and as Creel stated above, the American public was subjected to an intense barrage of propaganda messages. Of particular interest was the use of the oral tradition in the form of the "Four Minute Men," who were volunteer speakers in local communities who would lecture on the war at a moment's notice to any interested group wishing to acquaint itself with the "facts." The growing American film industry was enlisted to make propaganda movies, and the CPI encouraged the showing of these in neutral countries, while the fledgling radio medium was used to broadcast messages from the United States to the Eiffel Tower in Paris, and from there to most of the neutral European countries. The CPI also had commissioners in every foreign neutral and Allied nation whose job it was to disseminate daily news to the local press.

In the final assessment of the success of the CPI we must be careful to distinguish between the immediate results and the long-term effects on American society. As an agency of psychological warfare the CPI was extremely successful, and it created a war psychosis in the United States that went a long way in providing the moral and material support required by the armed services. However, when the war finally ended, and the Wilsonian concept of a war to "make the world safe for democracy" proved to be largely unfounded, the American public and especially the politicians began to question seriously both the tactics and the intensity of the CPI's propaganda activities. The "boosterism" mentality that accompanied so much of the domestic activities of the CPI when contrasted with the loss of so many American lives, especially in the face of the disillusionment with the settlement of the war, left a bad taste in the mouths of Americans. In turn this lead to a justified suspicion of the power of organized propaganda, and ultimately encouraged the pacifist and isolationist tendencies that existed in the United States for the next twenty years. As Linebarger (1954: 68) noted, "A more modest, more calculated national propaganda effort would have helped forestall those attitudes which, in turn, made World War II possible."

American military propaganda activities concentrated on morale and surrender leaflets because radio loudspeaker technology did not exceed the power of the megaphone by much at that time. Therefore, most communication with the enemy had to be in one of the most basic forms of all—the printed leaflet. The British and French had pioneered in this form of propaganda, but the Americans developed some of their own inventions, and balloons and airplanes were the chief methods of dispersement, but later special leaflet bombs and mortars were also used very effectively. The messages in these leaflets were essentially antimilitaristic and prodemocratic, stressing the class differences between the German leaders and the enlisted men (the same tactic as used in the Revolutionary War!), and also reminding German soldiers that American industrial might had now entered the war. The primary mission was to induce an attitude of surrender, and here the Americans really excelled for they were able to promise the half-starved German infantry first-class American food and care, and return to loved ones, all under the rule of international law. It soon became obvious that food was the most popular subject of appeal, for this had become an obsession with the starving German soldiers and civilian population.

Instead of attacking these issues directly by countering the information in the leaflets, the German high command attacked the whole concept of such demoralizing propaganda as being unethical, and stressed that German soldiers were expected to do their duty and would not be influenced by such messages. Of course this tactic failed and German soldiers surrendered in large numbers to the American and Allied forces in

the last months of the War. Once again, the German army's re-
luctance to get their hands dirty in psychological warfare cost
them dearly, but one must also point out that they had very few
propaganda issues with which to counter, for unlike the domestic conditions in Germany, there was very little deprivation and
starvation in the Allied countries, especially after America entered the war in 1917. Propaganda is most successful when it
has a firm footing in observable reality.

Atrocity Propaganda

Perhaps the most significant single feature of World War I
propaganda was the wide dissemination of atrocity stories as a
means of discrediting the enemy. Often called "hate propaganda," most of the atrocity stories concentrated on three types
of alleged cruelties: (1) massacre, such as the slaughter of the
Armenians by the Ottoman Empire, supposedly under the encouragement of the Germans; (2) mutilation, such as the goug-
ing out of the eyes of German soldiers; and (3) the mistreatment
of both soldiers and civilian populations by starvation or actual
torture. Such forms of propaganda are designed to stiffen the
fighting spirit of entire nations, to create fear of defeat, and also
as a more practical means to raise funds and encourage enlist-
ment to halt these inhuman acts. Ultimately, it also served the
purpose of prolonging the fighting and creating more severe
conditions for surrender.

There were literally hundreds of books and pamphlets devoted to the most graphic details of supposed atrocities committed by both sides. Stories emanating from Belgium had a
particularly strong influence in the Allied countries because of
the large number of Belgium refugees who fled to neutral nations in 1914. The popular notion comparing the German soldier to the "Hun" of old (the Huns were actually Mongols from
Central Asia), inspired by a careless remark made by the Kaiser
in 1899 when he admonished the German contingent off to fight
the Boxer Rebellion in China to "behave like Huns," became a
central theme of propaganda attacks against the Germans.
These atrocity stories, a few based upon real incidents but most
without foundation, formed the core of the anti-German propaganda aimed at the United States in the years before America
entered the war.

There were many atrocity stories that were widely circulated in the United States and other neutral countries; two have special significance. (Other atrocity propaganda stories have already been discussed in Chapter 4.) On October 9, 1915, Edith Cavell, a Red Cross nurse working in Brussels, was found guilty by a German court martial of helping British and French soldiers to escape into neutral Holland. She was sentenced to death and executed by a firing squad on October 12. She could have saved herself by professing ignorance of the law, but instead she openly admitted that many of the escapees had gone back to join their units; thus she was manifestly guilty of having committed a capital offense according to the German military code. This daughter of an English clergyman stated at her execution, "Standing before God and eternity, I realize this — patriotism is not enough. I must be free from hate and bitterness." These words were carved on the monument to Edith Cavell in central London (Read, 1941: 213). Edith Cavell became an instant martyr to the cause of propaganda and her "cold-blooded murder" was used to give credibility to the other atrocity stories coming out of Belgium. Even the supposedly neutral American press printed full accounts of the 50-year-old nurse's courage in the face of her executioners. In Britain even to this day Edith Cavell remains a symbol of courage and loyalty.

There is an interesting sidelight to this story that demonstrates the failure of the Germans to understand the value of propaganda. The French had shot several women spies, one of them as early as August 1914, and at least two after Edith Cavell's execution, but the Germans failed to use these events to their advantage, and they were not even reported in the American press. A later attempt by the Germans to make a propaganda event of the execution by the French of the Dutch-Javanese entertainer and professional spy Mata Hari seemed to lack appeal when compared to the death of the English nurse. (Of course, the Mata Hari story later achieved immortality through the efforts of Hollywood, which, in 1931, produced a movie about her exploits featuring the extremely popular actress, Greta Garbo.) In the United States and other neutral nations, the Germans were hard-pressed to counter their constant portrayal as a barbaric nation that readily executed women.

The other propaganda event of significance was the furor that surrounded the sinking of the luxury liner *Lusitania* on May 7, 1915, by a German U-boat—without any prior warning and with a loss of 1,198 lives, 128 of them American. Whether or not the sinking of the ship was justified by the fact that the ship was carrying arms did not seem to matter at the time, for both the British and American press used the incident to reinforce increasingly hostile attitudes toward German acts of atrocity. In one of those curious acts of history, just five days after the sinking to the *Lusitania*, the British Government issued their long-awaited Bryce Commission Report on the accuracy of the stories of German atrocities. This Committee, headed by a prominent British legal expert, had been formed in early 1915 as a result of a public demand to know the truth about the German outrages.

The final Report, which found "a compelling mass of evidence" to substantiate the atrocities, was translated into thirty languages and was widely circulated and reported in the United States (Read, 1941: 201-204). The findings of the Bryce Commission only served to accentuate the "barbarity" of the ship's sinking, despite the fact that the Germans may have had some justification for their actions during a state of war. Today there is still considerable doubt about the depositions taken by the Bryce Commission from Belgium refugees, and there is the suggestion that the commissioners were themselves caught up in the hysteria of war (Roetter, 1974: 47-48).

Reaction to World War I Propaganda

There is little doubt that propaganda was effective as a weapon of psychological warfare in World War I, but as indicated in Chapter 4, this must be viewed in its historical context. For the first time in history nations were forced to draw on the collective power of their entire populations by linking the individual to a larger societal need. As De Fleur and Ball-Rokeach (1982: 159) have pointed out, "It became essential to mobilize sentiments and loyalties, to instill in citizens a hatred and fear of the enemy, to maintain their morale in the face of privation, and to capture their energies into an effective contribution to their nation."

As a result, the general public indicated a response to mass media messages as never before, and this reaction reinforced already existing fears about the potentially dangerous role of the mass media in a mass society. The prevailing theories of psychology and the understanding of the way in which the mass media worked were relatively unsophisticated, and this lead to misinterpretation of how powerful the media really were. There was little appreciation of the specific social and political conditions that had made World War I propaganda so effective, and these incomplete perceptions colored much of the thinking about the mass media in general and propaganda in particular for the next twenty years.

THE INTERWAR YEARS, 1920-1939

The role of propaganda in the period between the two world wars can be characterized by three political developments: the Russian Revolution and the rise of the Communist Soviet Union; the strong isolationist impulse in the United States as a direct result of disillusionment with the outcome of World War I; and the rise of the fascist states, especially Nazi Germany. All three of these historical developments played a direct role in the outbreak of hostilities again in 1939, only this time all of the belligerent nations were aware of the necessity of both offering and countering propaganda in the strongest way possible.

The Emergence of Communist Propaganda

The philosophical underpinnings of the Russian Revolution lay in the adoption of an interpretation of the works of Karl Marx by a group of dissident Russian intellectuals, particularly Lenin and Trotsky. Ironically, it was the German General Ludendorff who arranged to have Lenin return to Russia from exile in Switzerland in 1917, specifically to sow the seeds of revolution that would end the war on the Eastern front, thus making more German troops available to confront the Allies in the West. Lenin finally succeeded in his Bolshevik Revolution in November 1917 when he overthrew the provisional government of Kerensky, which had earlier deposed Czar Nicholas II in March. The Bolsheviks came to power determined to create a new social order, but faced the immense task of transforming the thinking of a largely rural population of more than 170 million, many of whom were illiterate and most of whom were hungry.

To achieve their ends, the Soviet rulers erected an immense network of propaganda that included massive programs of political as well as practical education. Lenin mobilized every available form of communication (and entertainment) to meet this goal: the press, educational institutions, the arts, and even science all became part of the intensive internal propaganda system designed to play the central role in the creation of a Communist state. Controlled from the top, the arms of the Soviet propaganda machine reached into every aspect of Russian life, down to the local level where clubs and other quasi-social organizations received political education from trained propagandists. The establishment of reading rooms in even the smallest villages encouraged guided discussions, while films were accompanied by "question and answer" sessions. All of this was under the control and tight supervision of the Agitational-Propaganda Section of the Central Committee of the Communist Party, known as *Agitprop*, which was attached to every division of the Communist Party down to the smallest local cell (Maxwell, 1936: 61-79). While the internal political convulsions continued in Russia until the late 1950s, this intensive propaganda infrastructure was absolutely crucial to the establishment of the new Communist state. It was and continues to be the most extensive and long-lasting propaganda campaign in history.

The Communists used a variety of symbolic and political devices to enhance their propaganda program. Foremost among the political devices was the concept of the imminent threat or plot, much as had been used in the French Revolution, which allowed the threat of brutality or retaliation to be used against political enemies or merely those who questioned Party actions. The Hammer and Sickle was a strong visual symbol, and it received wide international recognition, but for many years the Soviet Union was restricted from lavish spectacle because of the spartan internal conditions. Even the *Internationale* was not played in the October uprising because the band did not know it; the *Marseillaise* was played instead! Today, of course, the Soviet Union engages in massive spectacles of military might, of civilian solidarity, and these symbolic displays have become a staple of worldwide Communist propaganda, signifying the importance of the collectivity over the individual. Because an articulated part of the Bolshevik program was to export Communism to all parts of the world—"the world Revolution"—Russian propaganda activities took on a worldwide dimension in the interwar period. In every country there sprang up national Communist parties, which in the period before the Stalinist purges of the mid-1930s were directly under the control of the Soviet Union, all aimed at establishing the international solidarity of the working class. Such sentiments had enormous appeal during the Depression, when unemployment, hunger, and general disillusionment with capitalism all contributed to a rise in the interest in communism in the Western democracies, especially inflation-wrought and war-weary Germany. Even in the United States the Communist Party and the "Popular Front" of pro-Soviet organizations attracted millions of members in the period 1935 to 1939, before the ill-fated Stalin-Hitler pact of August 1939 shattered their unity and created a schism with Moscow (O'Neill, 1982).

American Isolationism

As a direct result of their unsatisfactory experiences with the outcome of World War I, and lead by their politicians, the American people turned inward during the period 1920 to 1941. The "America First" movement gained in popularity as people seemed to want to turn away from the turmoil in Europe, and the severe effects of the Depression created a further impetus to concentrate on domestic issues. The reaction against propaganda was particularly virulent, as those responsible for creating the successful campaigns during the war seemed to be only too eager to explain how it was all done. George Creel published his book *How We Advertised America* in 1920, and this precipitated a lengthy (and somewhat justified) suspicion of propaganda. This fear was enhanced by the rise to power of Hitler, and the increased use of propaganda by the Nazi Reich and the other fascist states such as Italy. On the domestic scene, the emergence of prominent demogogues such as the ultraconservative Fr. Charles E. Coughlin, a priest whose fascist-like broadcasts gained wide attention (and considerable support) during the late 1930s, contributed to the concerns about the effects of propaganda.

The Institute for Propaganda Analysis was started in October 1937 with a grant from philanthropist Edward A. Filene, with Columbia University Professor Clyde R. Miller as the chief executive. According to Alfred and Elizabeth Lee, among the founding members of the Institute, propaganda analysis caught on so readily because "it provided a badly needed perspective for current affairs" (Lee and Lee,1979:viii). In one of its major publications, The Fine Art of Propaganda (1939), the Institute analyzed various aspects of propaganda, developing the seven "devices" or "ABC's of Propaganda Analysis." These were the following:

   • Name Calling: giving an idea a bad label, and therefore rejecting and condemning it without examining the evidence.
   • Glittering Generality: associating something with a "virtue word" and creating acceptance and approval without examination of the evidence.
   • Transfer: carries the respect and authority of something respected to something else to make the later accepted. Also works with something that is disrespected to make the latter rejected.
   • Testimonial: consists in having some respected or hated person say that a given idea or program or product or person is good or bad.
   • Plain Folks: the method by which a speaker attempts to convince the audience that he or she and his or her ideas are good because they are "of the people," the "plain folks."
   • Card Stacking: involves the selection and use of facts or falsehoods, illustrations or distractions, and logical or illogical statements in order to give the best or the worst possible case for an idea, program, person, or product.
   • Band Wagon: has as its theme "everybody—at least all of us—is doing it," and thereby tries to convince the members of a group that their peers are accepting the program, and that we should all jump on the band wagon rather than be left out (Lee and Lee, 1979).

This technique of analyzing propaganda was open to criticism, especially in that it can be very subjective in evaluation; however, this seven-point analysis remains with us today and can still be found in speech communication texts. With the advent of World War II, the subsequent Cold War, and then the Korean and Vietnam Wars, the Institute for Propaganda Analysis simply lost its reason for existence in the highly militarized atmosphere. Despite its demise, it serves as an ongoing symbol of the concern for the increased and sometimes subtle role of propaganda in our lives. American isolationism remained fairly strong even after war broke out in Europe in 1939; however, there is clear evidence through opinion polls that the American public was increasingly becoming pro-Ally, while at the same time they remained antiwar. Congress was reluctant at times to give President Roosevelt approval to supply Britain with arms, but gradually relented. The United States officially entered the war against Germany on December 11, 1941, four days after the Japanese attacked Pearl Harbor. Once committed in this fashion, the American public again became the target of massive propaganda campaigns both on the home front and in the armed services. (Some of these propaganda activities are examined in Chapter 3.) Since the end of World War II the isolationist impulse has periodically risen, but the coming of the atomic age has effectively prevented total withdrawal from the world arena, although many Americans still wish that isolationism was possible.

Hitler and Nazi Propaganda

One of the unexpected consequences of the somewhat hysterical anti-German propaganda of World War I was that it made many people, particularly politicians, suspicious of alleged atrocity stories emanating from Germany during the 1930s. The very success of the British propaganda efforts in 1914-1918 proved to be a serious handicap in getting the world to accept the reality of what was happening in Nazi Germany, and this created a disastrous delay in the public's awareness of the horrors of the concentration camps and other Nazi atrocities.

Hitler's place in the history of propaganda is assured, for as Thomson (1977: 111) notes, "Hitler shares with Julius Caesar and Napoleon Bonaparte, the distinction of not only making massive use of new methods of propaganda but also, of quite consciously and deliberately basing his entire career on planned propaganda." Goebbels, who became Hitler's Propaganda Minister and the mastermind behind the Nazi propaganda machine, described Hitler's propaganda principles, which he extracted from *Mein Kampf*, as

> a carefully built up erection of statements, which whether true or false can be made to undermine quite rigidly held ideas and to construct new ones that will take their place. It would not be impossible to prove with sufficient repetition and psychological understanding of the people concerned that a square is in fact a circle. What after all are a square and a circle? They are mere words and words can be moulded until they clothe ideas in disguise [Thomson, 1977: 111].

In *Mein Kampf* Hitler established several cardinal rules for successful propaganda: one should avoid abstract ideas and appeal instead to the emotions, which was the opposite of the Marxist concept; there should be constant repetition of just a few ideas, using stereotyped phrases and avoiding objectivity; put forth only one side of the argument; constantly criticize enemies of the state; and identify one special enemy for special vilification. Throughout the Nazi period Hitler and Goebbels stuck rigidly to these principles, and the world witnessed a mature, cultured people—the Germans—accepting one of the worst dictatorships in history and becoming party to a prolonged war and eventually the most heinous of all crimes, genocide.

Hitler had admired the propaganda efforts of the British in World War I, as well as the work of the poet-politician D'Annunzio, the short-lived dictator of Fiume in Italy, and the extroverted style and anti-Semitism of Karl Lueger, the Mayor of Vienna. A key to Hitler's thinking was that he saw the masses as "malleable, corrupt and corruptable," and open to emotional appeals; but especially he realized that propaganda could become much more effective if it was stiffened with a large dose of intimidation and terror (Zeman, 1973: xvi). Calling his political program National Socialism, Hitler immediately established a image that appealed to a wide section of the confused and demoralized German public. He promised to restore Germany to its former glory and to rid the country of the shackles imposed by the Versailles Peace Treaty, and thus rose to power with a skillful combination of power, spectacle, and propaganda.

Together Hitler and Goebbels probably understood the propaganda potential of the mass media better than anyone else alive, and they were in a perfect position to put their theories to the test. Their greatest advantage was the psychological condition of their audience, for the German Weimar government had failed to provide the leadership that would have restored German confidence and morale after 1918, and the German people were desperately searching for the answers to their political nightmare. Many of them turned to socialism and communism; National Socialism, with its emphasis on restoring the mythical Germany of the past and the perverse charismatic leadership provided by Adolf Hitler, offered an even more palatable alternative. Germany in the late 1920s and early 1930s supplied the perfect setting for the implementation of Hitler's schemes.

The Weimar Republic had an ineffective press, which was so diffused with small partisan papers that the Nazis were easily able to gain control of the newpapers in the period after 1925. Using the simple, nondoctrinaire approach, the Nazi newspapers *Völkische Beobachter* (Racist Observer) and later *Das Reich* preached the Nazi philosophy, especially anti-Semitism and anti-Communism, as well as providing information about the Nazi Party itself. But newspapers were not the main vehicle for Nazi propaganda, for the emotional appeals stressed by Hitler did not easily translate into written words. There were few journalists in Germany at this time with enough skill to compete with the fiery speeches from Nazi podiums.

It was with radio that the Nazis achieved their greatest success, and this medium was used extensively as the primary medium of official propaganda. The importance of radio was stressed when the Nazi government produced a cheap, one-channel radio set for the masses (the Völksempfanger), and eventually introduced compulsory installation of radios with loudspeakers in restaurants, factories, and most public places. During the war, there were even Radio Wardens who checked that people were listening to the right stations! As we have seen in Chapter 3, radio also became the primary medium for overseas propaganda activities, and Hitler used directed broadcasts to those European countries where he was trying to establish contact with German-speaking populations. Austria was to suffer particularly from a "radio war" in 1933, as Hitler attempted to incite the Austrians to overthrow their government. Radio was also extensively used to win the Saar Plebiscite in 1936, when Goebbels smuggled large numbers of cheap radios into the disputed territory in order to gain German support and to smear the anti-Nazi leader Max Brawn. On the day before the secret vote, German radio broadcast that Brawn had fled, and it was too late to counter this move so that even as Brawn was driven through the streets, he was called an imposter. Radio was also the perfect medium for communicating the almost religious fervor of Nazi spectacles, with the rhythmic chants of "Seig Heil," the enthusiastic applause, and the power of Hitler's or Goebbels' speaking style.

As we have already noted, the Germans did not have as much propaganda success with their use of the cinema—mainly because audiences were more attuned to escapist entertainment—and film propaganda, even when skillfully done, has a tendency to look too heavy-handed. This is especially true if the audience is aware that "this is a propaganda film." There were, however, some memorable German propaganda films, such as director Leni Riefenstahl's use of the Odin myth in the making of *The Triumph of the Will*; a film about the Boer War, *Ohm Krüger* which allowed the Germans to attack British colonialism; and *Jud Süss*, which was a subtle anti-Semitic examination of the influence of Jews on German life. Even more violent in its anti-Semitic attack was *Der Ewige Jude* (*The Eternal Jew*), depicting the worst racial stereotypes. However, the biggest box office attraction during this period, was the purely ence's rejection of blatant propaganda. Commercial Nazi propaganda films with rare exceptions failed to find strong overseas markets and therefore were limited in their influence. Some of the war documentaries, as indicated in Chapter 3, did create a fear of the German army in many neutral countries, but they also had the opposite effect of reinforcing opposition to German aggression in countries such as Britain and the United States.

Posters were also used extensively throughout the Nazi Reich; these usually featured bold colors, especially red, and used large, simplistic illustrations and heavy, dominating slogans. Hitler wanted to be an architect in his youth, and he always had an appreciation for the visual—he understood the importance of strong visual symbols. Especially in the period before the Nazis were able to dominate newspapers and radio, the poster became the primary source of propaganda, displaying especially the Nazi symbol of the swastika, the square-jawed pure Aryan Nazi stormtrooper, or anti-Semitic images of large-nosed Jews. These propaganda images became commonplace after Hitler come to power in 1932, and they contributed in no small measure to Nazi success (Zeman, 1978).

The Nazis used many propaganda devices, but one that they brought to the peak of perfection in the modern era was the spectacle. Under the supervision of Hitler's official architect, Albert Speer, these lavish public displays moved from being mere exhibitions of Nazi might to becoming propagandistic works of art, designed to evoke an outpouring of emotional fervor and support. These rallies also allowed the people of Germany to perceive Hitler in the context of a restored Germany, with strong overtones harking back to the Aryan myths of the past. Using dramatic lighting, controlled sound effects, and martial music, and with a cast of hundreds of thousands, the Nuremberg Rallies especially were centerpieces for the public affirmation of Nazi mythology, calculated to create the right degree of hysteria in the German people.

Finally, Nazi propaganda made extensive use of a wide variety of carefully designed symbols to emphasize their power and authority. These included the eagle, blood, marching—especially the goose-step—the "Heil" salute, the carrying of swords, the use of fire, the swastika, and the flag (Delia, 1971). Some symbols were more blatant than others, such as the skull and crossbones insignia worn by members of the Gestapo. Nazis were particularly adept at using architecture and sculpture as propaganda media, and Albert Speer masterminded the massive restructuring of Berlin and other large-scale construction projects ordered by Hitler to reflect his "Thousand Year Reich." Hitler apparently wanted to leave a monument to himself that would have dwarfed all such monuments from the past, including a triumphal arch that would have been 550 feet wide, 392 feet deep, and 386 feet high. Recanting after the war, Speer (1970) called this "architectural megalomania."

One major advantage that the Nazis had in the success of their domestic propaganda campaigns was total control over the country. By 1933, there were no competing propaganda messages of any consequence to distract the German public. The educational system, like the Russian, was an instrument of state policy and was geared to provide an ideological perspective of anti-Semitism and Nazi values. In fact, anti-Semitism became the underpinning of the Nazi propaganda campaign, as the Jews were blamed for everything that was wrong with Germany and the West. Jews were called decadent capitalists or godless Bolsheviks at the same time; it did not matter that much of the rhetoric was clearly contradictory, for Hitler's principles of propaganda required that a scapegoat be found, and anti-Semitism served both political and social ends. Through the persistent reinforcement of these messages, Hitler was able to achieve a fiery nationalism by convincing the German people that ridding themselves of Jews would create an undefiled, uncorrupt, pure Aryan nation. Socially, anti-Semitism was evoked to provide a rationale for German failure, as well as a reason to hope for a better future—once the problem had been taken care of. This was a classic propaganda ploy; Hitler demoralized Jews and mobilized hatred against them, providing a justification for his political and social policies.

In the long run Hitler's domestic propaganda campaigns were successful, and it was only defeat on the battlefield that finally ended the terror within Germany. In his recent book, *The War that Hitler Won*, Robert Herzstein makes a strong case for considering the overwhelming success of Hitler's propaganda efforts in the context of their times. Since 1945, we have concentrated on the loss of the war by the Nazis while ignoring their incredible propaganda victories in Germany and elsewhere. Even after the Allies had liberated a few concentration camps, German leaders were still advocating the extermination of Jews and Bolsheviks, and were blaming the loss of the war on these groups. Ultimately Nazism and its abhorrent racial philosophies could only be defeated on the battlefield (Herzstein, 1978).

WORLD WAR II

In many ways the propaganda efforts of the belligerent nations in World War II were predictable, following the discovery of the potential of psychological warfare in World War I. The major difference, as we have already noted in Chapter 3, is that radio now became the principal means of sending propaganda messages to foreign countries. The traditional propaganda media of pamphlets, posters, and motion pictures were again used, but with an increased awareness of the psychology of human behavior. On all sides psychologists were put to work on devising the best methods of appeal, taking into consideration specific cultural and social factors relative to the intended target audience. This was a far cry from the rather "buckshot" approach taken earlier, and indicated the seriousness with which psychological warfare was being waged. On both fronts—the European and the Pacific—American propaganda experts from the various agencies that were created to coordinate domestic and overseas propaganda activities were careful to use scientific methods where possible in devising their campaigns. In particular, there was to be little emphasis on atrocity propaganda, except where this served a deliberate purpose, such as President Roosevelt's delayed announcement of the Japanese execution of the American flyers shot down over Tokyo.

Both sides made much more extensive use of "white" and "black" propaganda through the medium of radio, as the new medium provided the ideal opportunity to establish contact over long distances without necessarily revealing the source of the message. Clandestine radio stations were established that broadcast both true and false information to the enemy, and special commentators were used to create the illusion of broadcasts coming from within their own countries. The British, through the services of the British Broadcast Corporation, were particularly adept at this, establishing several black propaganda stations aimed at both German domestic and military targets. These stations, by essentially broadcasting the truth about wartime conditions, were able to make a considerable impact on the German people, and often caused confusion on the military front (Roetter, 1974: 168-184). This emphasis on truth, which became the basic philosophy for the British Broadcasting system, proved to be an extremely powerful propaganda weapon, and by the end of the war the German civilian population was listening to these broadcasts in order to find out about conditions in their own country.

On the domestic front, in both Britain and the United States, extensive campaigns were devised to boost homefront morale. Particularly in Britain, where the German Luftwaffe had created chaos with their bombing raids, it was essential that the population be kept from panic. Again, the Ministry of Information, which was charged with this task, realized that truth was their greatest propaganda device, but their experts had a difficult time persuading their government to adopt this tactic. Eventually the Ministry won its argument that in fighting totalitarianism, Britain should not borrow its weapons of lies and censorship but instead should rely upon the sensibility and toughness of the British people, taking them into the government's confidence. In the long run, such propaganda tactics played an important part in maintaining the high morale of the British public, even during the darkest periods early in the war (McLaine, 1979: 11).

In the United States the problems were different, and the major emphasis was placed on providing a clear rationale to the American people as to why they were fighting the war in Europe. (There was no equivocation about why the Pacific War was necessary.) As mentioned in Chapter 4, it was deemed necessary to provide the American fighting man with an orientation to the reasons he was being asked to risk his life. The *Why We Fight* films, discussed in Chapter 4, were compulsory viewing for enlisted men, and the first of these, *Prelude to War*, was also shown to civilian audiences throughout the nation in 1943. It was these films that were the subject of important research into the effects of propaganda messages on specific audiences (see Chapter 4: 103-104). Utilizing all of the mass media, the Office of War Information (OWI), the organization charged with handling domestic propaganda before 1943, created immediate antagonism with what had always been a "free press." The American mass media were not used to being told what they could or could not do, and full cooperation with the government only came after a series of delicate negotiations. OWI officials were eager to have the domestic entertainment media use their considerable power to propagandize to the American public in a more blatant fashion than the media executives thought necessary. In the long run, the OWI reduced its demands in the face of congressional disapproval and suspicion that it was being used by President Roosevelt to further his own personal domestic policies. Allan Winkler (1978: 156-157), in his history of the OWI, suggests that the eventual success of the American propaganda campaigns, both domestic and abroad, was that they "sketched the war as a struggle for the American way of life and stressed the components—both spiritual and material—that . . . made America great."

The Cold War, 1945-1985

Once World War II was over, the world had entered a new age; people no longer entertained the naive concept that global conflict could be won or lost by conventional means, for now the frightening power of nuclear destruction loomed menacingly over the international scene. While wars of physical destruction continued, there were other types of wars to be fought as the world moved beyond its imperialist-colonial period, and many new nations fought for their rights in the global arena. This generated increased demands for more extensive propaganda activities, particularly as the two great world powers, Russia and the United States, sought to establish their political and cultural hegemony in the rest of the world.

In the struggle for international power, which has become a feature of modern politics, all nations have been forced to adopt new and permanent propaganda strategies as an integral part of their foreign policies. In fact, the use of international propaganda in its many forms is so ubiquitous that the foreign policy of most nations is geared toward both its generation and refutation on a continuous basis. In an age when instantaneous communication is the norm, nations have become conscious of creating and maintaining specific images that they hope to project to the rest of the world; and a vast amount of time, money, and human energy is spent on such activities. The astonishing growth of new communication technologies such as television satellites and transistor radios has created a worldwide audience for what were previously small-scale international activities. Increasingly world leaders are becoming astutely aware that their every action is being critically examined within this new electronic arena, and like the good actors that most politicians are, they are adjusting their postures and policies to make the most of their exposure.

Since the end of World War II there has been an enormous increase in the growth of new forms of propaganda activities, ranging from the traditional foreign policy pronouncements to more subtle, but no less effective, activities such as travel bureaus, sporting events, international trade exhibitions and world expositions, achievements in space and other technologies, and cultural phenomena such as art, fashion, and music. In fact, it would not be inaccurate to say that almost every aspect of human activity can be propagandized in the international arena. The Russians claim to have the oldest people in the world, the Scandinavians the lowest infant mortality rate, and the Americans the most automobiles per capita. All of these are used, in one form or another, as propaganda. The Olympic Games, in particular, has become a major propaganda event ever since Adolf Hitler used the 1936 Berlin games to showcase his Aryan Reich. In recent years, both the United States in 1980 and then the Russians in 1984 boycotted the Games as a means of propagandizing their displeasure over each other's foreign policies. The Russians went even further, claiming that "criminal elements" would make Los Angeles unsafe for their athletes, hoping to score international propaganda points against U.S. domestic conditions. Ultimately the Los Angeles Games proved to be the safest in recent years and also ran at a profit! At this point the Russians objected that the Americans had subverted the Olympic ideals into a "capitalist sideshow" — and thus are modern propaganda battles waged.

The emergence of these new communication technologies has often made it possible for those wishing to propagandize to make direct contact with their target audiences, and thus governments have much less control over the flow of information than was possible in the age of print. The consequences of this important historical shift are already noticeable as world public opinion gains influence. Also, there is increasing evidence of the frustration of unfulfilled rising expectations in the less-developed countries, which often manifests itself in hostile acts and bellicose propagandizing. We are also witnessing the emergence of new networks of common interest that cross international boundaries, such as terrorist organizations composed of members of the Irish Republican Army, the Palestine Liberation Organization, the Italian Red Brigade, and Japanese radicals, all funded by Libya with oil revenues largely from the European countries. The acts of terror that these various groups engage in are, in fact, their specific forms of propaganda for their differing causes. Capturing an American airplane or an Italian cruise ship can guarantee extensive media coverage that these groups could otherwise not afford. Clearly in cases such as these the terrorists misjudge the extent of worldwide sympathy for their cause, but these propaganda acts serve an important morale-building function for the groups themselves.

This new development in international propaganda activities creates a problem for open societies such as the United States and Great Britain. In recent years the issue of the rights of the free press have been questioned when these rights have run up against the necessity for the government to maintain some sort of secrecy. The U.S. Supreme Court decided by a 6 to 3 vote that the *New York Times* had the right to publish the Pentagon Papers in 1971, even though their exposure would result in an embarrassment for the government and its Vietnam policies. In a closed society such as the USSR there would have been no such public admission of government subterfuge, the press being under total control of the political system.

In open societies we are constantly faced with negative disclosures in the press that provide ammunition for propaganda attacks. This is one of the tributes that living in a free society extracts; and despite the apparent disadvantages, it seems as if there is greater public confidence in open societies where the public have some — albeit often skeptical — confidence in their news media. Although there is still a tendency "to kill the messenger" who brings the bad news, this is preferable to receiving managed news or no news at all. As an example, the Russians are often reluctant to report major catastrophes such as earthquakes, plane crashes, atomic accidents, or natural disasters such as floods or tornadoes. For reasons known only to the Communist psyche, such events are seen as a weakening of their image and a possible source of propaganda. It would be almost impossible in the West to "hide" such events from the media.

The emergence of this new international "media culture" places a great deal of importance on the shaping and channeling of information to gain the maximum advantage; in some ways it has become more important to say what a nation is doing than to really do it. At least we can be thankful for the fact that mass propaganda is now practiced through trade, travel, exchange of culture, and scientific and sporting achievements, and not through warfare. In the war of words that we are all subjected to, nations have taken to trying to "outpeace" each other!

ADVERTISING: THE UBIQUITOUS PROPAGANDA

There is little doubt that under any definition of propaganda, the practice of advertising would have to be included. Advertising is a series of appeals, symbols, and statements deliberately designed to influence the receiver of the message toward the point of view desired by the communicator and to act in some specific way as a result of receiving the message, whether it be to purchase, vote, hold positive or negative views, or merely to maintain a memory. Also, advertising is not always in the best interest of the receiver of the message (refer to Figure 1.1, p. 22). It is the *deliberateness* of the intention and the carefully constructed nature of the specific appeal that distinguish advertising from other forms of persuasive communication; also, in our society advertising is generally communicated at a cost to the communicator. Whether it be paid advertising in the traditional sense, or the production of leaflets or handbills on a small duplicating machine, advertising usually involves the cost of production and distribution. The advertiser (communicator) in turn hopes that this cost will be returned eventually in the form of some benefit such as the purchase of a product, the casting of a vote, or positive or negative feelings. In fact, advertising is the most ubiquitous form of propaganda in our society. It is found everywhere we look, almost everywhere we listen, and its pressure is felt in every commercial transaction we make.

The use of advertising as a means of informing the public about the choices and availability of goods and services is an integral part of the free-enterprise capitalist system. Although there have been some exceptions (the Hershey Chocolate Bar became a big seller, although it did not do consumer advertising until the early 1970s), advertising is the primary means of stimulating the sales of the products of our consumer-oriented society, and as such has a direct influence in the economy. However, there are many critics of advertising who point out that vast sums of money are spent on promoting an increasingly wider range of choices for an already overburdened market—after all, does our society really need to choose from more than thirty brands of toothpaste? The debate about the actual economic utility of advertising is also echoed by economists, who disagree about whether of not advertising increases the costs of goods—by creating a larger potential market, and thereby lowering unit costs or merely adding to the cost of producing and selling these goods. These arguments have existed ever since advertising became an essential part of modern capitalist economies in the nineteenth century (Pope, 1983).

Advertising also serves as the financial base for our vast mass communications network, for the structure of our commercialized media system is totally dependent on the revenues from advertising. Even our public broadcast systems depend to some extent on being underwritten by funds from the business sector. Although advertising may be considered an intrusion into our television viewing, magazine or newspaper reading, or enjoyment of the radio, we accept its existence because we understand its role in making possible our enjoyment of these media. If we really consider the actual structure of the commercial media system, it is the audience that is being delivered to the advertiser and not the other way around.

Institutional Propaganda

In our society advertising is institutional propaganda at its most obvious level. It serves as a constant reminder that we are being bombarded with messages intended to bring us to a certain point of view. Yet we can only absorb so much of what we are expected to, and so we have learned to cope with this enormous information overload. We may look, but not really see the television commercial; we may listen, but not really hear the radio jingle; and we leaf by print ads without paying attention. But every so often we do see or hear or read, and this is what is intended by the creators of advertising. From the more than 1,600 "messages" we are exposed to every day, we remember at most only about 80 (Heilbroner, 1985: 72).

In 1984, more than $67 billion was spent on advertising expenditures in the United States; this was for all types of advertising, from $500,000 commercials on the Superbowl telecast to the classified ads in the local neighborhood paper. There are more than 28,000 nationally advertised brands for sale in the United States (Heilbroner, 1985: 72). It is the job of the advertiser (and his or her appointed advertising agency) to make his or her brand stand out from the rest, and so we are inundated with advertising campaigns extolling the specific virtues of individual products.

The Science of Advertising

It is in this process of product differentiation that advertising propaganda is selective and often distortive in what it tells the consumer. The desire to appear to be different, or to be considered a superior product, or to provide faster, more reliable service encourages the use of hyperbole and exaggeration, and this in turn has created a nation of skeptical consumers. To overcome this growing skepticism, and to increase the chances of success in an already overcrowded marketplace, advertisers have resorted to a wide range of techniques from the most obvious to the very subtle to attract attention to their specific propaganda strategy. In the act of gaining the consumers' attention we are all too familiar with the blatancy of the bikini-clad woman on the car hood, but most of us are unaware of the effectiveness of the psychologically tested and then readjusted copy for a headache remedy seen on the nightly network news. Increasingly advertisers are resorting to a variety of scientific testing methods to maximize the expenditure of their advertising budgets by increasing the potential of their message getting through the morass, and this includes close demographic analysis of their target audience; an understanding of the psychological framework of receptivity for their message and whatever adjustments might be necessary to improve this; a study of the effectiveness of one specific message versus another specific message; and even the application of the psychology of color to shape the mood of the audience.

Despite all of this expensive scientific analysis, much of advertising remains ineffective and the list of failed products continues to grow. As we have noted many times in this book, not all propaganda is successful, for a variety of reasons. The "message" may not be convincing enough to warrant the consumer to change existing behavior (or purchase) patterns; or the product may not be seen as utilitarian or cost effective; or there might just be plain, old skepticism, for after all, advertising has a long history of being deceptive or distortive. Of course, advertising can also be extremely effective when the right combination of circumstances comes together, and there are many examples of advertising success stories. However, despite its proven effectiveness as a "mover of goods," or perhaps because of it, public attitudes toward advertising are often very negative. In many ways the consumer's experience with advertising has made him or her suspicious of all propaganda, and this might prove to be a healthy trend in our society. It will force advertisers and other propagandists to improve the quality of their messages and diminish the possibility of negative propaganda influence. If consumers are aware that they are being propagandized, the choice to accept or reject the message is theirs alone.

The Role of Advertising

In his important recent book *Advertising: The Uneasy Persuasion*, sociologist Michael Schudson (1984) suggests that advertising in the capitalist system serves the same function as the poster-art of authoritarian socialism, the state-sanctioned art of the Soviet Union. We are all familiar with those realistic posters of sturdy men and healthy women, working in wheat fields or factories and affirming the joys of socialism; in Schudson's interesting metaphor, advertising serves the same function, depicting equally healthy capitalists driving cars, smoking cigarettes, drinking beer, or wearing designer jeans, and essentially enjoying the materialist fruits of the free-enterprise system. As Schudson (1984: 215) notes,

> American advertising, like socialist realist art, simplifies and typifies. It does not claim to picture reality as it should be—life and lives worth emulating. . . . It always assumes that there is progress. It is thoroughly optimistic, providing for any troubles that it identifies a solution in a particular product or style of life. It focuses, of course, on the new, and if it shows signs of respect for tradition, this is only to help in assimilation of some new commercial creation.

Advertising in our society therefore has a symbolic and cultural utility that transcends the mere selling of merchandise, but "the aesthetic of capitalist realism—without a masterplan of purposes—glorifies the pleasures and freedoms of consumer choice in defense of the virtues of private life and material ambitions" (Schudson, 1984: 218).

Schudson's unique perspective on advertising provides us with insightful confirmation of precisely why advertising is the most plentiful form of propaganda found in today's society. Like the socialist-realist art it emulates, advertising serves as a constant reminder of the cultural and economic basis of our society. We do not always respond to all of the messages we receive, but its pervasiveness provides a sort of psychic comfort that our socioeconomic system is still working.

In the final analysis, advertising as propaganda has been largely responsible for the creation of the massive consumer culture in the twentieth century. Together with the growth of the mass media and improvements in transportation and communications, it is one of the forces that have contributed to the emergence of a "mass culture" (discussed in Chapter 3). Good or evil, honest or dishonest, economically vital or wasteful, advertising is with us as long as we choose to live in a capitalist economic system, the ultimate success of which is dependent upon a high level of consumption of the products of this system.

6

HOW TO ANALYZE PROPAGANDA

A ten-step plan of propaganda analysis includes identification of ideology and purpose, context, identification of the propagandist, investigation of the
structure of the propaganda organization, selection
of the target audience, understanding of media utilization techniques, analysis of special techniques to
maximize effect, audience reaction, identification
and analysis of counterpropaganda, and an assessment and evaluation.

The analysis of propaganda is a complex undertaking that requires historical research, the examination of propaganda messages and media, sensitivity to audience responses, and critical
scrutiny of the entire propaganda process. There may be a
temptation to examine the short-term aspects of propaganda
campaigns, but a true understanding of propaganda requires
analysis of the long-term effects. Propaganda includes the reinforcement of societal myths and stereotypes that are so deeply
embedded in a culture that it is often difficult to recognize a
message as propaganda.

As we said in Chapter 1, propaganda is a systematic attempt to
shape perceptions, manipulate cognitions, and direct behavior.
Its systematic nature requires longitudinal study of its progress.
Because the essence of propaganda is its deliberateness of
purpose, considerable investigation is required to find out what
the purpose is.

We have designed a ten-step plan of analysis that incorporates all of the elements of propaganda. This schema makes it difficult to study propaganda in progress because the outcome may not be known for a long time. On the other hand, to study propaganda in progress enables the analyst to observe directly media utilization and audience response in actual settings. The long-range effects may not be known for some time; thus analysis of contemporary propaganda may be a very long-range study. Chapter 7 has five case studies of propaganda, some of which are from the past, albeit recent, others are current and unfinished. We believe that contemporary propaganda is different from past propaganda mainly in the use of media. New technologies must be taken into account, for the forms of media and how they are used have always been significant in propaganda.

The ten stages of propaganda are as follows: (1) the ideology and purpose of the propaganda campaign, (2) the context in which the propaganda occurs, (3) identification of the propagandist, (4) the structure of the propaganda organization, (5) the target audience, (6) media utilization techniques, (7) special techniques used to maximize effect, (8) audience reaction to various techniques, (9) counterpropaganda, if present, and (10) effects and evaluation. These ten stages take into account the following questions: To what ends, in the context of the times, does a propaganda agent, working through an organization, reach an audience through the media while using special symbols to get a desired reaction? Further, if there is opposition to the propaganda, what form does it take? Finally, how successful is the propaganda in achieving its purpose?

THE IDEOLOGY AND PURPOSE OF
THE PROPAGANDA CAMPAIGN

The ideology of propaganda provides, according to Kecskemeti, "the audience with a comprehensive conceptual framework for dealing with social and political reality" (Pool et al., 1973: 849-850). In locating the ideology, the analyst looks for a set of beliefs, values, behaviors, and attitudes as well as ways of perceiving and thinking that are agreed upon to the point that they constitute a set of norms that dictate what is desirable and what should be done. An ideology contains concepts about what the society in which it exists is actually like. It states or denies, for example, that there are classes and that certain conditions are desirable or more desirable than others. An ideology is a form of consent to a particular kind of social order and conformity to the rules within a specific set of social, economic, and political structures. It assigns roles to gender, racial, religious, and social groups.

Ideology can be discerned from both verbal and visual representations that reflect preexisting struggles and situations, current frames of reference to value systems, and future goals and objectives.

The purpose of propaganda may be to influence people to adopt attitudes that correspond to those of the propagandist or to engage in certain patterns of behavior, for example, to contribute money, join groups, demonstrate for a cause, and so on. Propaganda also has as its purpose to maintain the legitimacy of the institution or organization that it represents and thereby ensure the legitimacy of its activities. Integration propaganda attempts to maintain the positions and interests represented by "officials" who sponsor and sanction the propaganda messages. Agitation propaganda seeks to arouse people to participate in or support a cause. It attempts to arouse people from apathy by giving them feasible actions to carry out. Kecskemeti said that agitation consists of stimulating mass action by hammering home one salient feature of the situation that is threatening, iniquitous, or outrageous (Pool et al., 1973: 849).

Mainly, the purpose of propaganda is to achieve acceptance of the propagandist's ideology by the people. Joseph Goebbels said that propaganda had no fundamental method, only purpose—the conquest of the masses.

THE CONTEXT IN WHICH
THE PROPAGANDA OCCURS

Successful propaganda relates to the prevailing mood of the times; therefore, it is essential to understand the climate of the times. The propaganda analyst needs to be aware of the events that have occurred and of the interpretation of the events that the propagandists have made. What are the expected states of the world social system (war, peace, human rights, and so on)? Is there a prevailing public mood? What specific issues are identifiable? How widely are the issues felt? What constraints exist that keep these issues from being resolved? Is there a struggle over power? What parties are involved, and what is at stake? It has been said that propaganda is like a packet of seeds dropped on fertile soil. To understand how the seeds can grow and spread, analysis of the soil—that is, the times and events—is necessary.

It is also important to know and understand the historical background. What has happened to lead up to this point in time? What deeply held beliefs and values have been important for a long time? What myths are related to the present propaganda? What is the source of these myths? A myth is a model for social action. For example, the mythology of American populism was based on a classic and good hero such as Abraham Lincoln who rose from a humble birth to a self-made lawyer to the White House. This hero is a Christ-like figure because he not only rose from humble beginnings, he also was martyred. The model for social action is that a person can rise above circumstances to become a leader who can make significant differences in people's lives. A myth is a story in which meaning is embodied in recurrent symbols and events, but it is also an idea to which people already subscribe. It is, therefore, a predisposition to act. It can be used by a propagandist as a mythical representation of an audience's experiences, feelings, and thoughts.

IDENTIFICATION OF THE PROPAGANDIST

The source of propaganda is likely to be an institution or an organization with the propagandist as its leader or agent. Sometimes there will be complete openness about the identity of the organization behind the propaganda; sometimes it is necessary to conceal the identity in order to achieve the goals set by an institution. When identity is concealed, the task of the analyst is a difficult one. It has been quite difficult to detect black propaganda until after all the facts are known. In black propaganda, not only is there deliberate distortion, but the identity of the source is usually inaccurate.

Some guidelines for determining the identity of the propagandist are found in the apparent ideology, purpose, and the context of the propaganda message. The analyst can then ask, "Who or what has the most to gain from this?" Historical perspective is also very valuable in making such a determination. Another aspect of identity determination is to look at the broader picture, for, generally speaking, propaganda that conceals its source has a larger purpose than is readily available.

When the propagandist is a person, it is easier to identify that person because propagandists usually have what Doob (1966: 274) called "verbal compulsions." Look for the person who speaks frequently and with authority. It is possible, however, for the person to be an agent or "front" for the actual propagandist, concealing the true identity of the leader or institution.

THE STRUCTURE OF THE PROPAGANDA ORGANIZATION

Successful propaganda campaigns tend to originate from a strong, centralized and decision-making authority that produces a consistent message throughout its structure. For this reason, there will be strong and centralized leadership with a hierarchy built into the organization. The apparent leader may not be the actual leader, but the apparent leader espouses the ideology of the actual leader. The analyst should investigate how it was that the leader got the position. The leader will have a certain style that enables him or her to attract, maintain, and mold the members into organizational units. The leadership style may include the mythic elements of the ideology.

Structure also includes the articulation of specific goals and the means by which to achieve them. Furthermore, in relationship to goals, there may be specific objectives and means to achieve them. Goals are usually long range and broader than objectives that are short range and more easily met. For example, a goal could be to stop the construction of nuclear power plants, whereas an objective could be to enlist the support of key figures in the community.

The selection of media used to send the propaganda message is another structural consideration. The analyst needs to look into the means of selecting the media. Often, where propaganda is distributed, the organization owns and controls its own media. Whoever owns the media exercises control over the communication of messages.

The analyst has to determine the makeup of the membership of the propaganda organization. There is a difference between being a follower and a member of an organization. Hitler (1939: 474-475) wrote in *Mein Kampf*, "The task of propaganda is to attract followers; the task of party organization is to win members. A follower of a movement is one who declares himself in agreement with its aims; a member is one who fights for it." The analyst might then ask, how is entry into membership gained? Is there evidence of conversion and apparent symbols of membership? Does new membership require the adoption of new symbols such as special clothing or uniforms, language, in-group references, and/or activities that create new identities for the membership? Are there rituals that provide mechanisms for conversion or transformation to new identities? Are special strategies designed to increase (or decrease) membership? What rewards or punishment are used to enhance membership in the organization?

The organization can be examined to find out if it has an apparent culture within itself. A culture is a system of informal rules that spells out how people are to behave most of the time. Values are the bedrock of a culture, thus propaganda will be based upon a complex system of values in its ideology that will be instrumental in achieving and maintaining all elements of its structure. Beliefs will be talked about; slogans will be used; everyone in the organization will agree with and consistently use these values in many ways. A culture also has heroes and heroines who personify the culture's values. Rituals are the systematic and programmed day-to-day routines in the organization, or they may be anniversary rituals that take place on a grand scale; for example, the May Day parade in Moscow or the inauguration of a president in Washington, D.C. Rituals provide visible and potent examples of what the ideology is.

There will also be a set of formal rules within the organization. The analyst should determine how the rules are sanctioned. Is there a system of reward and punishment? How are the rules made known? Who oversees the enforcement of the rules?

An organizational network becomes apparent through message distribution. How is the network used to foster communication? How is information disseminated from the leader to the membership? How is information transmitted to the public? Is there evidence that the public is denied access to information that is made available only to the membership or the organizational elite?

In order to obtain the data necessary to analyze the structure of a propaganda organization, the analyst should have access to sources that penetrate the organization. Previous investigators (Altheide and Johnson, 1980; Bogart, 1976; Conway and Siegelman, 1982) have either used assistants to feign conversion or have been members of the organizations at one time themselves. Often the verbal compulsions of the propagandists result in autobiographic treatments of their roles in the organization (Armstrong, 1979).

Structures of propaganda organizations also vary according to whether the communication is within the organization or directed to the public. The analyst may discern two different and separate structures, one for the hierarchy and the membership and one for the audience and potential members.

THE TARGET AUDIENCE

A target audience is selected by a propagandist for its potential effectiveness. The propaganda message is aimed at the audience most likely to be useful to the propagandist if it responds favorably. Modern marketing research enhanced by computer technology enables an audience to be targeted easily. Many facets of an audience are easily determined. Mailing lists can be purchased and coordinated with audience responses to media appeals. For example, if a person responds to a television pledge drive with a contribution, his or her name is put on a mailing list for future mail appeals from the same or other organizations who buy the list.

The traditional propaganda audience is a mass audience, but that is not always the case with modern propaganda. To be sure, mass communication in some form will be used, but it may be used in conjunction with other audience forms such as small groups, interest groups, a group of the politically or culturally elite, a special segment of the population, opinion leaders, and individuals. Bogart (1976: 56) points out that the United States Information Agency addresses itself to those in a position to influence others, that is, to opinion leaders rather than to the masses directly. He quotes a USIA report that says, "We should think of our audiences as channels rather than as receptacles: and "It is more important to reach one journalist than ten housewives or five doctors." Opinion leaders are a target for American propaganda abroad. In the Middle East, for example, the masses can be reached indirectly through reaching the culturally elite 10% of the population.

A distribution system for media may generate its own audience. A television program, a film, or a library may attract a supportive audience. Once that audience is identified, however, it too can be targeted.

Some organizations prefer a "buckshot" approach to a mass audience. Kecskemeti (Pool et al., 1973) claimed that strong propagandists could work the message media in a homogeneous way with a consistent message. Some audience members accept the message more eagerly than others; some reject it.

There are many variations of audience selection, and none should be overlooked by the analyst. It is useful to examine the propagandist's approach to audience selection, noting if there is a correlation between selection practices and success rate.

MEDIA UTILIZATION TECHNIQUES

At first, it may not seem difficult to determine how propaganda uses the media. The analyst examines which media are being used by the propagandist. Modern propaganda uses all the media available—press, radio, television, film, posters, meetings, door-to-door canvassing, handbills, billboards, speeches, flags, street names, monuments, coins, stamps, books, plays, comic strips, poetry, music, sporting events, cultural events, company reports, libraries, and awards and prizes. Some well-established honors function as propaganda—for example the Rhodes Scholarship, the Fulbright Awards Program, and the Soviet Friendship Scholarships. Use of tone and sound may have a conditioning effect. In 1950, Dobrogaev, a Russian psychologist, began working with speech tones and sounds for conditioning. In 1954, China began using loud speakers that broadcast official "truths" in city squares and gathering places. This is still being done in China today. A French fable reminds us, "Man is like a rabbit. You catch him by the ears."

The various messages coming from the same source over the media need to be compared to see if there is a consistency of apparent purpose. All output will be tied to ideology in one way or another. Describing the media usage alone is insufficient in drawing a picture of media utilization, for the analyst must examine the flow of communication from one medium to another and from media to groups and individuals. Evidence of multistep flow and diffusion of ideas should be sought. The relationship among the media themselves and the relationship between the media and people should be explored.

The main focus should be on how the media are used. The propagandist might show a film and pass out leaflets afterward. This type of practice maximizes the potential of the media. When an audience perceives the media, what expectations is it likely to have? What is the audience asked to do to respond to the message in the media? Does it seem that the audience is asked to react without thinking? Are the media used in such a way as to conceal the true purpose and/or identity of the propagandist?

Propaganda is associated with the control of information flow. Those who control public opinion and behavior make maximum and intelligent use of the forms of communication that are available to them. Certain information will be released in sequence or together with other information. This is a way of distorting information because it may set up a false association. Propaganda may appear in the medium that has a monopoly in a contained area. There may or may not be an opportunity for counterpropaganda within or on competing media. The media should have the capability to reach target audiences, or new technologies may have to be designed and constructed to do so.

The analyst should see what visual images are presented through pictures, symbols, graphics, colors, filmed and televised representations, books, pamphlets, and newspapers. Also, verbal innovations need to be examined for information, slogans, and emotional arousal techniques. The analyst should go beyond interpretation of the message to a closer scrutiny of the ways in which the message is presented in the media. What is the overall impression left with the audience? Essentially, how are the visual and verbal messages consistent with the ideology?

The selection of the media may be related to economics as well as to the most effective access to the audience. An audience that is located in a remote region without access to major media will have to be reached in appropriate ways. Sometimes the ways in which the messages are distributed require acceptance of innovations on the part of the audience. They may be asked to try new technologies or to participate in novel activities.

For analysis of media utilization, every possibility should be examined. Bogart (1976) tells of the faculty members in engineering and medicine at Cairo University who were so intensely sympathetic to communism that they would not come to the American library or read American material. They would, however, come to see a film about a new surgical procedure developed by an American physician or a film about an application of engineering to industry. The overt purpose of the film was to transmit valuable information, but the covert purpose was to get the faculty to see something better than any information they had gotten from any other source in their professional speciality. They were not expecting propaganda, but they absorbed a good impression of American science. Eventually, they started coming to the American library.

The analyst needs to be aware of unusual and unsavory media utilization as well. In 1954, for example, China began to send opium to Thailand to promote addiction, dependency, passivity, and lethargy.

SPECIAL TECHNIQUES TO MAXIMIZE EFFECT

We have deliberately chosen not to make a comprehensive list of propaganda techniques in the manner of the Institute for Propaganda Analysis (see Chapter 3). Propaganda is too complex to limit its techniques to a short list. There are certain principles, however, that can be elaborated upon to assist the analyst in examining techniques. Aristotle, in discussing rhetoric, advised the persuader to use "all of the available means of persuasion." Goebbels, in discussing propaganda, advised the propagandist that every means that serves the purpose of the conquest of the masses is good. Qualter, in discussing the techniques of propaganda, said that the common slogan of the four basic criteria of successful propaganda should be considered: it must be seen, understood, remembered, and acted upon.

We believe that propaganda must be evaluated according to its ends. Ends may be desired attitude states, but they are more likely to be desired behavior states such as donating, joining, and voting. They may also be aroused enthusiasm manifested in behavior states such as cheering, yelling, and so on.

Predispositions of the Audience: Creating Resonance

Messages have greater impact when they are in line with existing opinions, beliefs, and dispositions. Jacques Ellul (1965: 4) said, "The propagandist builds his techniques on the basis of his knowledge of man, his tendencies, his desires, his needs, his psychic mechanisms, his conditioning." The propagandist uses belief to create belief by linking or reinforcing audience predispositions to reinforce propagandistic ideology or, in some cases, to create new attitudes and/or behaviors. Rather than try to change political loyalties, racial and religious attitudes, and other deeply held beliefs, the propagandist voices the propagandee's feelings about these things. Messages appear to be resonant, for they seem to be coming from within the audience rather than from without. Lawrence Weschler, writing about martial law in Warsaw in 1982, quoted John Berger (1983: 69), the British art critic, who said, "Propaganda preserves within people outdated structures of feeling and thinking whilst forcing new experiences upon them. It transforms them into puppets—whilst most of the strain brought about by the transformation remains politically harmless as inevitably incoherent frustration." Of the obvious techniques to look for when analyzing propaganda techniques are links to values, beliefs, attitudes, and past behavior patterns of the target audience.

Messages that are supportive of rather than discrepant from commonly held views of the people are more likely to be effective. Yet the propagandist uses canalization to direct preexisting behavior patterns and attitudes. Once a pattern has been established among a target audience, the propagandist can try to canalize it in one direction or another.

When change does take place, it does so because of a multitude of factors related to the source of the message, the impact of opinion leaders, group interaction, the context in which the message is sent and received, and media utilization.

Source Credibility

Source credibility is one of the contributing factors that seems to influence change. People have a tendency to look up to authority figures for knowledge and direction. Expert opinion is effective in establishing the legitimacy of change and is tied to information control. Once a source is accepted on one issue, another issue may be established as well on the basis to prior acceptance of the source.

The analyst looks for an audience's perceived image of the source. How does the audience regard the source? Are the people deferential and do they accept the message on the basis of leadership alone? Is the propaganda agent a hero? Is there evidence that the audience models its behavior after the propagandist? How does the propagandist establish identification with the audience? Does he or she establish familiarity with the audience's locality, use local incidents, share interests, hopes, hatreds, and so on? During the Vietnam conflict, the Viet Cong would move into a hamlet and establish rapport with the local citizenry, taking their time to become integrated into the life of the hamlet. Soon they would enlist help from the villagers; for example, women would prepare bandages; boys would carry messages. Seeing that they were helping the Viet Cong, the villagers would experience cognitive dissonance and have to justify their own behavior by accepting the Viet Cong's view of the world.

Opinion Leaders

Another technique is to work through those who have credibility in a community—the opinion leaders. Bogart (1976: 102) tells how the USIA warned its agents not to offend the opinion leaders in other cultures. They were ordered to avoid taboos, curb criticism of respected leaders, and observe national pride. He said that Americans should sit down when being photographed with Asians in order not to emphasize their shorter stature. Above all, the agents were warned not to patronize opinion leaders in other cultures. The analyst should identify the opinion leaders and examine the ways in which the propagandist appeals to their status and influence.

Face-to-Face Contact

The analyst should look for evidence of the practice of supplementation through face-to-face contacts. For example, does the propaganda institution provide local organizations or places to go for "information"? Is the environment of the place symbolically manipulated? Traditionally, propagandists have provided listening stations, "reading huts," "red corners," libraries, and cultural events. Bogart said that the USIA provided cultural events that were free of political content but that had secondary effects on the people. USIA libraries are used as "bait" to get people to go in and hear lectures, see films, and listen to tapes. The USIA made special efforts to create a "pretty, inviting place" with flowers and comfortable furniture. One of the authors of this book, Professor O'Donnell, lived in Europe at one time and remembers the American centers and libraries as places to meet important American authors, smoke American cigarettes, drink good bourbon, and eat American food. At the time, these centers were a bit plusher and symbolized a "good life" more than native places did.

Group Norms

Group norms are both beliefs and values that are derived from membership in groups. They may be culturally derived beliefs or social and professional beliefs. Research on group behavior has shown that people will go along with the group even when the group makes a decision contrary to privately held beliefs and values (Karlins and Abelson, 1970: 41-67). The propagandist exploits people's conforming tendencies, and the analyst should look for examples of this. Conforming tendencies are also used to create a "herd instinct" in crowds. The propagandist may manipulate the environment to create crowded conditions to achieve a more homogeneous effect. It is common practice to hold large meetings in halls too small to accommodate the crowd in order to create the impression of a groundswell of support.

Reward and Punishment

Another way to get people to accept an idea "publicly" is through a system of rewards and punishments. A propagandist may even use threats and physical inducements toward compliance. "Propaganda of the deed" is when a nonsymbolic act is presented for its symbolic effect on an audience. For example, public torture of a criminal has been practiced for its presumable effect on others. Giving "foreign aid" with more of an eye to influencing a recipient's attitudes than to building the economy of a country is an example of symbolic reward.

Monopoly of the Communication Source

Whenever there is a monopoly of a communication source, such as a single newspaper or one television network, and the message is consistent and repetitious, people are unlikely to challenge the message. Weschler (1983: 69) says that in contemporary Poland people hear the same thing over and over again. "After a while," he said, "it does get through, and they find themselves thinking, Those Solidarity extremists really were bastards. But the strange thing is that this in no way affects their hatred of the government."

Visual Symbols of Power

The analyst should look at the media messages to examine the visual symbolization of power. Is there an iconographic denotation of power and ubiquity in visual presentations? For example, when a speaker stands in front of a huge flag, there is an emotional association transferred to the speaker. Sometimes a speaker will stand in front of a huge poster of him or herself. This symbolizes a larger-than-life feeling and creates a sense of potency.

Language Usage

Verbal symbolization can also create a sense of power. The use of language associated with authority figures such as parents, teachers, heroes, and gods renders authority to that which the language describes — "the fatherland," "Mother Church," "Uncle Sam." The propaganda agent who can manipulate sacred and authority symbols but avoid detection can define a public view of the social order. Propaganda uses language that tends to deify a cause and satanize opponents. Symbolization affects receivers according to associations that they make with the symbols. Again, it depends on the predispositions of the audience.

Exaggeration is often associated with propaganda. Goebbels said that outrageous charges evoked more belief than milder statements. There is a great deal of exaggeration associated with the language of advertising. *Everything* is the "best there is" and "satisfaction is guaranteed." The Russians called Americans "Imperialists" while referring to the Soviet Union as the "camp of peace and democracy."

Innuendo is also associated with propaganda. Implying an accusation without risking refutation by saying it causes people to draw conclusions. If one says, "The captain was sober today," an audience might draw the conclusion that he is usually drunk.

Arousal of Emotions

Propaganda is also associated with emotional language and presentations. Although this is sometimes true, there are many agents who feel that dispassionate reporting is more effective. The British Broadcasting Corporation has been known for objective and accurate reporting for years. There was outrage when the British government invoked for the first time a little-known clause in the BBC licensing agreement that gives the government the right to take over the BBC transmitters in times of crises. In 1982 during the Falklands invasion, a BBC-originated program came on the air in the guise of an Argentine radio program. On the program was "Ascension Alice," a sultry-voiced announcer who attempted to demoralize Argentine troops on the Falkland Islands. Alice reported that Argentine President General Leopoldo Galtieri said in a television interview that he was prepared to lose 40,000 men to defend the Falklands. She also played records that were sentimental Latin ballads and a rock song by Queen called "Under Pressure." The Associated Press said that the BBC also broadcast "clearly fake record requests from Argentine mothers for their boys at the front" (Dallas Morning News, 1982: 10A). Without explaining how they received the requests, they played messages such as a request from Ernesto's mother who said, "Look after yourself son and please come home safely soon." Conservative M.P. Peter Mills said, "We have to win the propaganda war. It's just as important as firing bullets and so far not enough ammunition has been made available" (Dallas Morning News, 1982: 10A).

Bogart (1976: 147) said that emotional propaganda may be appropriate for semi-literate people, but the USIA tried not to offend opinion leaders. He felt that reporting should not be heavy-handed. Instead of saying, "The Soviet Premier was lying again today when he said . . ." the Voice of America would report, "Comment of this subject points out . . ."

AUDIENCE REACTION TO VARIOUS TECHNIQUES

The analyst looks for evidence of the target audience's response to propaganda. If the propaganda campaign is open and public, the journalists will offer critical reaction to it. This should not be mistaken for the target audience's reaction. The analyst should look for evidence of target audience attitudes in opinion polls and surveys reported in the media.

The most important thing to look for is the behavior of the target audience. This can be in the form of voting behavior, joining organizations, making contributions, purchasing the propagandist's merchandise, forming local groups that are suborganizations for the main institution, and crowd behavior. The analyst looks for the audience's adoption of the propagandist's language, slogans, and attire. Does the target audience take on a new symbolic identity? If so, how do they talk about it? Over time, does the propaganda purpose become realized and part of the social scene?

COUNTERPROPAGANDA

In a free society where media are competitive, there is likely to be counterpropaganda. Where the media is completely controlled, counterpropaganda can be found underground. Under-

ground counterpropaganda may take as many media forms as
the propaganda itself. There are obvious forms of underground
counterpropaganda, such as handbills and graffiti, but another
important form of counterpropaganda is theater. Theater can
present an alternative ideology in the form of entertainment.
Bertolt Brecht, for example, used the stage to educate politically, to depropagandize. He used his position as playwrite as a
podium from which to educate. When his plays were broadcast
over the radio, a medium over which he had little control, he
"broadcast" counterpropaganda (Szanto, 1978: 197).

Counterpropaganda may become as active as propaganda itself. In this case, the analyst would examine it in the same ten
stages of analysis for propaganda. The analyst should also attempt to determine if it is clear to the public that counterpropaganda exists to oppose propaganda. Very often both
propaganda and counterpropaganda exist apart from mainstream ideology and the beliefs and behaviors of the general
public.

EFFECTS AND EVALUATION

The most important effect is whether the purpose of propaganda has been fulfilled or not. If not the overall purpose, then
perhaps some of the specific goals have been achieved. If there
has been a failure to achieve goals, the propaganda analyst
should try to account for the failure in his or her analysis.

Questions related to growth in membership should also be
examined as effects. The analyst must be careful about sources
in making determination of membership. Propaganda agents
traditionally inflate numbers regarding membership, contributions, and other goals.

Sometimes effects can be detected as adjustments in mainstream society. The analyst looks for the adoption of the propagandist's language and behaviors in other contexts. Legislation
may be enacted to fulfill a propagandist's goal, but it may be
sponsored by a more legitimate source.

Evaluation is directed to the achievement of goals but also to
the means through which the goals were adopted. How did the
selection of media and various message techniques seem to af-

fect the outcome? Would a different set of choices have altered the outcome? How did the propagandist manipulate the context and the environment? Would the outcome have been inevitable had there been no propaganda? If the public-at-large changed directions, what seems to account for the swing?

If the analyst can answer the many questions contained within these ten stages, a thorough picture and understanding of propaganda will emerge.

7

PROPAGANDA IN ACTION:
Five Case Studies

These five case studies were selected to provide examples of how propaganda has and is being used in our society. The subjects are (1) the banning of cigarette advertising on radio and television; (2) religion on television; (3) the Pueblo incident; (4) the abortion controversy; and (5) South African propaganda activities in the United States. Applying the analysis suggested in Chapter 6, each case study examines the propagandists, the audience, and the various techniques employed. The case studies demonstrate that propaganda is not always successful, and can be used in a variety of ways in modern society.

The ten stages of analysis are used in five case studies to illustrate the methods of analysis as well as how to apply them to what we consider to be five important examples of propaganda in our time. The case studies were chosen for the intensity of their propaganda as well as their relevancy in today's society. The only one of the case studies that can be said to be truly over is the one on the Pueblo incident. The others are current and in heightened phases of development. By the time this book is published, we fully expect that they will have entered new stages of development.

THE SMOKING CONTROVERSY: BROADCASTING, POLITICAL POWER, AND HEALTH

Not all of life's problems have happy endings, and not all propaganda case studies have clear, precise resolutions. This examination of the specific issues surrounding the campaign to remove cigarette advertising from the broadcast media shows that very often propaganda from one side is so powerful and well organized that it simply overwhelms the opposing forces. The tobacco lobby is still so powerful in the United States that it appears virtually untouchable in the halls of Congress; and yet inroads have been made, albeit small ones. Cities such as San Francisco have legislated no-smoking areas in the work place; companies such as Pacific Northwest Bell have banned smoking from their office buildings; and all over the United States restaurants are now creating smoke-free areas.

This case study demonstrates that sometimes it is the work of one person, aided by the right combination of political and social climate, that can effect changes, even in the face of a massive propaganda structure. This is not a classic case study of propaganda and counterpropaganda; it is an examination of how a combination of personal fortitude, legislative and political maneuvering, and some luck can bring about change. It should be emphasized that the tobacco interests did not really lose this battle; they merely altered their strategies, and their propaganda machine remains as strong and active as ever.

The Historical Context

On January 1, 1971, all cigarette advertising disappeared from American radio and television. No longer was the Marlboro man able to light up and show off his tatoo at the same time; the "cool" world of mentholated cigarettes with smoking couples always carefully depicted in a green pastoral setting ceased to exist; and the recently introduced line of "women's cigarettes" — Virginia Slims — could no longer entertain us with humorous vignettes depicting what happened to women who were caught smoking in the period before the 1930s. In the words of the Virginia Slims slogan, the fight against tobacco advertising on broadcasting had "come a long way, baby!" But to reach this point required a series of actions and reactions involving a complex mixture of groups and individuals, both in and outside of Congress, and the development of propaganda campaigns with literally billions of dollars at stake.

There are several ideological bases for the propaganda campaigns created by both sides of the smoking controversy. (In fact, the number of actual interest groups involved in this issue are too numerous to list, but for purposes of this study we will assume that there is a side in favor of smoking and the use of tobacco products, and a side opposed to the consumption of tobacco because it constitutes a health hazard and an environmental nuisance.) First, the tobacco interests in the United States constitute an impressive part of the nation's economy and have established themselves as an important force in American politics. The so-called tobacco coalition includes the eventual clientele who smoke more than $20 billion worth of tobacco products annually, the 22 states in which tobacco is grown, and the approximately 2 million jobs of varying types with a payroll of 30 billion supported by the tobacco industry, and the $22 billion contribution tobacco makes to the nation-wide tax base. The industry as a whole accounts for about 2.5% of the nation's Gross National Product. The beneficiaries of this multibillion dollar industry include manufacturers, advertising agencies, the mass media, farmers, tax collectors, and shopkeepers (Fritschler, 1983: 8). Clearly there is a lot of money and many other issues involved in any political decisions regarding smoking.

Second, tobacco has an almost mystical role in American history; it was one of the first American crops exported by the early settlers, and was once so valuable that it was even used as currency. This ties in with the third ideological perspective, which concerns the historical antagonism that has traditionally arisen between government and business, especially when the regulation of health or environment matters are the primary issue. In these instances, unless the advantages to the business community involved are very obvious, there is likely to be a great deal of politicking, and the myth of government interference in "free enterprise" is likely to be raised. Besides which, most Americans don't like to be told what to eat, drink, or smoke.

Fourth—and this is a very complex factor indeed—since 1933 the tobacco producers have been the beneficiaries of federal assistance through the Department of Agriculture, which operates a price support program and market quota rules that enforces a mandatory limit on production. These regulations have driven tobacco prices up and kept the supply down. The contradiction here is obvious, for as Fritschler (1983: 9) in his book *Smoking and Politics* notes, "For the proponents of these tobacco regulations to turn around and fight consumer-health regulation on the grounds that government regulation is unwarranted interference by big brother and bad for the economy is the kind of argument which makes rational people wince." The tobacco industry tends to slide by this conundrum in their anti-legislative philosophy; perhaps this is best exemplified by the statement by Jesse Helms, the conservative Republican senator from the major tobacco state of North Carolina, and a leader of the industry's fight against regulation, when he said, "In North Carolina, tobacco isn't a commodity, it's a religion." Thus we have a large, powerful industry, determined to preserve its privileges, facing continuous pressure from an equally determined, but much less powerful, somewhat uncoordinated group of individuals, together with various private and governmental health agencies, all of whom are concerned by the growing and very costly health menace that smoking has become.

The final ideological position is the consistent viewpoint put forward by the tobacco industry that, despite the thousands of studies that have established the connection between smoking and various physical ailments such as lung cancer, emphysema, chronic bronchitis, and even heart disease, that the actual causal link between smoking and these medical problems has not been clearly established. Although the health hazards of smoking had been pointed out in the mid-nineteenth century, it took a series of private and government reports between 1954 and 1964 to bring the matter into public arena for political debate. After the initial 1954 study reports done by a private group, the tobacco industry responded by the creation of the Tobacco Industry Research Committee (now called the Council for Tobacco-U.S.A.) which distributed fairly substantial funds for scientific research on the use of tobacco and its effects on health. While this served as a counterpropaganda move, in that the industry was now funding its own health-related research thereby demonstrating its concern, this organization was not in a position to directly counter the growing propaganda movement demanding some sort of regulation of public smoking. In 1958, the increased pressure was met head-on with the creation of the The Tobacco Institute, Inc., a lobbying public relations group that was supported by large contributions from the various factions making up the tobacco industry. The Tobacco Institute subsequently became the source of most of the industry's propaganda aimed at containing the disorganized array of health groups pushing for the labeling of cigarettes or other regulatory measures.

The Menace of Broadcast Advertising

The emergence of first radio and then television advertising proved to be of immense significance to the growth of the cigarette industry. The use of broadcast advertising was a major propaganda weapon in promoting smoking as an acceptable social behavior (the movies must also accept major responsibility here), and cigarette brands were widely associated in the public's mind with the sponsorship of many popular shows, and brands such as Lucky Strike, Camel, Philip Morris, and Chesterfield became symbols of entertainment as much as commerce during the era of the large radio networks. The emergence of television as a major advertising force in the 1950s brought into prominence such brands such as Kent, with its "micronite filter," and Winston, which "tastes good like a cigarette should," or the Old Gold lady dancing away inside her cigarette box, with only her arms and legs visible. Of all of these new television-promoted brands it was Marlboro, featuring the clean outdoors and the weathered features of the Marlboro Man in his cowboy hat and tatoo, that was most memorable, even though the actor involved later contracted lung cancer from cigarette smoking.

Television was used to promote filter cigarettes, with broad hints (often specific claims) that these were "healthier" than the unfiltered variety. In the late 1940s filter cigarettes accounted for 1.5% of the total market; by 1968 this had grown to nearly 75%. During this same period the number of different brands grew from a half dozen to more than thirty, in all shapes and sizes (Whiteside, 1970: 44). In the latter part of the 1960s the heavy promotion given to new brands of longer 100 millimeter cigarettes was particularly upsetting to those who were beginning to demand government regulation. In 1967, three years after the U.S. Surgeon-General had issued a report linking cigarette smoking to lung cancer and other medical problems, the tobacco manufacturers were spending about $217 million on television. In that same year the Public Health Service issued a report that found that "Cigarette smokers have substantially higher rates of death and disability than their non-smoking counterparts in the population."

Although the forces opposed to cigarette smoking lacked the structural organization to match the industry's propaganda, they were not without friends in the federal bureaucracy, as well as Congress. After a complex series of legislative steps, fought every step of the way by the tobacco industry, the Federal Trade Commission finally managed to get President Lyndon Johnson's signature on a bill requiring a health warning on cigarette packages on July 27, 1965. This bill also prevented the FTC from any further action against the tobacco industry for four years (the industry wanted a permanent ban), and was seen more as a victory for the propaganda efforts of the The Tobacco Institute than a positive health measure. The label was not seen as a serious threat to tobacco sales, whereas removing the FTC from the issue was seen as a major blow for the antismoking group. After examining this battle, one of the lobbyists for the antismoking side characterized the contest between the tobacco industry and the health people as being similar to a match between the Green Bay Packers and a high school football team. It is against this background that the rather unexpected fight to remove cigarette advertising from the broadcast media must be viewed.

The FCC and John Banzhaf III

A young New York lawyer, John Banzhaf III, was concerned about the tactics being used to advertise cigarettes, particularly "about the use of the public airwaves to seduce young people into taking up smoking without any attempt to tell the other side of the story on television and radio" (Whiteside, 1970: 46). He wrote a letter to WCBS-TV in New York asking for free time to be made available to present the health hazard side of the cigarette story. This request was denied, as Banzhaf had expected, so his next step was to file a petition with the Federal Communications Commission, pointing out that the Surgeon General's report and other scientific findings had shown a relationship between smoking and health, and, further, because this was a controversial issue of public importance, it was therefore proper for the FCC to order radio and television stations to provide reply time under the "Fairness Doctrine." This petition was presented early in January 1967, and on Friday, June 2, of that year the FCC—to everyone's surprise—ruled that its fairness doctrine did indeed apply to cigarette advertising on radio and television. The Commission dismissed Banzhaf's appeal for "equal time," offering instead a ratio of one antismoking message to three cigarette commercials. Everyone from the tobacco interests to Congress was caught off guard, but it was clear that there would be an appeal of the ruling.

Once he had achieved this major victory, Banzhaf expected that he could bow out, and that major private health organizations such as the American Cancer Society, the National Tuberculosis Association, and the American Heart Association—all known propagandists against smoking—would step in and take over. However, he quickly discovered that these groups had serious misgivings about alienating the broadcasters, upon whom they relied for free air time for their own causes and especially for fund-raising activities. The health group support for the FCC decision was quiet, unaggressive, and almost nonexistent during the period when the tobacco industry and the broadcasters appealed the FCC's ruling. Even Senator Robert Kennedy tried to intervene with the health groups on behalf of Banzhaf, but with no success. To their credit, the health agencies felt that the burden of the defense of the original decision lay with the FCC's own legal staff, and eventually they were proved correct. On November 21, 1968, the U.S. Court of Appeals held that the FCC could use its fairness doctrine to require free time for antismoking commercials because this decision was "a public-health measure addressed to a unique danger authorized by official and congressional action."

The result was that a series of antismoking commercials began to appear on radio and television, and this constituted the first major media propaganda campaign against the tobacco interests. The tobacco companies even tried to obtain "right of reply" to the antismoking commercials, but were turned down by the courts. The real importance of getting these antismoking commercials on the air was only realized later, when in February 1969 the FCC issued a public notice that it intended to propose a ruling to ban cigarette advertising from all radio and television broadcasting. This notice was filed four months before the end of the four-year moratorium on the ban that had prevented federal regulatory agencies from taking action against the tobacco industry. The FCC had put Congress on notice that if it did not act by July 1 of that year, the FCC would go ahead with its intentions, and tobacco advertising would disappear from the airwaves.

The tobacco lobby quickly swung into preparation, and several long congressional hearings were held to discuss the whole issue of cigarettes and health, and the proposed FCC action. The National Association of Broadcasters actively joined forces with The Tobacco Institute to combat the FCC's intention with a barrage of propaganda, claiming that the broadcast industry should be left to regulate itself. Eventually, however, cracks began to appear in this seemingly impregnable alliance, and on July 8, 1969, the NAB announced a plan to phase out all cigarette advertising from the air over a three-and-a-half-year period beginning on January 1, 1970. It is unclear exactly what prompted this decision, but it seems to have been inspired by the fear of having to air both pro and con advertising for tobacco products for the foreseeable future and who knew where this might lead with regard to other controversial products. It was far better to bite the bullet and get rid of cigarette advertising lest it contaminate other products. In any case, it was felt that in the three-and-a-half-year interim, the broadcast industry would easily find other customers only too eager to buy into the prime time programs or sporting events that would be made available by the removal of cigarette advertising.

The tobacco industry, stung by what they considered to be their betrayal by the broadcasters, went one step further and voluntarily agreed to end all broadcast advertising by September 1970. (Why drag out their impending demise on the air?) Eventually, now acting in a statesmanlike, responsible manner they moved the date up to January 1, 1970. The broadcasters who stood to lose more than $250 million a year for three years by this decision were now the injured party. Naturally the print media were elated at the prospect of all that additional advertising revenue coming their way.

Eventually, after much lobbying by all parties, a compromise was reached, and the final date of January 1, 1971 was set to allow the broadcasters one last crack at the revenue from the football bowl games on New Year's Day. (The tobacco industry had to get Congress to exempt it from antitrust action to act in a concerted manner like this.) Congress also managed to extract from the tobacco industry an agreement to strengthen the warning on the package to read: "Warning: The Surgeon General has Determined That Cigarette Smoking Is Dangerous to Your Health."

The Evaluation

Since 1971 there has been no cigarette advertising on radio or television; however, as Fritschler (1983: 141) pointed out, "The cigarette manufacturers were discovering that agreement with the antismoking people was not such a bad thing. The advertising budgets of the manufacturers dropped an estimated 30 percent in 1971, the first year of the television and radio ad ban, and gross sales were up 3 percent." The tobacco industry simply switched their advertising strategy, now purchasing more print, billboards, and sponsoring special sporting and other events that gave them clear identification in the media. Kool mentholated cigarettes sponsored a series of jazz festivals; Virginia Slims supported women's tennis tournaments, and numerous other events suddenly found tobacco sponsors.

The propaganda battle between the tobacco industry and the health interests did not cease with the Pyrrhic victory in 1971. Attempts have recently been made to show smoking as being "antisocial" and "unacceptable" to smart, young people; but the number of young smokers has shown no dramatic decrease. (In the fall of 1985, the Surgeon General, Dr. Koop, suggested that by the end of the century, smokers would find their behavior so socially unacceptable that they would have to smoke in private. Also, on the very day that this chapter is being finalized, a bill was introduced into Congress to consider placing health warning labels on other tobacco products such as chewing tobacco and snuff, and to ban the broadcast advertising of these products.) Of particular concern is the increasing amount of smoking among women of all age groups as women move out of the home and into the work force. With this increase in smoking has also come a concomitant rise in tobacco-related illness in women. As indicated earlier, some small victories have been achieved, but tobacco remains a powerful force in Congress, able to marshall impressive propaganda forces when required.

TELEVANGELISM AND BORN AGAIN POLITICS

An "evangelical-moralist" subculture has moved into a position of privilege, according to Martin E. Marty (1985), using Daniel Bell's term to describe the group that embraces evangelicalism, hypernationalism, and materialism. According to Marty, (1985: 14), these evangelical-moralists of the political far right had come from apparently nowhere to hold the most visible and assertive political position in American religion by 1984. Their leaders and the ranks identify with heroes, entertainers, and athletes, and they support competitive capitalism. They have had the ear and voice of President Reagan on occasion, and numerous other politicians—such as Senator Jesse Helms of North Carolina—enlist their support. This religious-moralist-political movement is, according to Conway and Siegelman (1982: 43), "big-money, high-technology Christianity," and its most visible manifestation is on television.

The evangelical preachers who broadcast over vast cable and satellite hookups are making very effective use of the latest communications technologies. These televangelicals, as they are called, have more than 60 syndicated television programs by satellite to cable systems. There are 36 television stations with full-time religious schedules, some of which broadcast 24 hours a day. Furthermore, religious telecasters buy commercial television time, usually on Sundays. There is virtually no home in the United States that the electronic church cannot reach. Combined with computer-assisted direct mail, television is used by this movement to enlist financial and political support from millions of people.

The ideology of this group is a combination of conservative religion and conservative politics. The religious ideology is based on a literal interpretation of the Bible as a supreme authority and acceptance of Jesus Christ as a savior. Politically, the group supports values with "pro" categories such as pro-life, pro-family, pro-America, and pro-God. It advocates a male-dominated society with women assuming the biblical roles of wives and mothers. Social programs such as welfare are thought to undermine the moral fiber of the community. Communism is seen as a purveyor of godless atheism. A strong military and capitalism along with accumulation of wealth are considered central to American society.

One important ideological expression is "secular humanism," defined as "man's attempts to solve his problems independently of God" (Hadden and Swann, 1981: 85). Crime, rebellious youth, divorce, and drug addiction are blamed on secular humanism. The religious right claims that secular humanism controls state and national governments, the mass media, public education, colleges and universities, textbooks, the American Civil Liberties Union, the National Organization for Women, and the Ford Foundation. Secular humanism is the target enemy for all speakers on the religious right.

The mythology of the religious right encompasses a traditional, moral community with an authoritarian church, family, and state in the midst of material prosperity. It sentimentalizes a past of moral rectitude that never existed. This myth is important because it depicts modern society as a state of decay and decline, thus drawing lines between a religious and national good versus irreligious and unpatriotic evil. Televangelists such as Jerry Falwell offer people an easy choice: "We want to bring America back . . . to the way we were" (Combs, 1984: 82).

The professed purpose of the religious right is evangelism, that is, reaching the masses with a message of Christian faith, personal counseling by telephone and mail, and supporting those who wish to be "born again." At the same time, the masses are asked to contribute money, form lobbying groups to support conservative political candidates, and become activists against abortion, gay rights, pornography, sex education, feminism, gun control, busing, civil rights, welfare, labor unions, socialism, and communism. The actual purpose appears to be to establish a conservative power base that has little, if anything, to do with religion. The "religious" right seeks control of state and national governing bodies, and it needs a large voting and lobbying base of support.

Before the mid-1970s, the religious right had been politically submerged, unorganized, and quiescent. Discontentment with the social developments of the 1960s and 1970s, such as civil rights and legalized abortion, along with "born again" President Jimmy Carter, apparently encouraged a religious revival. Although activism had not been encouraged, leaders were being trained, networks of communication were being established, and political organizations were being formed. The religious right joined forces with the political right, but, as Hammond (1985: 60-61) pointed out, there would have been a Moral Majority with or without a clergyman at its helm.

A keystone event occurred on April 28 and 29, 1980 when approximately 200,000 people gathered in Washington, D.C., for the "Washington for Jesus" prayer meeting. A total of 75 speakers and entertainers, such as Pat Boone, spoke, sang, and prayed for the nation. Organizers Pat Robertson, head of the Christian Broadcasting Network (CBN), and Bill Bright, founder of Campus Crusade for Christ, stationed people in the crowd according to their congressional districts. Letters were sent to members of Congress inviting them to contact the rally's representatives so they could learn "how we want you to vote" (Hadden and Swann, 1981: 129). A few months later, on August 22, several televangelists including Jerry Falwell participated in the National Affairs Briefing in Dallas where Ronald Reagan, candidate for the presidency, spoke. By then, the news media had made the public aware of a religious right that had moved into the political arena.

For the most part, propaganda agents for the religious right are preachers. They are not the old-time television preachers who have been on the air for years, such as Oral Roberts, Rex Humbard, and Jimmy Swaggart, for these men do not tend to be political. They are newcomers such as James Robinson who preaches from the Religious Roundtable against homosexuals, sex education, and abortion; Jim Bakker, host of the PTL ("Praise the Lord") Club, a Christian talk show; Robert Schuller of the "Hour of Power," broadcast from the Crystal Cathedral in

Los Angeles; and Jerry Falwell, star of "The Old Time Gospel Hour" and founder of the Moral Majority, Inc., a lobby that has sought to influence legislation and elections at local, state, and national levels. Falwell travels approximately 300,000 miles a year to speaking engagements and Moral Majority rallies. He has been on the "Today" show, "Donahue," "Nightline," and the covers of *Newsweek* in 1980 and *Time* in 1985. He is an opportunist who never misses a chance to link the religious right to national and international issues, including world hunger and support for apartheid in South Africa.

Another agent is Marion G. "Pat" Robertson, a Yale Law School graduate and former businessman, who is host of the *700 Club*, a 90-minute religious talk and news program that is on the air daily. Robertson is also the president of CBN, which broadcasts 24 hours a day and aims to become the fourth commercial television network in America. Robertson has a black cohost, Ben Kinchlow, and together they become spiritual anchormen who comment on the news, conduct interviews with politicians and entertainers, pray, and offer prophecies.

Behind the scenes of the religious broadcasters is a small group of men who help finance and organize the political right. Richard Viguerie and John Terry Dolan of the National Conservative Political Action Committee (NCPAC) are the chief publicists, fund raisers, and organizers behind attempts to unseat liberal incumbents in Congress. NCPAC raises millions of dollars to defeat its ideological enemies and elect its loyalist supporters. Paul Weyrich is the force behind the Committee for the Survival of a Free Congress and founder of Christian Voice, the organization that issues the *Morality Index,* better known as the "Report Card," which gives scores on the number of times members of Congress voted "correctly" on key moral issues.

The major structure that holds the religious right together is the use of modern communication technology. Television, telephones, and direct mail, assisted by computer banks of information on the audience, enable the religious right to have frequent contact with the masses. The formation of small cell-block groups such as local Bible study groups, Christian schools, and missionary organizations is urged. Converts to the cause are encouraged to seek positions in education, government, and the media and to develop their abilities to influence others. Lobbying groups are formed to monitor legislation and government appointments. The religious right owns and controls its own media, financing it largely from its membership through donations. It is difficult to determine how large the membership is because Falwell and others exaggerate its size. Falwell claims that the Moral Majority has two to three million members, yet *The Moral Majority Report* newsletter has a circulation of 482,000 (Horsfield, 1984: 153). Research indicates that there is a potentially large audience comprising older Americans who regularly watch television. The research indicates that the target audience seeks personal inspiration, companionship, and support (Horsfield, 1984: 118-124). There is also a lunatic fringe of racial and religious bigots who want to commit excesses such as burning books and records, and they have become emboldened by the rhetoric of the religious right (Hadden and Swann, 1981: 173).

It is through the various mass media that a "moral community" has formed through vicarious media experiences. Nielsen polls indicate that religious television reaches 13.7 million people (Conway and Siegelman, 1982: 42). Its format includes church services, talk shows, soap operas, soft rock music, and game shows. Messages are designed for television, for they are delivered quickly, simply, and with entertainment. Adroit use of the media enables people to "join" the electronic church, for they are encouraged to call on toll-free telephone numbers for counseling and support.

Pat Robertson said, "We feel we introduced 'two-way television'" (Armstrong, 1979: 107). He commands 83 phone-in counseling centers through which, in 1980, 10,000 volunteers made contact with almost two million callers (Conway and Siegelman, 1982: 58). When someone calls in, his or her name and address goes into computer banks that aid in direct mail campaigns for donations. After a call is made, a pamphlet, a free lapel pin, or a written prayer is sent to the caller. A few weeks later, an appeal for money is sent along with offers for books, records, religious art, and bumper stickers. This merchandise is also offered for sale in commercials during the television programs. Membership in the 700 Club and other "organizations" creates a sense of belonging as well as an obligation to contribute regularly. Those who respond regularly become a special target audience who will be asked to contribute toward building funds and other special projects. Some are spotlighted for bequests, for the religious right has trust departments and its own life insurance policies. 500,000 letters a week are sent out from a pool of 4.5 million names. Once a person's name is on the mailing list, political mail is sent as well. It has been estimated that about $500 million is sent in yearly in response to television and direct mail campaigns (Conway and Siegelman, 1982: 42), and it is all tax free.

Other forms of media utilization are newsletters, magazines, radio programs, books written by the ministers, cookbooks with recipes for "faith hamburgers" and "love beans" written by the ministers' wives, phonographs and cassette tapes, petitions, voting drives, and local rallies. On September 3, 1985, Jerry Falwell spoke at Cole Park in Dallas to a large crowd in an antipornography rally against the 7-11 stores that sell *Playboy, Hustler,* and other "adult" magazines. The Southland Corporation that owns 7-11 stores is a major supporter of the Jerry Lewis Telethon for muscular dystrophy and had just presented Lewis with a check for $1 million on Labor Day, the day before Falwell appeared in Dallas. The 7-11 stores' slogan is "Thank heaven for 7-11." Falwell said at the rally, "Why thank heaven for 7-11?" The most predominant symbol at the rally, which was well-covered by the local media, was the cross, prominently displayed and carried by many people. Because Falwell had recently spoken out in favor of the South African government, counterdemonstrators appeared at the rally carrying signs that said, "Apartheid is obscene." The antiapartheid demonstrators and the antipornography demonstrators engaged in verbal conflict and scuffling. Seven months later, in April 1986, Southland Corporation stopped selling adult magazines at its 8500-store 7-11 chain.

Falwell's propaganda techniques are well-known to American audiences. He uses exaggeration, especially concerning the size of his support group. He uses colorful language and false association. He speaks of "babykillers" in reference to abortion, of "godless communists," and "homosexual perverts." He has snappy punchlines, such as, "God created Adam and Eve, not Adam and Steve!" when talking about homosexuality, and "Jesus was not a pacifist. He was not a sissy" when talking about national defense (Conway and Siegelman, 1982: 68). People either love him or hate him.

Audience response is strong enough to keep the broadcasts on the air. Contributions are signs that people support the religious right in fairly large numbers because the contributions are sent in small sums, often as little as five dollars. National Religious Broadcasting claims that 115 million Americans tune in every week (Conway and Siegelman, 1982: 42), but Arbitron estimated the total number of persons viewing all 66 syndicated religious programs to be about 20.5 million (Hadden and Swann, 1981: 61). Arbitron does not include cable systems; thus its figures may be on the low side.

There is little evidence of counterpropaganda. Christian leaders oppose the religious right. A statement entitled "Christian Theological Observations on the Religious Right Movement" was released by fifteen Protestant denominations. Norman Lear, creator of "All in the Family" and other television programs, has organized "People for the American Way" in an effort to promote religious pluralism and television spots that denounce televangelists. In Falwell's hometown, Lynchburg, Virginia, the minister of the First Presbyterian Church gives anti-Falwell sermons with titles such as "Could Jesus Belong to the Moral Majority?"

Although they took credit for the election of Ronald Reagan and the defeat of George McGovern in 1980, research indicates that the religious right has had little influence on national elections (Horsfield, 1984: 152-155). There is no reason to assume that they could not be an influence in future elections. The religious right tends to coalesce around certain issues with effectiveness, and that plus their effective use of the media could influence future elections.

THE PUEBLO INCIDENT

On January 23, 1968, a tiny U.S. navy ship, the USS Pueblo was hove to in international waters, approximately 18 miles off the hostile coast of North Korea, near the important port of Wosnan, which was used by both the North Korean fleet and Soviet submarines. Some of the 83 crewmen were measuring the temperature and the salinity of the water in keeping with the ostensible role of the Pueblo as a hydrographic survey ship, but it was an open secret that the real mission of the Pueblo was to act as an electronic "watchdog" for the U.S. armed services and the CIA. The Pueblo was on a spy mission similar to that conducted by Soviet "trawlers" off the coast of non-Communist countries, and was equipped with some of the most sophisticated electronic sensing devices available. Its role was to scoop up every electronic signal for miles around, as the world's superpowers played their accepted surveillance games.

Suddenly a Soviet-built North Korean torpedo boat bore down on the Pueblo and, after asking for the American ship to identify itself, signaled "Heave to, or I will open fire." Thus began a series of events that, for the next eleven months, proved to become one of the more bizarre propaganda wars in the Cold War period. When the torpedo boast first appeared, Commander Lloyd M. Bucher was not overly disturbed because he had expected to be harassed; this was normal procedure for such spy ships. But the actual threat to open fire was something new, and, although concerned, he proceeded to maintain his course. An hour later three more Korean boats arrived as well as two MIG jets, and the Pueblo was ordered to follow this small flotilla. When Bucher became aware that the Koreans were serious about boarding his vessel he radioed his plight to his home base, and immediately ordered the destruction of equipment and documents. As the American vessel tried to escape it was fired on point-blank by the Koreans, wounding the Commander and eleven crewmen, one fatally. The Pueblo was taken into tow and brought into Wosnan harbor, while the might of the American armed services seemed helpless to do anything about it.

Back in the United States President Johnson was faced with an extremely difficult decision; already under pressure because of the increasing domestic disenchantment with the Vietnam War, he resisted the temptation to order immediate military retaliation. In Congress there was a strong reaction, as senators and members of Congress demanded everything from an outright declaration of war to the bombing of Wosnan harbor or the impounding of all Korean ships. After consultation with his advisors Johnson agreed to a limited call-up of air units, and then went on nationwide television to explain his position to the American public. In the developing propaganda war, Johnson was determined to disprove his popularly held image as "war maniac" by acting firmly, but calmly, emphasizing negotiation through the United Nations and other diplomatic means. Within minutes after the president's speech, the cameras switched to the U.N. Security Council, where U.S. Ambassador Arthur Goldberg was briefing the Security Council on the incident.

The Propaganda Stream

The North Koreans did not miss the opportunity to exploit Commander Bucher for propaganda purposes, and Radio Pyongyang, the official voice of North Korea, broadcast a "confession" from the commander, which he delivered in a strangled, listless voice that even his wife failed to recognize at first. The North Koreans were oblivious to the fact that to the rest of the world this confession was an obvious fake, and an analysis of its contents showed that it was written in the dialectic pidgin prose favored by some Communist writers. At one point Bucher said, "A lot of dollars would be offered to the whole crew members of my ship and particularly I myself would be honored for a good job." Another example was: "I have no excuse whatsoever for my criminal act as my ship intruded deep into the territorial waters of the Democratic People's Republic of Korea and was captured by the naval patrol crafts of the Korean People's Army in their self-defense action while conducting the criminal espionage activities. My crime committed by me and my men is entirely indelible" (*Time,* 1968: 16). Even some Communist bloc countries such as Czechoslovokia did not believe Bucher's confession, and the Pentagon labeled it as "a travesty of the facts."

The North Koreans quickly established a pattern of using a series of false confessions by individual crewmen to justify their actions, in which the United States was constantly portrayed as an imperialist bully, and a "paper tiger" whose bluff had been called by a smaller country with great success. While the United States continued the difficult process of diplomatic negotiations (because few nations wished to act as intermediaries with the often irrational North Koreans), the propaganda from Pyongyang poured out in a never-ending stream. Photographs of handwritten statements of Pueblo crewmen confessing their guilt as "war mongers" were constantly made available to the world press. There were also newsfilms of Commander Bucher appealing to the U.S. government to apologize for its "aggression" against North Korea, and the revelation of documents that supposedly showed that the Pueblo was deliberately ordered to operate within North Korean territorial waters. Because this was a major story, the world press were eager for news, and unwittingly encouraged the North Koreans by publishing everything made available to it; in the meantime, the United States had little of a concrete or visual nature to contribute, except to try through diplomatic channels to obtain the release of the 82 prisoners. The inherent contradiction was that although the North Koreans were using the crudest forms of propaganda, the sophisticated nature of modern mass communication nevertheless continued to provide them with an international audience.

Perhaps the saddest photographic images were those of the crew in captivity, which the Koreans carefully constructed and posed to show the "imperialists" suitably humbled, and yet supposedly healthy and safe in the "humanitarian" People's Republic of North Korea. In actual fact the crew members were constantly beaten or tortured into making these propaganda confessions or appearances. But the crew had the last word, for they were often able to use subtle signals to discredit their own confessions. In one famous photograph eight grinning members of the crew outwitted their captors when nobody noticed that three of the captives were wigwagging an internationally recognized signal of obscenity with their middle fingers. The Communist functionaries had used the picture to advertise the home comforts of their jail, but the propaganda backfired when the world press with some glee pointed out what the picture really meant. The sailors responsible paid dearly for their act by being tortured and beaten, but they were also elated by their feat of making fools of their captors, and success at providing a very newsworthy form of counterpropaganda.

The valiant counterpropaganda efforts of the captured crew did not stop there for on other occasions navigation charts prepared for the Koreans showed the Pueblo running at a speed of 2,500 miles per hour. A still more elaborate signal was buried in a confession in which the crew declared that it really did not matter how far the Pueblo penetrated North Korean waters because "penetration, however slight, is sufficient to complete the act." That statement, as every red-blooded sailor knew, is the definition given in the Uniform Code of Military Justice for rape! (*Newsweek*, 1969: 30).

The North Korean Motivation

When the Pueblo incident is examined in detail, it is not absolutely clear why the North Koreans were so willing to risk incurring the retaliation of the American military for what in the long run turned out to be a relatively unsuccessful propaganda campaign. There is little doubt that they were encouraged in this exploit by the Russians, who were eager to see the Americans engaged on another Asian front to increase the military pressure in Vietnam. To his credit, President Johnson resisted the military solution despite the public's and Congress's growing impatience with the protracted affair.

The incident received worldwide attention, but clearly the Koreans were aiming their propaganda mainly at Asian countries, especially South Korea, trying to make the United States "lose face" with its allies. They hoped to create a crisis of confidence with the United States' inability to defend its own military installations, let alone those of other countries. The North Koreans also used the incident to boost their own prestige, as well espousing the inherent moral and military superiority of the Communist system. As long as the crew were prisoners the Koreans were able to command international media attention, and they made maximum use of their opportunities. However, from all the available evidence it appears that most countries were skeptical about the propaganda campaign, but this did not stop the North Koreans from issuing "confessions" and news releases.

Between January and September the stream of anti-U.S. venom continued, but there was evidence by the end of September that the North Koreans had milked all possible propaganda value out of the Pueblo affair, and were interested in ending it quickly, while still seeking to gain maximum advantage for their humanitarian actions in releasing the "criminal aggressors." In December 1968, Major General Gilbert H. Woodward, the head of the negotiating team at Panmunjon (the site of the "peace talks" since the end of the Korean War in 1953), signed a document—written by the North Koreans—in which, on behalf

of the U.S. Government, he admitted that the Pueblo had vio-
lated North Korean territorial waters. The document went on to
apologize for the intrusion, acknowledge the truth of the crew's
confessions, and promise not to violate North Korean waters
again. But before he signed the document, Woodward, with the
foreknowledge of the Koreans, denounced the document as a
tissue of lies. With his jaw tensed he said, "My signature will not
and cannot alter the facts. I will sign to free the crew and only to
free the crew." Two-and-a-half hours after the signing, Commander Bucher and his crew limped across the 250-foot bridge
that separates North from South Korea, and the body of the
dead crewman followed in a hearse.

The Ironic Twist

The men returned home on December 23, as the North Koreans hoped to gain continued propaganda advantage from the
world press for acting in a humanitarian manner by releasing
the men at Christmastime; however, historical events are not always so easily managed, for on the same date the Apollo 8
spacecraft had been launched and was heading for the moon. It
was this event that captured the headlines, and live television
pictures of the spacemen were viewed by hundreds of millions
throughout the world, completely eclipsing the Korean hopes
for a propaganda coup. For the first time in history people were
able to see pictures from the mysterious far side of the moon,
and viewers were thrilled to look back onto their own planet
from the vantage point of the earth's satellite. The Apollo 8
spacemen were the first to orbit the moon, and this voyage con-
firmed that it was only a matter of time before humans would
be walking on the moon itself. These dramatic events in space,
watched by families home for the holidays, took the immediate
drama out of the Pueblo crew's release and undercut the North
Korean's last attempt at propagandizing the incident. It has
never been made public as to whether the negotiated release of
the prisoners was deliberately timed to coincide with the moon
shot. Whatever the U.S. government's intentions, the end result
was that for those crucial few days, thanks to the crew of the
Apollo 8, the United States became the international hero"
(Thum and Thum, 1972, 16-20).

An Evaluation

The Pueblo incident clearly illustrates that in an age of instantaneous media coverage a deliberately created international incident can be turned into a tool for propaganda purposes. Despite all of its existing military strength, the United States wisely chose not to counter the constant propaganda by force, but conducted its negotiations through diplomatic channels. The North Koreans miscalculated in that most of the world's sympathies eventually were with the captured Americans, but even this did nothing to bring about their release. In the final evaluation, it was the North Koreans who were embarrassed, especially when the truth of their treatment of the captured crew was revealed in the official navy investigaton of the incident. At that point it was the United States that went on the propaganda offensive, providing information for the world press, although the public seemed to have lost interest in the incident once the crew were returned. Since the Pueblo incident there have been many similar events deliberately created for propaganda purposes.

FETAL VISION:
THE ABORTION CONTROVERSY

A vitriolic debate has been going on for the past twenty years over the single issue of whether or not abortion should be legal. Propaganda on both sides of the debate has produced one of the most bitter and intractable disputes on the American scene. The sides are clearly drawn, but the participants on each side represent a diverse array of interests and organizations. The issues are clearly moral, legal, and political, but the means of settling the dispute over the issues has been far from clear.

The ideology of both sides in the abortion controversy has evolved and solidified in twenty years. Indeed, the names commonly used to describe each faction reflect each group's ideology. The antiabortion side is generally called "prolife" and is often specifically known as "Right-to-Life." The proabortion side is most frequently known as "prochoice," although this name is not as well-known or as widely used as the other side's "prolife."

The dominant ideology of those who oppose abortion has to do with human life defined as fetal life with the mandate that the fetus must be protected as a human life. Abortion terminates the life of the fetus; therefore, the prolife group wants all abortions to be illegal. This group believes that it is wrong to take what they refer to as an "innocent human life." In the name of humanity, these people are "striving to retain the dignity of human life in all stages" from inception to the grave (Stewart et al., 1984: 128). They feel that once abortion becomes morally acceptable, euthanasia, infanticide, and eugenics would not be far behind. In the late 1970s, the ideology expanded to include the values of family, home, and children, especially as defined by the religious fundamentalists and the far right. Women were charged with the duty of protecting unborn children for the sake of perpetuating social family structures. Women who wanted to terminate pregnancies were characterized as using abortion to solve personal problems. The rationale for legalized abortion has been depicted as a utilitarian ideology that solves the problem of an unwanted child or some hardship for the mother-to-be. The ideology of the prolife group draws the line between its ideology as morally right and its opposition's ideology as utilitarian.

The ideology of those who support legal abortions has evolved over the years. At first, abortion was a feminist issue linked to discrimination against and male oppression of women. Abortion was later viewed as a constitutional right as well as a woman's right to have control over her own body. Maintaining that abortion is a personal matter, those who supported legalization stated their dominant ideology as "choice," that is, having a choice over whether or not to bear a child after conception had taken place. Furthermore, the prochoice group does not believe that a fertilized egg is a human life. They deny that the fetus is a person on biological grounds and thereby deny that the fetus has human rights.

The abortion controversy began in 1963 when Pope John XXIII convened a group to study birth control. Three years later, this group advocated the support of contraception including artificial birth control. Pope Paul VI rejected this recommendation and adopted a traditional birth control report. Having formally rejected artificial birth control, the Catholic Church in

America lobbied against the sale of contraceptives. In 1973, when abortion became legal, the same group began to protest legalized abortion.

On January 22, 1973, the U.S. Supreme Court decided in the case of *Roe vs. Wade* and *Doe vs. Bolton* that (1) a woman's constitutional right of privacy precludes a state from prohibiting her from obtaining an abortion on demand during the first trimester of pregnancy, (2) that a state could regulate abortions during the second trimester only for the purpose of protecting the woman's life, and (3) that a state could regulate abortions during the third trimester to preserve the life of the child. Thus the Supreme Court viewed fetal life as human only after the first six months of pregnancy. This decision, in effect, legalized most abortions.

Shortly after the Supreme Court decision, the National Conference of Catholic Bishops, Family Life Division, created the National Right to Life Committee. Eventually the committee became less controlled by the church and more by political conservatives. In the late 1970s, an organization called the Library Court, a new-right group made up of representatives from fifty organizations that discussed social issues, decided to combine several issues and conduct a campaign against Planned Parenthood, sex education, and "abortifacient" contraception (a coined term for contraceptives that induce abortion, such as the IUD), with abortion being the focal point. The Library Court was joined by political conservatives and together they set up the Life Amendment Political Action Committee (LAPAC). This coalition then launched American Life Lobby, which became the largest antiabortion group in the United States. Its strategy advisor was Paul Weyerich, of Christian Voice, the organization that issues the *Morality Index*; and Richard Viguerie of NCPAC helped with direct mail.

There are five types of groups that have solidified to oppose abortion: political conservatives, religious fundamentalists, Roman Catholics, the Moral Majority, and the far right. They may disagree on other issues, but antiabortion is one issue that unites them. Their purpose is to make abortion unlawful once again. At first they wanted to get a constitutional amendment passed that would define human life as beginning at the moment of conception and that prohibited the termination of pregnancy except in situations in which the mother's life is in certain danger. Such an amendment would have the effect of overturning the Supreme Court's decision in *Roe v. Wade* and would preclude further court and legislative actions to liberalize abortion. Massive political pressure was mobilized to move such an amendment. In June 1983, when the U.S. Senate defeated an antiabortion amendment, the Director of LAPAC accused the National Right to Life Committee of handing the prolife movement the greatest single setback in its history. With strife and disagreement in its ranks, the prolife movement escalated its activities and adopted another purpose: to provide political support for conservative appointees to the Supreme Court. A conservative Court, the group believes, would overturn *Roe v. Wade*.

Another purpose of the prolife group is to use government "to end the hedonism built into American life over the past generation. Their prime aim is to shut down the sexual carnival and make government use its muscle to establish the old time religion" (Lake, 1984: 434). This purpose links abortion with sexual immorality and suggests that women who want abortions are guilty of promiscuity. One Congressman, John McCollister from Nebraska, linked a deterioration of values with an increase in abortions: "Amid our material affluence, we are experiencing a deterioration of those personal values held by our people that made us great. Broken homes, deserted families, empty churches, and lines at X-rated movies are signs of our times. Consequently, we've seen over the past ten years, mushrooming illegitimate births and abortions" (Lake, 1984: 433-434).

The prochoice group has had as its purpose to maintain the legalization of abortion and to defend abortion in the face of prolife attacks. Groups such as the National Organization of Women and Planned Parenthood have taken a watchdog stance to protect women's rights to abortions, but specific groups such as the National Abortion Rights Action League and the Religious Coalition for Abortion Rights are actively seeking support and membership. The latter group claims that abortion is a religious issue because many religions favor abortion and would, therefore, be infringed upon should it be made illegal once again.

The American public-at-large has been the target audience for both sides of the controversy, with special emphasis placed on the voting public. Elected representatives at state and national levels become specific target audiences whenever legislation regarding abortion is proposed. Massive letter-writing campaigns have been organized to put political pressure on politicians. One group, the Concerned Women of America (CWA), has a network of 600,000 women who support the prolife/profamily side. Known as "chain and prayer leaders," they inundate government agencies and elected officials with letters, telegrams, and phone calls. Televangelists such as Jerry Falwell, Jimmy Swaggert, and Pat Robertson encourage the CWA from their television pulpits.

Another form of eliciting public support has been the use of full-page newspaper advertisements with hundreds of names of local citizens, particularly opinion leaders, who are opposed to abortion. These names are usually acquired after Sunday masses at Roman Catholic churches, but they are not identified as Catholics in the ads. In fact, prolife fliers that are mailed to homes and distributed at fairs, churches, and shopping centers describe the antiabortionists as "nondenominational" and a "nonprofit, nonsectarian group of concerned citizens" (Stewart et al., 1984: 129). Quotations from scripture and clergy rarely appear in prolife literature. Sources of information in prolife literature are medical, scientific, and philosophic in support of fetal life being human life.

One of the continuing goals of the prolife supporters is to "prove" that the fetus is a human being; therefore, abortion violates the most basic and fundamental human right—the right to life. Leaflets with titles such as "Love and Let Live" or "We Care, We Love, We Are Pro-Life" include pictures of fetuses having identifiable and functioning human characteristics. Charts demonstrate how quickly the "baby" or "child" comes into existence after conception. The Indiana Right to Life organization stated in a "President's Report" to its membership, "Once people are aware that the heart of an unborn child beats at just 18 days after conception and that termination of pregnancy really refers to abortion, not birth, then people want to know what they can do to restore protection to the unborn child" (The Communicator, December 1978: 2).

Prolife literature is notorious for full-color photographs of tiny bodies in buckets and trashcans with accompanying accounts by nurses or doctors telling about how they had to smother or bash in the head of an aborted fetus because it refused to die. One leaflet entitled "The U.S. Supreme Court Has Ruled that It's Legal to Kill a Baby" poses the question: "Have we ever, in a civilized society given to one person (the mother) the complete right to kill another (the baby) in order to solve the first person's personal problem?" The Lafayette, Indiana, *Journal and Courier* (January 22, 1979: A8) ran a newspaper advertisement entitled "Eagles, Beagles, Babies, and 'There Oughta Be a Law'" featuring large pictures of a bald eagle, two beagle puppies, and an unborn fetus. The caption beneath the pictures read: "Ours is a peculiar society. We have laws protecting wildlife and dogs, but not defenseless human beings." The ad goes on to tell that there is a $5000 fine for stealing one eagle egg plus one year in jail or both, that Congress passed a law prohibiting the use of dogs for chemical, biological, or radioactive warfare materials, and yet "While these laws protect the life and rights of eagles and beagles, last year more than 1,000,000 unborn babies were terminated through abortion on demand. Terminated means killed. Killed without penalty" (*Journal and Courier,* 1979: A8).

Other newspaper advertisements cite historical figures and documents to establish that our country's history supports the protection of fetal life. One advertisement entitled "A Declaration of Respect for Life" cites the second paragraph of the Declaration of Independence in which "life, liberty, and the pursuit of happiness" are named as unalienable rights, which prolifers extend to the fetus. Another advertisement cites Thomas Jefferson's statement, "The care of human life and happiness—and not their destruction—is the first and only legitimate object of good government."

In an out-and-out appeal to voters, the Indiana Right to Life Political Action Committee reports that the abortion issue transcends any other issue:

> Would you vote for: members of Congress who in the past have been indicted for misuse of public funds (remember no one was killed?)—or did that disqualify them from holding public office?

Would you vote for: a candidate who would do nothing to stop, or who would endorse legal child abuse or torture?—or would that disqualify him or her from holding office?

Then would you vote for: Any person running for public office who either agrees with, who has publicly stated that he or she will do nothing to stop, or will resist any effort to stop the killing of over one million innocent pre-born babies a year—or does such active (or passive) approval of this killing disqualify such a person from holding office? [Stewart et al., 1984; 127]

Perhaps one of the more innovative, and certainly expensive, propaganda techniques of the prolife movement has been the establishment of pregnancy crisis centers. There are more of these centers than abortion clinics (of which there are 5500 existing); these centers advertise hotline numbers in copy that suggests that they may be abortion centers. Some centers may give only pregnancy tests. While a woman waits for the results, the center has her watch slides of aborted fetuses or the film, *The Silent Scream,* a scientifically undocumented film designed specifically to appeal to the emotions by suggesting that the fetus is able to experience pain during an abortion. If the woman's pregnancy test is positive, the center offers to help her by giving her clothing, finding a family to stay with, part-time work, and adoption assistance. One of the oldest of these clinics is Birthright, founded in 1968 by Louise Summerhill, a Canadian Catholic. Denise Coccioloni, the national director, said there are 510 centers in the United States and 85 in Canada that see 500,000 women a year. The Pearson Foundation, organized in 1969 by Robert J. Pearson, has its headquarters in St. Louis with 130 centers in the United States. Pearson intends to establish 1000 more centers in the next five years. The Pearson clinics pass themselves off as abortion clinics, but feature slide shows on fetal development instead. Its direct mail pitch says that when a woman visits a clinic thinking that it is an abortion clinic, "to her surprise, it is not an abortion clinic at all." The Christian Action Council, made up of conservative Protestant churches, opened its first crisis center in 1980 and now has 155 centers with 700 more planned. They give pregnancy tests, offer help in arranging for families to stay with, and part-time work. They give no information on birth control. Jerry Falwell instigated the "Save-a-Baby" program in 1984. He wants to establish 1000 centers now with a goal of 10,000 centers in the future. This project, which claims to have counseled 18,000 women, has a 24-hour-a-day hotline.

Recently, prolife supporters have adopted more militant strategies. They picket abortion clinics and doctors' homes. Using bull horns and harrassment of clinic patients, they claim to be shutting down abortion clinics. The Pro-Life Action League, headed by Joseph Scheidler, holds vigils at what they call "abortuaries" and send couples out to talk women out of abortions.

Such protest tactics have brought charges from the prochoice side that call the prolife supporters "anti-choice fanatics" who resort to violence and "prove just how little is really meant by the 'right to life' catchphrase" (Stewart et al., 1984: 124). In answer to such charges, Dr. J. C. Willke, the President of the National Right to Life Committee, charged his followers: "Let us witness peacefully in work, in picketing, by sit-ins, in letters, by prayers, and at the ballot box. It is they who live by violence and the modern sword, the suction curvette. Violence is not our way" (Stewart et al., 1984: 130).

How successful has the antiabortion movement been? Attempts to pass an abortion amendment have failed, but the Hyde Amendment, passed in 1978, cut off most federal funds for abortions. Actually, both sides in the controversy have been successful in getting the public to understand and accept key values from both sides. National polls and some legislative outcomes have indicated that the national understanding of abortion recognized the undesirability and desirability of abortion for its roles in protecting women, in protecting fetal life, and family structures (Railsback, 1984: 418). The public can compare the propaganda on both sides, comprehend their values, and know about their practices. In a sense, it is a tribute to an open society that the major outcome thus far has been enlightenment of the public on both sides of the issue.

SOUTH AFRICA AND THE "MULDERGATE AFFAIR"

As a complex, multiracial society, South Africa (officially the Republic of South Africa since 1960) has had a troubled history in the twentieth century. However, when the strictly Calvanist, white supremacist Nationalist Party was elected in 1948, they introduced the concept of *apartheid,* or complete segregation of the races, which has made South Africa a political pariah in almost every country in the world. By gradually introducing various political and social restrictions, they strengthened the power of the white minority while increasingly denying basic civil rights to the majority nonwhite racial groups. (The current population of South Africa is approximately 6 million whites to 23 million nonwhites of various racial groups.) Not since Hitler's anti-Semitic laws in the 1930s had any country attempted to officially establish such restrictive and repugnant racial policies, and by the late 1970s South Africa was finding itself becoming more and more isolated within the world community.

The problem for the West was that the white government of South Africa was staunchly anti-Communist, and the country itself was situated in a vital geographic position at the foot of the African continent, which commanded the sea lanes into the Indian Ocean. The importance of the sea route around the Cape of Good Hope had been demonstrated dramatically when the Suez canal was closed following the Israeli-Arab war in 1973; besides which, the large tankers plying their trade from the Persian Gulf to the United States and Europe were forced to go around the Cape because of their extraordinary length. Another major moral dilemma is the fact that South Africa produces more than half of the world's gold supply, and is by far the major supplier of such vital minerals such as platinum, vanadium, chromium, and other precious metals so necessary for today's technologies. Because of South Africa's long previous membership in the British Commonwealth, there were also strong cultural connections with the English-speaking nations, sharing such activities and media as sports (which is particularly important to South Africans), books, magazines, motion pictures, and, since 1976, television programs. (One of the authors of this book, Dr. Jowett, grew up in South Africa and remembers with great pleasure as a child listening to American-produced radio serials such as *Superman* in the 1940s and 1950s.)

Thus South Africa was an integral part of the West, and yet its abhorrent racial policies were becoming increasingly difficult for its political friends, particularly Britain and the United States, to justify and accept. Especially since the Civil Rights

Movement in the United States had brought an end to obvious racial injustices in this country, the restrictive South African racial laws were beginning to receive attention in the American press with increasing frequency in the 1970s. (In Britain there had been a strong anti-South African lobby since the early 1960s.) It is within the historical context of the accelerating negativity associated with South Africa that this case study must be understood.

The Muldergate Affair

In February 1974, a plan was formulated by a group of six men close to South African Prime Minister John Vorster. Led by the urbane Eschel Rhoodie, who had spent more than a dozen years overseas as an information officer for the government, they decided to go on the propaganda offensive. As Rhoodie later described this meeting, he told the group, "I want you to approve not an information asset but a propaganda war in which no rules or regulations would count" (Rothmyer, 1980: 455). His plan was agreed to, and a secret fund was established to finance Rhoodie's operations for the next five years. By his own account, he helped to orchestrate between 160 and 180 secret projects through 1978, at a cost that approached $100 million. What Eschel Rhoodie did for the South African Government was not all that unusual, for as we have already noted, widespread propaganda activities are normal practice for most governments; however, the extent of these operations, and the fact that all of the details were later revealed for public scrutiny, makes this a unique case study.

In 1978, when a series of circumstances caused the opposition press in South Africa to begin to investigate some of Rhoodie's unusual expenditures on trips and other activities, many of the details of the massive propaganda "war" became public, becoming known in South Africa as the "Muldergate Affair" because it caused the resignation of Rhoodie's immediate superior, Minister of Information, Connie Mulder, and subsequently led to the retirement of Prime Minister Vorster. Rhoodie fled to Europe, where he was extradited from France and returned to South Africa to face trial for fraud. The government established a special board of inquiry known as the Erasmus Commission to examine the whole affair, and Rhoodie was sentenced to six years in prison. He was later successful in his appeal against this sentence, and returned to Europe, were he lives today. The Erasmus Commission was particularly biased in its findings, going out of its way to hide the official involvement of the South African government, but the flamboyant Eschel Rhoodie had no hesitation in telling the world press about his propaganda successes. In his 900-page book defending his own reputation, *The Real Information Scandal* (1983), he provides an enormous amount of detail concerning every aspect of his propaganda work for the Information Ministry. Although critics have correctly pointed out that it is sometimes difficult to substantiate his claims, this volume provides fascinating reading for students of international propaganda. As Rhoodie (1983: 1) notes in the opening paragraph, "*The Real Information Scandal* is about propaganda warfare, political deceit, treachery, cowardice, courage and love; about callous and malicious journalism, the abuse of government power and administrative terrorism."

The range of propaganda activities undertaken by the South African government during this period ranged from wining and dining members of congress to bankrolling the purchase of American and foreign newspapers covertly, sponsoring phony academic conferences, and even providing expensive golfing junkets for American business people in South Africa. The purpose of all of this was to create a more favorable image for South Africa in the world's press, and especially to reach those opinion leaders, such as politicians and business people who were in a position to mold public opinion. A good example would be the role of the Michigan publisher, and friend of former president Gerald Ford, John McGoff. McGoff owned the Panax chain of about forty small-town newspapers, which was apparently in some financial difficulty. In 1974 McGoff offered to buy the ailing *The Washington Star* for $25 million; however, $10 million of that was going to come from Rhoodie's secret fund. McGoff was outbid for the *Star,* but he later bought *The Sacramento Union* for $8 million. Later he added to his holdings in Texas and California, and even made an unsuccessful bid for the short-lived New York *Trib.* The Erasmus Commission noted that McGoff took another $1.7 million in 1975 to purchase a half-interest in UPITN, the second largest news-film producer and distributor in the world. (The other half was owned jointly by United Press International and Independent Television News of Britain.)

As Karen Rothmyer (1980: 456) points out, there is little clear evidence that either Panax or McGoff's personal holdings were effective long-term propaganda tools for putting forward the position of the South African government, although McGoff did encourage his editors to publish more stories favorable to South Africa. However, Rhoodie notes that the motivation behind financing the purchase of *The Washington Star* was to counteract the enormous influence of *The Washington Post* and The *New York Times*. Had the bid by McGoff been successful, then the *Star* would have established a South African desk "to run significant articles on South Africa" as well as an "Africa Desk" to "make sure Washington learned more about how the rest of Africa went about regulating its affairs" (Rhoodie has a lengthy account of the *Star* incident on pp. 382-388).

The purchase of *The Sacramento Union* was considered prudent because, according to Rhoodie (1983: 387), "California was the most populous state in the USA . . . [and it] . . . could bring additional support to conservative politicians such as Mr. Ronald Reagan." However, McGoff was never given formal permission to use South African financing to finalize the purchase, and he was eventually forced to sell the newspaper to pay back half his debt and to prevent knowledge of his involvement with the South African government becoming public in the United States. Nevertheless, the findings of the Erasmus Commission made McGoff's role very clear. The Securities and Exchange Commission and the Justice Department were both interested in whether or not McGoff acted as an unregistered foreign agent for South Africa.

In the period 1974 to 1978 the South African government used several public relations firms to put forward its position to the American public. One of these was the prestigious and politically well-connected firm of Sydney S. Baron and Company, which was paid more than $650,000 a year plus expenses for their services. In an interview Baron noted, "Every client can't be Disneyworld . . . Clients have problems, and problems are challenges . . . South Africa is a very challenging one" (Stone, 1979: 390). Baron performed the usual public relations activities of preparing background stories and press releases on South Africa, but one of his main contributions was to organize three large conferences sponsored by the South African Trade Organization that brought together about 300 top American business executives to hear Gerald Ford and former Treasury Secretary William Simon argue on behalf of investing in South Africa. The late Sydney Baron was incidentally also a good friend of John McGoff, and did public relations work for the Panax company.

There were many unsubstantiated rumors concerning the extent to which secret South African funds were funneled to U.S. politicians sympathetic to that country's cause. In a series of tapes made by Rhoodie in Europe in 1978, he hinted strongly that a $250,000 campaign contribution had been made to Roger Jepsen, a conservative Republican from Iowa, to assist in his defeat of Senator Dick Clark, chairman of the African Subcommittee of the Senate Foreign Relations Committee and an outspoken critic of South African apartheid policies. Clark was indeed defeated in this election in 1978. Rhoodie also hinted that secret South African funds had in 1976 helped defeat Senator John Tunney of California, another strong critic of South Africa. According to Rhoodie, Baron had promised that if his current South African public relations contract was renewed, he would "see to it" that neither Clark nor Tunney was reelected. Baron apparently suggested to Rhoodie that "it is better you should not know" how the money was spent in these senatorial races. In fairness, it should be pointed out that Rhoodie had serious doubts that Baron was really able to do anything substantial to bring about the defeat of these two anti-South African senators, and there has never been any proof that illegal contributions were made (Rhoodie, 1983: 174-175). However, the fact that the South African government was willing to carry its propaganda war to the extent of meddling in foreign elections should not be too surprising; it is fairly common practice in this propaganda age.

There were other innovative propaganda techniques used by the Ministry of Information involving internationally known South African personalities. The famed artificial heart pioneer, Dr. Christian Barnard, was used as an intermediary between the South African government and American labor leader George

Meany to prevent a boycott of South African shipping in American ports by American labor unions. Meany, the respected head of the AFL-CIO, agreed to send a fact-finding team to South Africa instead. On other occasions, Barnard used his worldwide popularity to speak on behalf of a more tolerant attitude toward South Africa's complex problems. (It should be noted that Barnard has often been very critical of the South African government for its strict racial policies.)

One of the greatest golfers in the history of the game is the South African Gary Player, and he too has been used as a propaganda tool by the South African government as part of Rhoodie's grand plan. Between 1975-1978, when investors were beginning to consider taking their money out of South Africa, Player was requested to write letters to carefully selected top executives of major companies in the United States, such as McDonnell Douglas, Union Carbide, Bank of America, and others, inviting them to play golf with him for a full week in South Africa. All expenses were paid by the secret fund, including compensation for Player's absence from the U.S. professional golf circuit. The thrill of playing with one of the greatest in the game was enough inducement for these board chairs and other chief officers to come to South Africa, where they were often joined on the golf course by the prime minister, who was an avid golfer. As Rhoodie (1983: 181-187) noted, a personal invitation from Gary Player was worth ten invitations from the foreign minister. Many of these top industrial leaders later wrote letters to the U.S. government speaking in glowing terms about South Africa and requesting a more tolerant government policy toward that country. In a hostile world the South African government was using every positive propaganda opportunity it found, and Gary Player, who has also been critical of the policies of apartheid, suddenly found himself in the middle of the Muldergate Affair.

The Evaluation of the Campaign

It is difficult to assess the target audience's reaction to the entire campaign because it was so extensive in scope; however, as we have seen, clearly some of it worked, and the South African government was able to bring about a favorable impression of itself when it counted. Other techniques did not work, and only resulted in embarrassment for all involved, such as the McGoff affair and the blatant attempt to "buy" the American media. What the South Africans could not prevent was the constant pressure of world opinion against an increasingly unwieldy political apparatus and repugnant racial policies. The racial unrest within South Africa itself began to be seen nightly on American television sets, and no amount of golf or free trips to what is one of the most beautiful countries on the globe could prevent increased pressure from special interest groups who now countered with their own propaganda.

Starting in 1984, American liberals had themselves arrested for trespassing at the South African Embassy in Washington; South African sports teams were actively discouraged or prevented from playing anywhere in the world (they had already been thrown out of the Olympic Games since 1960), and even Gary Player was harassed by spectators during tournaments in the United States and Britain. The archconservative, fundamentalist preacher Reverend Jerry Falwell with a large television following found that even his considerable powers of persuasion were useless when, after his visit to South Africa, he failed to stem the growing tide of divestment, and this has proved to be one of the few setbacks in his controversial career. His usually faithful flock was divided on his position because what they saw on television, and read in the newspapers did not match his biased perspective. His support of the racist South African minority government once again raised the issue of his support of segregationist policies in the 1950s and 1960s. Even President Ronald Reagan, whose policy of "constructive engagement" had been the official administration's position for five years, was forced by congressional pressure to take a harsher stance against the South African government, much to that government's surprise and dismay.

It is clear that the current South African government has maintained their "larger mentality" (closed-mindedness) about the correctness of their racial policies. While they are still wary of a repeat of the Muldergate Affair, they are sophisticated enough to understand and appreciate the power of the American media to mold public opinion where there is an absence of counterinformation. Therefore they have continued their propaganda efforts. However, since the Muldergate Affair, the opposition to apartheid, both inside and outside of the country, tried to seize the initiative that the brief information gap had provided to saturate the American media with their side of the story, and this has now escalated into a major confrontation.

However, according to recent reports there is evidence that there is widespread sympathy for the white South African minority in the United States. There has been a definite shift in propaganda strategies from a behind-the-scenes manipulation to confronting South Africa's critics publicly, and trying to make a case the public can understand in the American context. In forums that range from Rotary and Kiwanis Clubs to committee rooms on Capitol Hill to religious television programs, South Africa's defenders are stressing that American values and methods cannot be imposed on a system that has a very different demographic and racial makeup; that change is occurring and cannot take place overnight; that South Africa is the West's "best friend" in Africa, and the last real anti-Communist bastion on that continent; and that divestment will only harm those it is intended to help the most, while destroying a viable economy and endangering the supply of precious metals vital to the security of the "free world" (Ungar, 1985: 3B).

Apparently many Americans are listening sympathetically, for as Rep. James Symington, a Democrat from Missouri noted: "There is a mystic chord of *deja vu*. . . . For many Americans, looking at South Africa is like getting into a time machine" (Ungar, 1985: 3B). For their part, the South African propagandists play on this natural U.S. sympathy. The South African ambassador to the United States, Herbert Beukes, noted the similarity between the people who emigrated to the United States from Europe and those who went to South Africa. "They had the same religious base and pioneer spirit. They wanted to escape from colonial rule and believed in a free-market system." Beukes asked, "Isn't it possible that you recognize in South Africa something of yourselves?" (Ungar, 1985: 3B).

As this case study is being written the South African government is being forced to make concessions to its nonwhite majority population that would have been unthinkable only six months ago. The U.S. government continues to reassess its position in the face of increasing pressure from many sections of American society, while others plead for time, tolerance, and understanding. This is one propaganda case study that appears to be without an immediate ending, and should provide students of the subject with interesting data for many years to come.

HOW PROPAGANDA WORKS
IN MODERN SOCIETY

Propaganda is a form of communication and can, therefore, be depicted as a process. A model of the propaganda process includes the social-historical context, a cultural rim made up of government, economy, events, ideology, and myths of society, the propaganda institution, the propaganda agents, media methods, the social network, and the public. Generalizations about propaganda in modern society are based on the events and concepts discussed throughout the book.

This chapter presents a model of propaganda and several generalizations that have evolved from the events, ideas, and concepts that have been discussed in previous chapters. This chapter also reaffirms our position that propaganda is a form of communication that can be depicted as a process.

MODEL OF THE PROCESS OF PROPAGANDA

As one looks at the model of propaganda (Figure 8.1, p. 211), it can be seen that it depicts the development of propagandistic communication as a process within a social system. The model is complex because, as we have seen in the preceding chapters, propaganda itself is complex. The process of propaganda takes

the form of a message flow through a network system that includes propaganda agents, the media, and a social network,
originating with an institution and ending with the possibility of
response from the public or a target audience within the public.
The message flow is contained within a cultural rim that is itself
placed within a social-historical context. The model therefore
depicts the necessity of examining the process of propagandistic communication within the multitude of features contained
within a social-historical-cultural framework. The flow of propaganda from institution to public has several canals that feed
into or are fed by the elements of the cultural rim, to and from
the institution itself, to and from the media, and to and from the
public. This indicates that, as propaganda occurs, it has a potential impact on the culture at any point during the process, and,
of course, the culture has, in turn, an impact upon the process of
propaganda.

SOCIAL-HISTORICAL CONTEXT

Propaganda as a process is socially determined. The social-
historical context provides a heritage that gives a propagandist
motivation and even a "style" of communication. In order to
understand how propaganda works, we must consider how the
existing social-historical context *allows* it to work. The propaganda that emerges is the product of forces established long before the activity originated and is controlled by those forces.
That is why the uses and methods by which propaganda
emerges differ from society to society.

The propagandist is influenced by past models through allusions to historical figures, methods, and impulses for current
propaganda activity. For example, the idea that freedom is
worth dying for was the basis for Patrick Henry's "Give me Liberty or Give Me Death" speech in the time of the American
Revolution. The same idea provided the impulse for the
anti-Communist slogan, "Better Dead Than Red" almost 200
years later. In another culture, the Middle East, present-day
propaganda can be traced back to the social-historical context
of the origins of Mohammedanism in the seventh century and
the subsequent spread of the Islamic religion. Thirteen centuries later, Mohammed's charge to his disciples to convert the in-

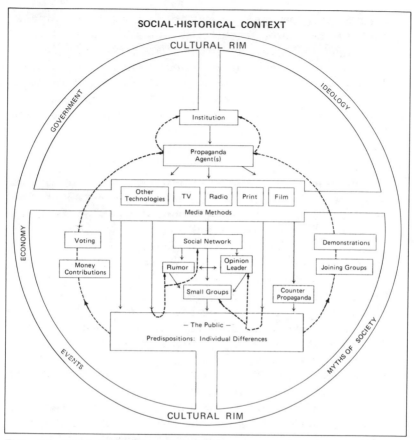

Figure 8.1 Model of the Process of Propaganda

fidels and be willing to die fighting for the faith still shapes the content that takes form through modern technologies. When the Palestinians commit what Americans may think are "suicidal" acts, they do so believing that a death for the cause will assure them a place on the right hand of God. Each incident of propaganda is, thus, historically based; yet each act of propaganda also takes place at a specific time in history and is a product of its time. It is highly unlikely that the propaganda of Adolf Hitler would have worked in Germany during a time of prosperity. Time, both past and present, shapes the internal dynamics of the model.

The flow of propaganda to and from an institution depends upon the conditions of the times and upon the availability of the media. For example, conditions in the 1950s in America tended to be more restrictive than the 1960s due to the Red Scare and McCarthyism. In the sixteenth century, Martin Luther's ability to reach his audience was made possible by the development of the printing press. If the times and the conditions are right, to paraphrase Nietzsche, the propagandist is a hero who does nothing but shake the tree when the fruit is ripe.

CULTURAL RIM

Culture includes the social-historical context. We have depicted culture within the social-historical context only for purposes of clarifying the concepts presented here. In the model, the elements of culture are depicted as a rim surrounding the flow of propaganda with canals leading to and from the process and the cultural rim. The cultural rim is the infrastructure that provides the material context in which messages are sent and received. How propaganda is developed, used, and received is cultural specific. The elements of a culture—its ideologies, societal myths, government, economy, and specific events that take place—influence propaganda. Take, for example, whether a society is open or closed. A closed society such as the Soviet Union controls the media, preventing messages from the "outside" from coming into the system. American newspapers cannot be freely sold. Russians are forced to rely on the *Pravda* for news and tend to be skeptical and suspicious of what they read. Likewise, the Soviet Union prevents the news of certain kinds of events, such as airplane crashes, earthquakes, and other disasters, from reaching the international audience.

An open society, on the other hand, tends to have more flexible, accessible media systems that accept or reject messages without having to refer to higher authorities all the time. In the fall of 1985, the American Broadcasting Company and the producers of the program *20/20* chose to reject a program segment about the death of Marilyn Monroe and a connection with Robert Kennedy because of the producer's personal friendship with the Kennedy family. The British Broadcasting Corporation, however, chose to broadcast the story. In open systems, the variety of channels in the media, competing images, and easy access to them tend to make audiences less suspicious, but also more discerning and concerned about the potential for propaganda.

The economy dictates the flow of propaganda relative to the sale or consumption of goods. Advertising certainly dictates the structure of the mass media system in the United States. In the nineteenth century, the economy even dictated the attainment of literacy. If a nation needed laborers, it was less likely to support education of the masses.

The culture is a system of formal and informal rules that tell people how to behave. People's behavior, in turn, can alter the culture by creating new societal myths or changing ideologies.

THE PROCESS OF PROPAGANDA

Institution

An institution generally initiates and fosters propaganda due to its organizational and financial powers. The propaganda may be to maintain the institution's legitimacy, its position in society, and its activities. An institution that is outside of the established order may also initiate propaganda to agitate in order to demonstrate support for a counterideology or concern over an issue. Institutional affiliation may not be revealed by the propagandists, who may act as "fronts" or agents for the source. This is often the case during wartime or for espionage activity.

Propaganda Agents

Propaganda agents are the people who facilitate messages directly and through the media for an institution. Sometimes they are powerful and charismatic figures; other times they are bureaucrats or low-keyed disseminators of information. Their purpose is to send out ideology with a specific objective to a target audience for the benefit of the institution but not necessarily for the good of the receiver. There is likely to be a hierarchy of agents with a chain of command to ensure that the message will be homogeneous.

Media Methods

The propaganda agents select and use the available media to send the message to the target audience. The development of new technologies affects the nature of propaganda and has been seen to be the major factor in the use of propaganda. Short-wave radio has enabled the major governments of the world to broadcast ideology to remote places. Cable and satellite television has enhanced religious television, giving it access to virtually every American home. Direct mail and the storage and speed of computer usage has produced a steady and regulated stream of messages to target addresses.

Media utilization is vital to a propaganda campaign. Access to and control of the media literally means access to and potential control of public opinion. The type of media selected by the propagandist is appropriate to the audience that needs to be reached. Media are used to disseminate information to the membership of a propaganda organization as well as to those whose support is solicited. Where the media are not owned, the propagandist runs the risk of the information being filtered through the media or being released in an inappropriate fashion.

The media message should be homogeneous with a consistency of purpose in order for the propaganda to be effective. Less control over the media means less control over the homogeneity of the message.

Mass media has become so extensive and influential that it affects the culture. Thus, although the propagandist's intent is to reach a target audience, the media usage can influence culture along the way to the target audience. Likewise, the culture influences the media. An open society allows competing messages to come from the media, thus the propagandist's message, when mediated by unsympathetic or critical people, can be diffused. On the other hand, the worldwide media is avaricious for sensational news. This enables propagandists to receive worldwide exposure at no cost. Certainly, the Palestinian hijackings of airplanes and ships and the subsequent media coverage have promulgated messages that otherwise would have remained unheard or unseen. Conversely, media coverage of a competing event can completely diffuse the impact of a propaganda event, such as when the North Koreans released the Pueblo crew while the media covered Apollo 8's journey to the moon.

Media also affect the propaganda agents and the institution. Too much exposure may be harmful, causing the propagandist to have to change strategies. Unwanted publicity can lessen the credibility of an agent or institution. The peculiarities of the medium itself may not be understood well enough. Richard M. Nixon discovered that television caused him to appear unshaven and unattractive in the 1960 debates with John F. Kennedy because he wore improper makeup and the wrong color suit. Before his 1968 campaign appearances on television, Nixon hired Johnny Carson's makeup man to make sure that his appearance was appropriate for the televised image.

Sometimes the target audience receives the message directly from a medium or combination of media; sometimes selected audiences function as channels of communication to broader audiences through a social network.

Social Network

A social network is made up of the following: opinion leaders who may influence an audience because of their position within the social network; small groups of people that may include opinion leaders and/or propaganda agents; and people who facilitate rumors innocently or deliberately throughout a social network. In the multistep flow of communication, a social network receives information from the media that is, in turn, disseminated throughout a community by leaders within it. Likewise, the public may receive information from the media and carry it back to the opinion leaders for explanation or confirmation.

As we have seen, in institutions such as the United States Information Agency, information may be sent directly from the propaganda agent to opinion leaders, sidestepping the media altogether. Although the process model of propaganda depicts the flow of information from the propaganda agent through the media to the social network, it is possible for the message to bypass the media and go directly to opinion leaders or small groups. For the most part, however, the media are used heavily by agents of propaganda with the social network coming into play as a mediating influence.

The Public

The propagandist's audience may be the general public or a segment of the public targeted for a specific set of responses. As we have seen in previous discussions, the predispositions of the audience are canalized by the propaganda message, having the effect of resonance. Media experiences create shared experiences, thus the public may form "communities" related to the propaganda message. For example, the abortion controversy has created moral communities among those who oppose abortion.

Public response to propaganda messages takes many forms. The public may fail to receive a message; it may choose to ignore it; it may be skeptical and suspicious; it may take sides for and against; it may respond in desired ways. Desired behavioral responses are voting, contributing money, purchasing products, joining groups, engaging in demonstrations, and putting pressure on elected officials through letters, telegrams, and phone calls. Such responses can be observed and measured, enhancing the propagandist's effectiveness. The same responses can also be fed back into the cultural rim, creating new events, affecting the economy, creating new myths, electing new government officials, and altering ideology over time.

The model of the process of propaganda is an interactive and cyclical model with each segment having the potential of interacting with another. Propaganda is a communicative form with potential to create change. This book has demonstrated changes throughout history, but, more important, it should equip the reader with the ability to recognize and evaluate propaganda in modern society. We have learned some things about propaganda in writing this book, and the following generalizations, though few in number, may constitute new ways of looking at a very old subject.

GENERALIZATIONS

(1) Propaganda creates and is created by strange and powerful bedfellows. Special interests cause groups that are normally diverse to unite in a common cause. The abortion controversy has brought the far right and the Roman Catholics together. The antipornography movement has united the Moral Majority and feminists.

(2) Propaganda serves an informative function in that it tells people how to behave. Because people turn to the media in or-

der to understand events and find out what to do about them, they unwittingly expose themselves to propaganda and may become naive supporters of an invisible institution.

(3) Even when it is obvious that a message is propaganda, people will respond favorably to it. Knowledge that communication is propagandistic does not necessarily neutralize people's reaction to it.

(4) People tend to divide into opposing camps in response to propaganda, and public "communities" are formed that create powerful "armies" to fight for and support a cause. The media can instantly transmit information, and the community responds with instantaneous reactions.

(5) New technologies are powerful allies of propagandists. Computer technology has created an unexpected force in direct mail propaganda. People's predispositions are easily identifiable, making them easy targets for propaganda.

(6) External propaganda may be created for internal consumption. The Pueblo incident turned out to mean more as morale boosting for the North Koreans than anything else. Ridiculed by the rest of the world, the North Koreans used their propaganda for their own country.

(7) Propaganda is not an evil thing. It can only be evaluated within its own context according to the players, the played upon, and its purpose.

This brief examination of propaganda has, we hope, made you more aware of how much this activity has shaped our lives, and helped to form the attitudes we have on so many subjects. Propaganda by itself is a natural outgrowth of the development of sophisticated media of communication; it will always be with us, in one form or another, and, we, as individuals can accept or reject it as we wish. We should not fear propaganda, for in a free society, somewhere, somehow, alternate message systems always appear. As long as people care, propaganda's powers are controlled; if we give up our rights to free speech, for whatever reason, then we lose control to those who control the propaganda systems. In the long run, freedom of speech in a free, open society is the greatest deterrent to the misuse of propaganda.

REFERENCES

ABELMAN, R. and K. NEUENDORF (1985) "How religious is religious television programming?" Journal of Communication 35, (Winter): 98-110.

ALLPORT, G. W. (1935) "Attitudes," pp. 798-884 in C. Murchison (ed.) The Handbook of Social Psychology. Worcester, MA: Clark University Press.

— — —(1968) "The historical background of modern social psychology," pp. 1-80 in G. Lindzey and E. Aronson (eds.) The Handbook of Social Psychology, Vol. 1. Reading, MA: Addison-Wesley.

ALTHEIDE, D. L. and J. M. JOHNSON (1980) Bureaucratic Propaganda. Boston: Allyn and Bacon.

ARMSTRONG, B. (1979) The Electronic Church. Nashville: Thomas Nelson.

ARONSON, E. (1980) The Social Animal. San Francisco: W. H. Freeman.

BAILYN, B. (1967) The Theological Origins of the American Revolution. Cambridge, MA: Harvard University Press.

BANDURA, A. (1977) Social Learning Theory. Englewood Cliffs, NJ: Prentice-Hall.

BARRETT, E. W. (1953) Truth is Our Weapon. New York: Funk and Wagnalls.

BEM, D. J. (1970) Beliefs, Attitudes and Human Affairs. Belmont, CA: Brooks/Cole.

BERELSON, D. (1966) Reader in Public Opinion and Communication. New York: Free Press.

BIDDLE, P. R. (1966) "An experimental study of ethos and appeal for overt behavior in persuasion." Ph.D. dissertation, University of Illinois, Urbana.

BLUMER, H. (1933) Movies and Conduct. New York: Macmillan.

BOGARDUS, E. S. (1925) "Measuring social distance." Journal of Applied Sociology 9: 299-308.

BOGART, L. (1976) Premises for Propaganda. The United States Information Agency's Operating Assumptions in the Cold War. New York: Free Press.

BOHN, T. (1977) An Historical and Descriptive Analysis of the "Why We Fight" Films. New York: Arno Press.

BONNER, R. J. (1933) Aspects of Athenian Democracy. Berkeley: University of California Press.

BOSTER, R. J. and P. MONGEAU (1984) "Fear-arousing persuasive messages," pp. 330-375 in R. N. Bostrum and B. H. Westley (eds.) Communication Yearbook 8. Beverly Hills, CA: Sage.

BRAMSON, L. (1961) The Political Context of Sociology. Princeton, NJ: Princeton University Press.

BROWN, J.A.C. (1963) Techniques of Persuasion: From Propaganda to Brainwashing. Baltimore: Penguin Books.

BROWNE, R. W. (1850) The Nichomachean Ethics of Aristotle, Volume II. (trans.) London: H. G. Bohn.

BROWNFIELD, A. C. (1984) Washington Inquirer (May 4): 6.

BRUNTZ, G. G. (1938) Allied Propaganda and the Collapse of the German Empire in 1918. Stanford, CA: Stanford University Press.

BUMPUS, B. and B. SKELT (1985) Seventy Years of International Broadcasting. Paris: Unesco.

BURKE, K. (1973) The Philosophy of Literary Form. Berkeley: University of California Press.

CARLSON, J. (1983) "Crime-show viewing by pre-adults: the impact on attitudes toward civil liberties." Communication Research 10 (October): 529-552.

CARY H. (1854) Plato: Works of Plato, Vol. 1. (trans.) London: H. G. Bohn.

CHOUKAS, M. (1965) Propaganda Comes of Age. Washington, DC: Public Affair Press.

COOPER, L. (1932) The Rhetoric of Aristotle. (trans.) New York: Appleton-Century-Crofts.

CHRISTENSON, R. M. and R. MCWILLIAMS [eds.] (1967) Voice of the People: Readings in Public Opinion and Propaganda. New York: McGraw-Hill.

COMBS, J. E. (1984) Polpop: Politics and Popular Culture in America. Bowling Green, OH: Bowling Green University Popular Press.

COMSTOCK, G. (1980) Television in America. Beverly Hills, CA: Sage.

CONWAY, F. and J. SIEGELMAN (1982) Holy Terror: The Fundamentalist War on America's Freedoms in Religion, Politics and Our Private Lives. New York: Doubleday.

CREEL, G. (1920) How We Advertised America. New York: Harper & Row.

CUSHMAN, D. P. and R. D. MCPHEE (1980) Message-Attitude-Behavior Relationship: Theory, Methodology, and Application. New York: Academic Press.

CZITROM, D. J. (1982) Media and the American Mind. Chapel Hill: University of North Carolina Press.

DAVISON, W. P. (1971) "Some trends in international propaganda." Annals of the American Academy of Political and Social Science 398 (November): 1-13.

DE FLEUR, M. L. and S. BALL-ROKEACH (1982) Theories of Mass Communication. New York: Longman.

DELIA J. (1971) "Rhetoric in the Nazi Mind: Hitler's theory of persuasion." Southern Speech Communication Journal 37, 2: 136-149.

DICKENS, A. G. (1968) Reformation and Society in Sixteenth Century Europe. New York: Harcourt Brace Jovanovich.

DONDIS, D. (1981) "Signs and symbols," pp. 71-86 in R. Williams (ed.) Contact: Human Communication and Its History. New York: Thomas and Hudson.

DONNERSTEIN, E. AND N. MALAMUTH [eds.] (1984) Pornography and Sexual Aggression. New York: Academic Press.

DOOB, L. W. (1948) Public Opinion and Propaganda. New York: Henry Holt and Company.

Editor (1937) "Editorial Foreword." Public Opinion Quarterly 1 (January): 3.

EDWARDS, W. (1954) "The theory of decision making." Psychological Bulletin 51: 390-417.

ELLUL, J. (1965) Propaganda: The Formation of Men's Attitudes. New York: Knopf.

EMERY, E. and M. EMERY (1984) The Press and America. Englewood Cliffs, NJ: Prentice-Hall.

EWEN, S. and E. EWEN (1982) Channels of Desire: Mass Images and the Shaping of American Consciousness. New York: McGraw-Hill.

FESTINGER, L. (1957) A Theory of Cognitive Dissonance. Stanford, CA: Stanford University Press.

FIELDING, R. (1972) The American Newsreel. Norman: University of Oklahoma Press.

FISHBEIN, M. and I. AJZEN (1975) Beliefs, Attitudes, Intentions, and Behavior: An Introduction to Theory and Research. Reading, MA: Addison-Wesley.

FRITSCHLER, A. L. (1983) Smoking and Politics. Englewood Cliffs, NJ: Prentice-Hall.

FURHAMMER, L. and F. ISAKSSON (1971) Politics and Film. New York: Praeger.

GERBNER, G., L. GROSS, N. SIGNORELLI, M. MORGAN, and M. JACKSON-BEECK (1979) "The demonstration of power: violence profile no. 10." Journal of Communication 29 (Summer): 177-196.

GRAFF, H. J. [ed.] (1981) Literary and Social Development in the West. Cambridge: Cambridge University Press.

GRANDIN, T. (1939) The Political Uses of Radio. Geneva: Geneva Research Center.

GREENBERG, B. S. [ed.] (1980) Life on Television. Norwood, NY: Ablex.

HADDEN, J. K. and C. E. SWANN (1981) Prime Time Preachers: The Rising Power of Televangelism. Reading, MA: Addison-Wesley.

HALE, J. (1975) Radio Power. Philadelphia: Temple University Press.

HAMMOND, P. E. (1985) "The curious path of conservative Protestantism." Annals of the American Academy of Political and Social Science 480 (July): 53-62.

HEILBRONER, R. L. (1985) "Advertising as agitprop." Harper's (January): 71-76.

HERZSTEIN, R. (1978) The War that Hitler Won. New York: G. P. Putnam's Sons.

HESS, S. and M. KAPLAN (1975) The Ungentlemanly Art. New York: Macmillan.

HORSFIELD, G. (1984) Religious Television: The American Experience. New York: Longman.

HOVLAND, C. I. and W. MANDELL (1952) "An experimental comparison of conclusion drawing by the communicator and by the audience." Journal of Abnormal and Social Psychology 47: 581-588.

HOVLAND, C. I., I. L. JANIS, and H. H. KELLEY (1953) Communication and Persuasion: Psychological Studies of Opinion Change. New Haven, CT: Yale University Press.

HOVLAND, C. I., A. A. LUMSDAINE, and F. D. SHEFFIELD (1949) Experiments on Mass Communication Vol. 3, Studies in Social Psychology in World War II. Princeton, NJ: Princeton University Press.

HUNT, E. L. (1925) "Plato and Aristotle on rhetoric and rhetoricians," pp. 3-60 in E. L. Hunt (ed.) Studies in Rhetoric and Public Speaking. New York: Century.

JONES, D. B. (1945) "Hollywood war films." Hollywood Quarterly 1, 1: 1-19.

Journal and Courier (1979) "Eagles, beagles, babies, and 'there oughta be a law.'" A8.

JOWETT, G. (1976) Film: The Democratic Art. Boston: Little, Brown.

— — —(1982) "They taught it at the movies: films as models for learned sexual behavior," pp. 209-221 in S. Thomas (ed.) Film/Culture. Metuchen, NY: Scarecrow Press.

JOYCE, W. (1963) The Propaganda Gap. New York: Harper & Row.

KARLINS, M. and H. I. ABELSON (1970) Persuasion: How Opinions and Attitudes are Changed. New York: Springer.

KATZ, E. and T. SZECSKO [eds.] (1981) Mass Media and Social Change. Beverly Hills, CA: Sage.

KECSKEMETI, P. (1973) "Propaganda," pp. 844-870 in I. D. Pool et al. (eds.) Handbook of Communication. Chicago: Rand McNally.

KELMAN, H. C. and C. I. HOVLAND (1953) "'Reinstatement' of the communicator in delayed measurement of opinion change." Journal of Abnormal and Social Psychology 48, 3.

LAKE, R. A. (1984) "Order and disorder in anti-abortion rhetoric: a logical view." Quarterly Journal of Speech 70 (November): 425-443.

LAND, R. E. and D. O. SEARS (1964) Public Opinion. Englewood Cliffs, NJ: Prentice-Hall.

LANG, J. S. (1979) "The great American bureaucratic propaganda machine." U.S. News and World Report (August 27): 43-47.

LASKI, H. J., et al. (1970) Where Stands Democracy: A Collection of Essays. Freeport, NY: Books for Libraries Press.

LASSWELL, H. (1927) Propaganda Technique in the World War. New York: Knopf.

— — —(1935) Propaganda and Promotional Activities. Minneapolis: University of Minnesota Press.

— — —(1938) "Foreword," pp. v-viii in G. G. Bruntz, Allied Propaganda and the Collapse of the German Empire in 1918. Stanford, CA: Stanford University Press.

— — —and D. BLUMSENSTOCK (1939) World Revolutionary Propaganda: A Chicago Study. New York: Knopf.

LASSWELL, H. D., D. LERNER, and H. SPEIER [eds.] (1980) Propaganda and Communication in World History (Vols, 1-3) Honolulu: University of Hawaii Press.

LAZARSFELD, P. L., P. BERELSON, and H. GAUDET (1948) The People's Choice: How the Voter Makes Up His Mind in a Presidential Campaign. New York: Duell, Sloan, and Pearce.

LAZARSFELD, P. F. and F. N. STANTON [eds.] (1944) Radio Research, 1942-43. New York: Duell, Sloan and Pearce.

LEE, A. M. and E. B. LEE (1979) The Fine Art of Propaganda. San Francisco: International Society for General Semantics.

LEE, C. (1980) Medial Imperialism Reconsidered: The Homogenization Of Television Culture. Beverly Hills, CA: Sage.

LERNER, D. [ed.] (1951) Propaganda in War and Crisis: Materials for American Policy. New York: G. W. Stewart.

— — —and L. M. NELSON [eds.] (1977) Communication Research: A Half Century Appraisal. Honolulu: University Press of Hawaii.

LIEBERT, R. M., J. M. NEALE and E. S. DAVIDSON (1973) The Early Window: Effects of Television on Children and Youth. New York: Pergamon Press.

LINEBARGER, P. M. A. (1954) Psychological Warfare. New York: Duell, Sloan, and Pearce.

LIKERT, R. (1932) A Technique for the Measurement of Attitudes. Archives of Psychology. New York: No. 140.

LIPPMANN, W. (1922) Public Opinion. New York: Free Press. (reprinted 1960, Macmillan)

LOWENTHAL, L. (1949) Prophets of Deceit: A Study of the Techniques of the American Agitator. New York: Harper.

LOWERY, S. and MELVIN L. De FLEUR (1983) Milestones in Mass Communication Research. New York: Longman.

MacCUNN, J. (1906) "The ethical doctrine of Aristotle." International Journal Of Ethics 16: 301.

MANNHEIM, K. (1943) Diagnosis of Our Time. London: Routeledge, Kegan, Paul.

MARTIN, L. J. (1971) "Effectiveness of international propaganda." Annals of the American Academy of Political and Social Science 398 (November): 61-70.

MARTY, M. E. (1985) "Transpositions: American religion in the 1980s." Annals of the American Academy of Political and Social Science 480 (July): 11-23.

MARWELL, G. and D. R. SCHMITT (1967) "Dimensions of compliance-gaining behavior: an empirical analysis." Sociometry 30, 3: 340-364.

MAXWELL, B. W. (1936) "Political propaganda in Soviet Russia," pp. 61-79 in H. L. Childs (ed.) Propaganda and Dictatorship. Princeton, NJ: Princeton University Press.

McBRIDGE, S. (1980) Many Voices, One World. New York: Unipub.

McLAINE, I. (1979) Ministry of Morale: Home Front Morale and The Ministry of Information in World War II. London: George Allen and Unwin.

McCROSKEY, J. C. (1969) "A summary on the effects of evidence in persuasive communication." Quarterly Journal of Speech 55, 1: 169-176.

McGUIRE, W. J. (1964) "Inducing resistance to persuasion: some contemporary approaches," in L. Berkowitz (ed.) Advances in Experimental Social Psychology, Vol. 1. New York: Academic Press.

— — —(1969) "The nature of attitudes and attitude change," pp. 136-314 in G. Lindzey and E. Aronson (eds.) The Handbook of Social Psychology, Vol. 3. Reading, MA: Addison-Wesley.

McQUAIL, D. (1975) Communication. New York: Longman.

MERTON, R. (1968) Social Theory and Social Structure. New York: Free Press.

MEYERHOFF, A. E. (1965) The Strategy of Persuasion: The Use of Advertising Skills in Fighting the Cold War. New York: Coward McCann.

MITCHELL, M. (1970) Propaganda, Polls, and Public Opinion: Are the People Manipulated? Englewood Cliffs, NJ: Prentice-Hall.

NAISBITT, J. (1982) Megatrends. New York: Warner.

NELSON, R. A. (1981) "Propaganda," in M. T. Inge (ed.) Handbook of American Popular Culture, Vol. 3. Westport, CT and London: Greenwood.

— — —(forthcoming) Propaganda: A Reference Guide. Westport, CT: Greenwood.

Newsweek (1969) "Out of Hell into Heaven." 72 (January 6): 28-31.

NORDENSTRENG, K. (1982) "U.S. policy and the Third World: a critique." Journal of Communication 32 (Summer): 54-59.

NORDENSTRENG, K. and H. I. SCHILLER (1979) National Sovereignty and International Communication. Norwood, NJ: Ablex.

NYE, G. P. (1941) "Our madness increases as our emergency shrinks." Vital Speeches 7 (September 15): 722.

O'DONNELL, V. and J. KABLE (1982) Persuasion: An Interactive Dependency Approach. New York: Random House.

O'NEILL, W. L. (1982) A Better World. New York: Simon & Schuster.

PACKARD, V. (1957) The Hidden Persuaders. New York: D. Mckay.

PAYNE, D. [ed.] (1965) The Obstinate Audience. Ann Arbor, MI: Foundation for Research on Human Behavior.

POOL, I. D., F. W. FREY, W. SCHRAMM, N. MACCOBY, and E. B. PARKER [eds.] (1973) Handbook of Communication. Chicago: Rand McNally.

POPE, D. (1983) The Making of Modern Advertising. New York: Basic Books.

PRATKANIS, A. R. and A. G. GREENWALD (1985) "A reliable sleeper effect in persuasion: implications for opinion change theory and research," pp. 157-173 in L. S. Alwit and A. A. Mitchell (eds.) Psychological Processes and Advertising Effects. Hillsdale, NJ: Lawrence Erlbaum.

QUALTER, T. H. (1962) Propaganda and Psychological Warfare. New York: Random House.

— — —(1985) Opinion Control in the Democracies. New York: St. Martin's Press.

RAILSBACK, C. C. (1984) "The contemporary American abortion controversy: stages in the argument." Quarterly Journal of Speech 70 (November): 410-424.

RANDALL, R. S. (1968) Censorship of the Movies. Madison: University of Wisconsin Press.

READ, J. (1941) Atrocity Propaganda, 1914-1919. New Haven, CT: Yale University Press.

RHOODIE, E. (1983) The Real Information Scandal. Pretoria: Orbis, S. A.

ROETTER, C. (1974) The Art of Psychological Warfare, 1914-1945. New York: Stein and Day.

ROGERS, E. M. and F. F. SHOEMAKER (1971) Communication of Innovations: A Cross-Cultural Approach. New York: Free Press.

ROLOFF, M. E. and G. R. MILLER [eds.] (1980) Persuasion: New Directions in Theory and Research. Beverly Hills, CA: Sage.

RONALDS, F. S., Jr. (1971) "The future of international broadcasting." Annals of the American Academy of Political and Social Science 398 (November): 31-80.

ROSENTHAL, S. P. (1934) Changes of Socio-Economic Attitudes Under Radical Motion Picture Propaganda. Archives of Psychology. New York: No. 166.

ROTHMEYER, K. (1980) "The South African lobby." The Nation (April 19): 455-457.

RUBIN, B. (1973) Propaganda and Public Opinion: Strategies of Persuasion. Columbus, OH: Xerox Education.

SCHILLER, H. I. (1970) Mass Communications and American Empire. New York: Augustus M. Kelly.

SCHREINER, S. A., Jr. (1977) The Condensed World of Reader's Digest. New York: Stein and Day.

SCHUDSON, M. (1978) Discovering the News. New York: Basic Books.

— — —(1984) Advertising, the Uneasy Persuasion. New York: Basic Books.

SERENO, K. and C. D. MARTENSEN (1974) Foundations of Communication Theory. New York: Harper & Row.

SHAW, J. F. [trans.] (1873) "On Christian doctrine," in Rev. M. Dodds (ed.) The Works of Aurelius Augustine, Bishop of Hippo. Edinburgh: T. and T. Clark.

SHIBUTANI, T. (1966) Improvised News. Indianapolis: Bobbs-Merrill.

SMITH, B. L. (1958) "Propaganda," pp. 579-588 in D. L. Sills (ed.) Encyclopedia of the Social Sciences, Vol. 12. New York: Macmillan.

SPEER, A. (1970) Inside the Third Reich. New York: Macmillan.

SPEIER, H. (1950) "The historical development of public opinion." American Journal of Sociology 55 (January): 376-388.

——— and M. OTIS (1944) "German radio propaganda to France during the Battle of France," pp. 208-247 in P. Lazarsfeld and F. Stanton (eds.) Radio Research, 1942-1943. New York: Duell, Sloan and Pearce.

STARR, M. E. (1977) "Prime-Time Jesus." Cultural Correspondence 4 (Spring): 19-26.

STEWART, C. J., C. A. SMITH, and R. E. DENTON (1984) Persuasion and Social Movements. Prospect Heights, IL: Waveland Press.

STONE, P. H. (1979) "Muldergate on Madison Avenue." The Nation (April 14): 390-393.

SZANTO, G. H. (1978) Theater and Propaganda. Austin: University of Texas Press.

The Communicator (1978) "President's report." p. 2.

The Dallas Morning News (1982) "British enlist 'Alice' in Propaganda War." (May 23): 10A.

THOMAS, W. I. and F. ZNANIECKI (1918) The Polish Peasant in Europe and America, Vol. 1. Boston: Badger.

THOMSON, O. (1977) Mass Persuasion in History: Edinburgh: Paul Harris.

THUM, G. and M. THUM (1972) The Persuaders: Propaganda in War and Peace. New York: Atheneum.

THURSTONE, L. L. (1929) The Measurement of Attitudes. Chicago: University of Chicago Press.

Time (1968) "In Pueblo's wake." 91 (February): 11-17.

TRIANDIS, H. C. (1977) Interpersonal Behavior. Monterey, CA: Brooks/Cole.

UNGAR, S. J. (1985) "South Africa: polishing a tarnished image." The Houston Post (October 15): 3B.

VALINS, D. (1966) "Cognitive effects of false heart-rate feedback." Journal of Personality and Social Psychology 4, 4: 400-408.

WANGER, W. (1941) "The role of movies in morale." American Journal of Sociology 47 (November): 378-383.

WESCHLER, L. (1983) "A state of war—I." The New Yorker (April 11): 45-102.

WESTLEY, B. H. and M. S. MACLEAN, Jr. (1977) "A conceptual model for communications research," pp. 73-82 in K. K. Sereno and C. D. Mortensen (eds.) Foundations of Communication Theory. New York: Harper & Row.

WHITESIDE, T. (1970) "Cutting down." New Yorker 46 (December): 42-95.

———(1971) "Selling death." New Republic 164 (March 27): 15-17.

WILKERSON, M. M. (1932) Public Opinion and the Spanish-American War. Baton Rouge: Louisiana State University Press.

WINKLER, A. (1978) The Politics of Propaganda: The Office of War Information, 1942-1945. New Haven, CT: Yale University Press.

WISAN, J. E. (1934) The Cuban Crisis as Reflected in the New York Press. New York: Columbia University Press.

WISH, H. (1950) Society and Thought in Early America. New York: David McKay.

ZEMAN, Z.A.B. (1973) Nazi Propaganda. New York: Oxford University Press.

———(1978) Selling the War: Art and Propaganda in World War II. London: Orbis.

ZIMBARDO, P., E. EBBESON, and C. MASLACH (1977) Influencing Attitudes and Changing Behavior. Reading, MA: Addison-Wesley.

INDEX

ABOUT THE AUTHORS

Garth Jowett is currently Professor of Communication at the University of Houston, having served as Director of the School of Communication from 1980 to 1985. He obtained his Ph.D. in communications history from the University of Pennsylvania, and has served as Director for Social Research for the Canadian Government Department of Communications, and was a former consultant to various international communications agencies. He has published widely in the areas of popular culture social history, and the history of communications. His major book, *Film: The Democratic Art* (1976), is considered to be the standard social history of moviegoing; and his volume in Sage's CommText Series, *Movies as Mass Communication* (with James M. Linton), is a unique and widely appreciated study. He has recently completed a book on popular culture, and is currently at work on a social history of television in America. He is the advisory editor of the Garland Press Film Dissertation Reprint Series, and is on the editorial boards of several communication and film journals.

Victoria O'Donnell is Professor and Chairperson of the Division of Communication and Public Address at North Texas State University. She received her Ph.D. from The Pennsylvania State University. She has published articles and chapters in a wide range of journals and books on topics concerning social influence, the social effects of media, Southern women in film, television and myth, British politics, and Nazi propaganda. She is also the author (with June Kable) of *Persuasion: An Interactive-Dependency Approach* (Random House, 1982). She is currently writing a book on analyzing media. The recipient of numerous research grants and honors, including being named Honor Professor at North Texas State University. She was chosen to be a Danforth Foundation Associate and a Summer Scholar of the National Endowment for the Humanities. She has taught in Germany and has been a visiting lecturer at universities in Denmark, Norway, and Sweden. She has also served as a private consultant to the U.S. government and many American corporations.